"A HEART WRENCHING AND CHILDREN. A MUST READ FOR AND MEMBERS OF OUR CRIMINAL JUSTICE OF THE LIVES DESCRIBED, HOPEFULLY WILL BEGIN TO DISPEL SOCIETY'S PREJUDICE OF ADDICTION AS A CHOICE, BUT RATHER ADDICTION AS A DISEASE. THESE TRAGEDIES CAN BEFALL ANYONE OF US. IF BUT ONE LIFE CAN BE SAVED BY THIS WORK, THE SECOND WILL SURELY FOLLOW".

- NEIL YESTON, MD, FACS, FCCP, VICE PRESIDENT ACADEMIC AFFAIRS, HARTFORD HOSPITAL, ASSISTANT DEAN, GRADUATE MEDICAL EDUCATION, PROFESSOR OF SURGERY, UNIVERSITY OF CONNECTICUT SCHOOL OF MEDICINE.

"I FOUND THE BOOK TO BE POIGNANT, HEARTFELT AND SURPRISINGLY ENCOURAGING. THE COURAGE, HONESTY, SADNESS AND STRENGTH OF THESE PARENTS OVERWHELMED ME."

- DR. WANDA BETHEA, PSYCHOLOGIST AND LIFE COACH, ADJUNCT PROFESSOR FLORIDA TECH AND WEBSTER UNIVERSITY, MELBOURNE, FLORIDA

"*I AM YOUR DISEASE (THE MANY FACES OF ADDICTION)* IS A MOVING BOOK AND PASSIONATELY WRITTEN. IT IS TOLD BY THE PEOPLE WHO LIVED IT---THOSE AFFECTED BY ADDICTION---THE ADDICTS AND THEIR FAMILIES. IT IS WROUGHT WITH PAIN AND TEMPERED WITH HOPE. IT IS WELL WORTH THE READ."

- ALYCE LAVIOLETTE, AUTHOR OF *IT COULD HAPPEN TO ANYONE; WHY BATTERED WOMEN STAY.*

"THIS IS A BOOK THAT I RECOMMEND FOR PARENTS, GRANDPARENTS, YOUTH, COLLEGE STUDENTS, EDUCATORS AND BUSINESS LEADERS. THERE IS A MESSAGE FOR ALL OF US ON ITS PAGES. IF WE TAKE HEED, ADDICTION WILL NO LONGER BE "SILENT," WE WILL HAVE TAKEN ACTION! IT IS MY HOPE THAT ALL WHO READ THE BOOK WILL INVOLVE OTHERS SO THAT THE TOPIC MAY BE RAISED AND DISCUSSED OVER AND OVER AGAIN - AND MOVE US CLOSER TO REDUCING THE NUMBER OF LIVES LOST AND LESSENED DUE TO DRUG ADDICTION. THE AUTHORS HAVE SUCCEEDED IN CREATING A VOLUME THAT IS ALARMING, REALISTIC, INFORMATIVE AND, HOPEFULLY, AN IMPETUS FOR CHANGE!"

- DR. DAVID G. CARTER, SR., CHANCELLOR OF THE CONNECTICUT STATE UNIVERSITY SYSTEM. FORMER PRESIDENT OF EASTERN CONNECTICUT STATE UNIVERSITY AND PAST CHAIR OF THE AMERICAN ASSOCIATION OF STATE COLLEGES AND UNIVERSITIES

"A MOST HEARTWRENCHING AND HEARTWARMING BOOK OF LIFE STORIES FILLED WITH COMFORT AND DISCOMFORT. THE COMMON THREAD IS THE PAIN OF THE VICTIMS OF ADDICTION UNTIL DEATH, AND THE CONTINUED LINGERING PAIN OF THE FAMILY AND FRIENDS LEFT BEHIND. A MUST READ BOOK FOR ALL THOSE SHARING THAT PAIN."

- EILEEN DUNN, M.DIV., D.MIN. RESIDENTIAL TREATMENT SPIRITUAL DIRECTOR & PASTOR

"I AM YOUR DISEASE (THE MANY FACES OF ADDICTION) IS A VERY DIFFICULT BOOK TO READ. THESE ARE TRUE-LIFE HORROR STORIES. ANYONE WHOSE LIFE HAS BEEN TOUCHED BY ADDICTION WOULD PROFIT FROM READING THIS. AND ANYONE WHO SUSPECTS THEIR CHILD IS FLIRTING WITH ADDICTION SHOULD PUT IT ON HIS OR HER NIGHTSTAND TONIGHT."
 - CATHY MATHIAS, FREELANCE BOOK REVIEWER FOR FLORIDA TODAY

"I AM YOUR DISEASE IS A BOOK FILLED WITH EMOTION. IT'S ABOUT REAL FAMILIES WHO LOST A CHILD TO THIS DISEASE CALLED ADDICTION. EACH PARENT HAD TO RELIVE THEIR CHILD'S DEATH, SO THEY COULD TELL THEIR STORY. THE ONLY HOPE THEY HAVE LEFT IS THAT MAYBE THEY CAN SAVE SOMEONE ELSE'S CHILD. THIS BOOK SHOULD BE READ BY EVERY PARENT AND CHILD."
 - LYNNE COPELAND (BRISTOL PA)

"WHEN I GOT MY COPY OF THIS BOOK AND BEGAN TO READ, I JUST COULD NOT PUT IT DOWN. I EXPLAINED TO MY 12-YEAR-OLD, 6TH GRADER GRANDSON WHAT THE BOOK WAS ABOUT AND HE STARTED READING IT AND UNDERSTOOD WHAT HE WAS READING. PARENTS AND CHILDREN ALIKE WOULD BENEFIT FROM THIS BOOK. IT TOUCHED ME DEEPLY LIKE NO OTHER BOOK I HAVE EVER READ."
 - KATHY MILLER, WEST MELBOURNE, FLORIDA

"THIS BOOK PROVES THAT THE DISEASE STRIKES ANY FAMILY AND DOESN'T DISCRIMINATE. THESE WERE THE KIDS NEXT DOOR. THE FOOTBALL, BASEBALL, BASKETBALL SPORTS JOCKS, CHEERLEADERS, THE HONOR STUDENTS, NURSES, MUSICIANS, ARTISTS, COLLEGE GRADUATES, TEACHERS. YES, IT CAN HAPPEN IN YOUR FAMILY AND THIS BOOK TELLS EACH PARENT'S AND CHILD'S STORY WITH SUCH RAW, TRUE EMOTION THAT IT IS A MUST READ FOR EVERY PARENT AND CHILD."
 - SANDRA LACAGNINA, ANGELS OF ADDICTION, MEMPHIS, TN

"THIS BOOK IS A MUST READ FOR PEOPLE STRUGGLING WITH ADDICTION, THE PEOPLE WHO ARE WATCHING THEM HELPLESSLY AND FOR THOSE OF US WHO HAVE LOST A CHILD TO THIS HORRIBLE DISEASE. THIS BOOK WILL OPEN THE EYES OF THE WORLD AND LET THEM KNOW THAT THESE ARE LOVED CHILDREN FROM GOOD HOMES, WHO MADE A WRONG CHOICE FOR WHATEVER REASON, AND GOT CAUGHT IN THE JAWS OF THE MONSTER CALLED ADDICTION."
 - CHRISTINE TOZZO, SARASOTA, FLORIDA

"I STRONGLY RECOMMEND THIS BOOK, NOT ONLY FOR PARENTS BUT FOR KIDS LIVING IN OUR SOCIETY WHERE PEER PRESSURE CAN CONTROL AND CONVINCE EVEN THE MOST EDUCATED, LOVED, INDIVIDUAL. DRUGS DO NOT DISCRIMINATE, PLEASE DON'T BE THE NEXT TO WRITE YOUR OWN TRAGIC STORY!"
 - CAROL DIGIANTOMMASO, NORTH READING, MA

"THERE ARE A LOT OF BOOKS AVAILABLE THAT EXPLAIN THE CLINICAL EFFECTS OF ADDICTION BUT NONE ARE AS GRIPPING AND TOUCHED ME LIKE THIS BOOK DID. THIS BOOK SHOWS ADDICTION AND ADDICTS IN A DIFFERENT LIGHT. IT SHOWS HOW ADDICTION DOESN'T DISCRIMINATE. IT KNOWS NO BOUNDARIES. THE RICH, THE POOR, THE EDUCATED THE NONEDUCATED ALIKE. ADDICTION TOUCHES ALL OF US AND LEAVES A MARK ON SOCIETY. I HOPE THAT EVERY SCHOOL, LAW ENFORCEMENT AGENCY AND EVERYONE ELSE READS IT TO UNDERSTAND THAT GOOD PEOPLE BECOME ADDICTED. IT'S EVERYONE'S DISEASE."
- KAREN VENTIMIGLIA CHESTERFIELD TWP, MI

"I AM YOUR DISEASE (THE MANY FACES OF ADDICTION) IS FULL OF TRUE STORIES BY PARENTS WHO NEVER COULD POSSIBLY IMAGINE IN THEIR WILDEST NIGHTMARES THAT THE CHILDREN WHO THEY ADORED MORE THAN THEIR OWN LIVES, WOULD HAVE TO BURY THEM LONG BEFORE THEY HAD A CHANCE TO LIVE THEIR LIVES TO THE FULLEST, TAKING WITH THEM THE VERY SPIRIT OF THEIR PARENTS' LIVES, AND WHO WILL NEVER BE THE SAME AGAIN!!! FROM THE 1ST PAGE TO THE LAST, YOU WILL BE KEPT SPELLBOUND BY THE BOOK'S HONESTY AND IT'S HEART."
- AGNES SPARNECHT, DEERFIELD BEACH, FLORIDA

"THIS BOOK IS POWERFUL AND EYE-OPENING. TRULY, IT IS A "MUST HAVE" FOR ANYONE WHO MIGHT EVER COME INTO CONTACT WITH A DRUG-ADDICTED INDIVIDUAL OR THEIR DISTRAUGHT FAMILIES. THAT WOULD INCLUDE EVERY PARENT, EVERY DOCTOR, EVERY MINISTER, EVERY COUNSELOR, EVERY TEACHER, EVERY NURSE, EVERY SCHOOL NURSE, AND EVERY POLICE OFFICER, ETC."
- SUE SHIELDS, BUCKS COUNTY, PA

"THIS BOOK IS A MUST READ FOR EVERY PARENT, GRANDPARENT AND TEENAGER. YOU THINK IT CAN NEVER HAPPEN TO YOU BUT ADDICTION CAN AFFECT EVERYBODY. THESE TRUE STORIES, WRITTEN BY PARENTS AND SIBLINGS OF CHILDREN THAT HAVE DIED FROM ADDICTION, WILL LEAVE YOU BREATHLESS AND EMOTIONAL, BUT IT IS A STORY WHICH MUST BE TOLD. I HAVE NEVER READ A BOOK AND BEEN AFFECTED LIKE I WAS AFTER READING THIS."
- PAUL JOSEPH, BOARD OF DIRECTORS
  WWW.FAMILIESCHANGINGAMERICA.ORG

"THIS BOOK IS A MUST HAVE FOR ANYONE WHO HAS CHILDREN, IS CONSIDERING HAVING CHILDREN OR KNOWS ANYONE WHO HAS CHILDREN. "I AM YOUR DISEASE" IS REAL - THE TRULY HEARTBREAKING STORIES TOLD THROUGH TEARS AND ANGUISH BY REAL PEOPLE WHO HAVE SUFFERED THE WORST POSSIBLE LOSS. WITH GREAT HONESTY AND EMPATHY SHERYL LETZGUS MCGINNIS OFFERS HOPE THAT THE STIGMA SOCIETY PLACES ON DRUG ADDICTION WILL CHANGE "
- LISA CAPPIELLO BROOKLYN, NY

I AM YOUR DISEASE

THE MANY FACES OF ADDICTION

SHERYL LETZGUS MCGINNIS WITH HEIKO GANZER, LCSW, CASAC

Outskirts Press, Inc.
Denver, Colorado

The opinions expressed in this manuscript are solely the opinions of the author and do not represent the opinions or thoughts of the publisher. The author represents and warrants that s/he either owns or has the legal right to publish all material in this book. If you believe this to be incorrect, contact the publisher through its website at www.outskirtspress.com.

I Am Your Disease
The Many Faces of Addiction
All Rights Reserved
Copyright © 2006 Sheryl Letzgus McGinnis with Heiko Ganzer
R 2-3

Cover Artwork courtesy of Amy Zofko.
a2zdesigns@earthlink.net
All Rights Reserved. Used With Permission.

This book may not be reproduced, transmitted, or stored in whole or in part by any means, including graphic, electronic, or mechanical without the express written consent of the publisher except in the case of brief quotations embodied in critical articles and reviews.

Outskirts Press
http://www.outskirtspress.com

ISBN-10: 1-59800-699-1
ISBN-13: 978-1-59800-699-5

Library of Congress Control Number: 2006936392

Outskirts Press and the " OP" logo are trademarks belonging to
Outskirts Press, Inc.
Printed in the United States of America

Could This Be Your Child?

CONTENTS

Dedication and Acknowledgements
Foreword
"I Am Your Disease"
Part One   DRUGS

Scott Graeme McGinnis, RN　　　　　　　　　　　1
"Mom Nobody Wakes Up One Day And Decides
To Be An Addict."

Keith Tedesco　　　　　　　　　　　　　　　　17
"My Nine Days Of Hell."

Jason Anthony Barganier　　　　　　　　　　　25
"Once Upon A Child."

Mike DiGiantommaso　　　　　　　　　　　　47
"My Son's Journey Towards Destruction."
"Just For Fun."

Lang Jackson Hitchcock　　　　　　　　　　　55
"I Don't Need Therapy. God Will Get Me Through This."

Michael Murphy　　　　　　　　　　　　　　59
"My Son's Deadly Choice."

Jeffrey Scott G.　　　　　　　　　　　　　　　65
"I Have Hurt And Shamed Myself On Numerous Occasions
Although My Actions Shall Not Dictate My Eternity."

Samantha Sandler　　　　　　　　　　　　　69
"My Beautiful Daughter And Friend."

James Byron Keaton 77
"Relax Mom. It Ain't That Bad. You Worry
Too Much."

Katie Kevlock 83
"This Is Bigger Than Me, Mom. It's A
Monster I Can't Control."
"A Girl Named Katie."

Josh Joseph 93
"A Life Too Fast."

Johnny Paul King 101
"My Precious Johnny Angel."
"The Moment My World Crashed."

Wade McLeod Grussmeyer 111
"My Greatest Loss."

Vernon Creamer, Jr. 135
"In Loving Memory Of Vernon."

Eddie Anthony Cappiello 141
"So Little Time."

Jennifer Carol Lee 157
"A Bright Star Now."

Brett M. Tozzo 161
"Through The Years With My Son,
Brett. Heaven Sent, Heaven Bound.

John Konewal 169
"You're In The Arms Of An Angel."

Dennis Konewal 171
"Gone But Never Forgotten."

Robby Nunes   175
"I Hope You Have The Time Of Your Life."

Lenny Orlandello, Jr.   183
"An Angel's Face.'

Bobby Mehlberger   187
"My Bobby."

Kara Edelman   191
"A Mother's Greatest Fear."

Brandon James Hagner.   195
"Broken Dreams, Lost Promise."

Gino Ventimiglia   199
"Shattered Lives."

Mark Daniel Bauer   205
"Living A Parent's Worst Nightmare."

Matthew Guastamacchia   211
"In A New York Minute, Everything Can Change."

Donald Charles Parent   215
"My Precious Son."

Justin Luke Scancarello   223
"Forever Justin In My Heart."

David Dill   225
"For The Love Of David – Our Bright And Shining Star."

Cindy's story   231
"And I Don't Take Drugs."

Ricky Aaron Phillips   235
"Until You Beat This Thing Called Addiction,

It Will Destroy
All Until It Is Fiction."

Joseph Smerker 249
"My Beautiful Son."

Ricky Weldon, Jr. 253
"The Beginning Of A Bad Dream."

Jason Eugene Mitchell 257
"My Precious Angel Jason."

William Elliott Sommer 261
"Losing Will."

Shauna Patricia Mikula 265
"My Daughter, My Best Friend."

David Charles Hall 269
"My Honey Boy."

Keith Montambo 273
"Ignorant Of The Truth."

Sara Jo Corbett 283
"You Are So Beautiful To Me."

Random thoughts and poems 286
    A Mom's Thought
    Comet People
    I Never Thought I Could
    Grief Wish List
    Mr. And Mrs. Crystal Meth
    Ms. Heroin
    Nothing Really Ever Dies
    My Mom Lies
    It's OK To Let Me Go Mom
    Another Mom's Thought
    The Missing Page
    Death Be Not Proud
    I Lost My Child Today
    Will You Go Or Will You Stay?
    The 'Everything We Could' Brigade
    The Invisible Cord
We Remember Them
    Kids' Thoughts on Peer Pressure
    Fentanyl and Heroin: A deadly mix
    Some Gentle Suggestions and Tips on Coping
    In Memoriam

Part Two Gambling   340
Afterword   353
Grief Support Sites   359

DEDICATION
&
ACKNOWLEDGEMENT

To my two sons, Dale and Scott, who have given me so much happiness and joy. Dale, our first born, who lives near us and Scott, our baby, who lives in our hearts forever and ever. To my husband, Jack, for his continued, loving, unwavering support and understanding during the long hours spent at the keyboard and ignoring the housework. To my dad, Jack, or as we call him, Jack The Good, a.k.a. Mr. 6 for 6, former semi-pro baseball player, and to my late mother, Iris, a great Australian beauty and lady.

A big Thank You to my son Scott's then girlfriend Amy Zofko, an outstanding professional graphic artist and dear friend, for all of her hard work on the book covers. It couldn't have been done as well without you Amy, and I am awestruck by your talent. It's no wonder that your art work has been displayed on the Mir Space Station and that you have won so many prestigious awards.

Also, my heartfelt thanks to everyone who opened up their hearts, as painful as it was, to share their personal heartbreak and to give us a glimpse into their painful journey through their emotional roller coaster of life now without their loved ones. I walk with them, beside them, and even in their grief, they reach out to pick me up when I fall.

To the many thousands of children who are no longer with us because they were young and made an error in judgment and especially to the children whose stories are told herein. They were the light of their parents' lives and that light shall not be extinguished in death. Their flame burns brightly in the hearts of the parents and siblings who face each day without them.

A special thank you to all of you who work diligently trying to educate people about the Disease of Addiction, who try to erase the stigma of a drug-related death, to let our children rest in the peace and dignity that they were so often denied in life.

A thank you also to the addicted persons who struggle every hour of every day, trying to reclaim their lives from the Addiction Monster. It is an uphill battle, yet they trudge along, with hope in their hearts and an incredible fortitude, with their only tool being their overwhelming need to slay the monster.

A special thank you to Heiko Ganzer, whose invaluable contribution to this book opened my eyes to the problem of gambling, especially among our youth today. As Heiko so accurately points out, "An addiction is an addiction."

To everyone struggling with addiction, I applaud your efforts for each day that you make it through clean and sober. For all of you who are not giving in to the pressure to do drugs, I applaud you. I wish you all well, my friends.

I AM YOUR DISEASE
(The Many Faces of Addiction)

By Sheryl Letzgus McGinnis

(With Heiko Ganzer, LCSW, CASAC)

This book is lovingly written and dedicated to bereaved parents everywhere, who have lost a child to the disease of addiction, to those who have lost their life to this horrible life-sucking disease, and to children and young adults everywhere who may be on the threshold of doing drugs.

It is our hope that the reader will come to understand addiction and what it does to a family, to understand the pain that our children suffered and that the families that they leave behind still suffer.

It is so easy to adopt the attitude of *well this was their choice. Nobody forced the drugs on them. They made their bed, let them lie in it.* Yes, our children did make this choice. But we have to remember the key word here…children!

Not all children will make this choice but if they do and they have addiction in their family history and in their own genes, then that one bad choice may lead to a lifetime (indeed it can be a very short lifetime) of suffering and struggle every day of their lives…all because of one bad choice as a child!

We, the parents in this book, ask society not to judge us, not to compound our suffering by stigmatizing our children and us. The pain we bear from losing a child is something so profound and devastating that we are brought to our knees by it. To be looked at askance by our neighbors, friends and even family members just deepens the hurt that we feel and further maligns our children who are not here to defend or explain themselves.

We, who have suffered so, try our best to conceal our heartache from the world. We put on The Mask and smile and go about our daily lives. While we may be smiling on the outside, sadly we are crying on the inside.

In these pages you will read the heartfelt memories and experiences of parents who have suffered the ultimate loss: The death of a child. It has been said that the death of a spouse is the loneliest experience, but the death of a child is the saddest.

These stories are gripping, compelling, and brutally honest. (Please note that some names have been changed but the stories and events are accurate).

One important purpose of this book is to reach out to parents, and children everywhere, to let you know that, no matter how hard you try, no matter how much you love, no matter how vigilant you are, no matter how protective you are, no matter how trustworthy your children are, no matter how studious they are, no matter how bright they are, no matter how involved they are in music or sports or their church or community, no matter what values and morals were instilled in them…this can still happen in your family! No matter what! Believe it!

Some of these stories are short because it is all the bereaved person was able to bring up out of their gut, and put to pen and paper, without being overwhelmed by grief in the retelling of their story. Other stories are longer because some of the bereaved just can't stop when it comes to expressing their feelings about their lost child and/or the effects that the deaths have had on them. To some, writing their story and that of their child is cathartic and cleansing. To most, it is a very painful journey back in time that tears at their heart just to remember it, let alone to put it out there before everyone.

It is this author's fervent wish that young people will read this book, that our government representatives will read it, that parents, teachers, mental health professionals, the clergy, and especially people who think "not in my family," will read it.

In other words we want to get the word out to everyone because the disease of addiction affects us all, not just the addicted person and the addicted person's family, but the very fabric of our society, our nation, and our world as a whole.

The drug problem, and this includes alcohol, is pandemic. One has only to turn on the TV or radio or pick up the evening newspaper to find story after story of drug abuse, its dire consequences, and the futility experienced by everyone who tries to combat this scourge.

The author has also invited middle school students to write their experiences and opinions of the pervasive drug problem. What our children have to say may surprise you, and open your eyes to how our children view drugs and life in general.

The stories that follow are from people from all over our country, from different backgrounds, religions, ethnicities, different parenting techniques and philosophies, different life-styles, and different socioeconomic levels, all bonded together by one profound, life-altering experience; the devastating loss of a child.

You will also hear from some of the deceased in the form of poems they have written, stories they have written, and their profound feelings that will reach out and grab your heart and twist it into a huge knot and cause a sadness that will not be denied.

Our children must be told the truth about drugs. We cannot make up scary stories just to obtain a particular result. Children see through our lies, and will discount anything that we say if they have previously been lied to. Education will be our salvation.

It is never too early to start an on-going dialogue with our children about drugs, but it can be too late!

Kids, it's never too late to talk to your parents about drugs. If you feel that you can't talk to your parents, please find another responsible adult, perhaps a favorite uncle or aunt, or favorite teacher or even the parents of a good friend. Believe me, we can be a lot more understanding than you think. We have your best interests at heart when we beg you to never do drugs. We've been around a lot longer, and have seen and learned so much.

We want you to live! We don't want to watch you destroy your life and your future. Youth is fleeting. It's a time of learning and experiencing, a time to prepare you for your future. There won't be much of a future though if you destroy your youth with drugs.

Ask any adult if they would like to be a young kid again. Chances are the answer will be a resounding No! As much as we extol the virtues and joys of childhood, the carefree, devil-may-care existence, the truth is that childhood can be very hard. You may feel that drugs are the way out of your unhappy existence. They are not. Ultimately, they will only add to your sadness.

Whatever choices you make today will follow you long after you've left childhood like the ripples of a receding wave. A lot of bad choices can be undone and as adults we're very thankful for that. Everybody makes mistakes in their life. However, some bad choices can never be undone; choices that lead to AIDS and drug addiction.

I know you think that this can never happen to you! Let me tell you a little about the Addiction Gene. Scientific research is showing that there is indeed an addiction gene. How do you know if you have the gene? At this present time, there is only one way of knowing if you have the gene. Unfortunately, when you find out, it's too late. You're addicted!

When you have pawned all of your possessions, sold everything you have, been kicked out of school, or dropped out, or have lost job after job, have lost what little self-esteem you had, had encounters with the police and judicial system, lied through your teeth to everyone, hurt the ones who love you the most, have stolen from everyone you could including your own family, and friends, have disregarded all of your moral training and values, have lost all interest in previously healthy, enjoyable activities, doing whatever you can to obtain your next high, then you are addicted!

Perhaps not all of the above apply to you now. But most of them, if not all, will eventually define you. You will lie with impunity. You can steal the rings off your poor mother's fingers and look her in the eyes and say no, it wasn't you. You will no longer know truth from fiction. Your whole world will be dedicated to the next score. Nothing else will matter. That all-important high is all that matters in your life now. You are consumed by the dangerous quest for drugs and eventually the drugs will consume you. The drugs will have total power, and control of your life. There will be nothing that you can do to prevent this, nor will you want to. Any rational thought of leading a good, productive, clean life has been stolen from you by drugs. Drugs will mean more to you than your own parents or other loved ones or anything that you ever valued in life.

Please pay close attention to the following narrative, "I Am Your Disease." It is a composite of many drug addicts compiled by Heiko Ganzer, Psychotherapist, who is a Licensed Clinical Social Worker, and Certified Addictions and Substance Abuse Counselor with Phoenix Psychotherapy. You can read more about Mr. Ganzer and his efforts to help addicted people by logging on to: http://www.heiko.com/

To the parents of a child lost to addiction who are reading this book, I offer my heartfelt condolences. We suffer a double whammy. Not only do we suffer the loss of our child, we suffer the stigma from the community, of having lost a child to drugs. The "Not my child" parents and the "Well, if they had been raised properly none of this would have happened" parents, are ignorant of the facts of addiction. They don't mean to deliberately hurt us. They just need to be educated that yes, this can happen even to their sweet, adorable children.

This book is filled with stories of children with promise, children who were loved and nurtured by their parents and family and friends, parents who did everything that our society says to do, to raise bright, intelligent, kind, caring and compassionate children. You will read about these children's ordeals, their struggle to break free of the Addiction Monster. They are my children…your children…anybody's children.

I AM YOUR DISEASE

I Am Your Disease by the Anonymous Addict

(Written by Heiko Ganzer, LCSW, CASAC)

Well, hello there! I cannot believe I have really been talked into doing this: Telling you about myself (which obviously you as clients either don't know, or won't accept). I am going to let you know how I operate; what my strategies are, how I win, (and I love to win!).

My initial reaction was—Why should I disclose them to you? After thinking it over, it came to me that as usual, many people will read this and not consider this information anyway, so I have nothing to lose. I mean, what the heck. Why shouldn't I divulge this stuff—who's really gonna pay attention? After all, this information has been available for many years and only a few gave a damn about it. Heck, many people, even after reading this, will still foolishly continue to take me on "their" way (how this makes me chuckle).

AA/NA/GA people try to tell them things; they won't accept it. Professional counselors tell them these things; they won't accept it, but OK, you want to hear the truth directly from the horse's mouth? Read on. They teach you that I am a disease. (I snicker because many people won't even accept that!). People fail to strongly impress upon you what kind of disease you are up against. Words like progressive, and insidious have little impact on you so let me tell you what I'm all about—I AM YOUR DEADLIEST ENEMY!

I make AIDS look minuscule compared with the devastation I have caused and intend to continue to impact on humanity. I conduct my business of mutilation and destruction in a very business-like, highly productive, orderly manner that results in me being extremely successful! I have an insatiable desire to torture, maim and destroy. I am totally vicious! I am brutal! I have perfected my skills of deception to an art form!

Early on, in the beginning of my attack on you, I can make myself almost invisible. I take you down ever so slowly and skillfully at first because I sure as heck don't want you to become aware of me. That might frighten you away.

I am the Master of Manipulation! As my progression becomes more visible, I most emphatically am not going to let your frustration and anger be directed at me. No, no, no! I tell you it's the job, it's your spouse, and it's the kids. God forbid you should ever wise-up that it's ME. So I have you lash out at the only people who really care about you.

How I revel as I see you thrashing about throwing powder-puff punches at the world. I continually whisper outright lies in your ear and incredibly, you buy right into them. Remember when I told you "THIS TIME IT WILL BE ALRIGHT!" or "SURE YOU WENT OVERBOARD IN THE PAST, BUT THAT WON'T HAPPEN AGAIN" and my all-time classic—" YOU CAN DO IT YOUR WAY. YOU DON'T NEED ANY HELP!" Each time I lie to you, and you listen to me, I betray you. Look at your track record chump! My paramount reason for being on this earth is to make certain you never achieve your full potential or enjoy the things you deserve.

I see you start project after project, but I keep you from completing them so you rarely ever enjoy a feeling of accomplishment. I keep you chasing two rabbits at the same time and grin as I watch your dreams of tomorrow become unfulfilled promises of yesterday.

With the young I damage your potential, destroy your initiative. What pleasure I get from stunting your emotional growth, and converting you into a "never-wuz." With older people I remove the enjoyment of your autumn years, and make you into a "has-been." I adore screwing up parents. Instead of you moving forward with your lives, I suck you dry with worry and concern about the fate of your kids. In the face of all logic, reasoning and just plain common sense, Mr./Mrs. Compulsivity, you keep listening to me, and your reward for foolishly doing this is that I BETRAY YOU AGAIN, AND AGAIN, AND AGAIN!

Beginning to get the picture, Pal? I'm not exactly what you would call Mr. Nice Guy! I am a high-tech conversationalist! I just love to convert beautiful, sensitive, caring productive people into self-centered, omnipotent blood-sucking leeches who day-by-day drain their loved ones emotionally, physically, and financially. I give you selective hearing; so you hear only what I want you to hear! I give you tunnel vision; so you see what I want you to see! I roundly applaud myself as you begin to stumble through life as I prevent you from hearing and growing. How you delight me as you continually permit me to twist your thinking! By the way, pal-o-mine, I not only get a big boot out of messing you up, I am without peer when it comes to wrecking everyone who cares about you and whom you care about.

I convince you, of course, that you are only hurting yourself, no one else! As things begin getting a little tackier (that's called PROGRESSION), and unbelievably you still listen to me, I advance more rapidly within you. I cheer you on as you make emotional yo-yo's out of those who still stand at your side. Of course, you mean all those wonderful promises you make to them like "NO MORE, NEVER AGAIN," etc.

I make damn sure you never carry them out by enticing you to have just one card game, one drink, one joint, one line, or just make one little old bet. You'd better believe I don't want you wising up to the fact that I am breaking the spirit of the other people in your life; that I am causing them TEN TIMES the amount of pain and sorrow that I'm dishing out to you.

Under my influence—I grin when you say things you would not have said, I smile softly as you begin not doing things you should. I chuckle as I witness you doing things you never would have done, and I let out a real belly laugh as you begin doing unthinkable things that inflict horrible pain on those you love which now cause you even higher levels of guilt, remorse, and shame. I become ecstatic every time I witness those tears running down the faces of defenseless individuals and children who you are threatening and terrorizing (your very own spouse and kids).

I must admit I am thrilled to my toes as I rip the very life out of the people around you. Get a load of this—the target that gives me the greatest satisfaction in destroying are YOUR KIDS! I am delighted by every opportunity to keep getting them so upset and off balance by what is going on that they do not stand a chance of growing up without being severely scarred. Look at the millions, yes millions, of untreated ACOA's ACOG's, I've got romping around this country all screwed up! How I chuckle when you say "YOU'LL DIE" IF YOU DRINK, BET OR USE AGAIN! First of all you know damn well you don't really believe that, (just look at your past track record).

I do not kill people; well, sometimes I do, but when that happens it really ticks me off; obviously I socked it to that person too hard. Heck, when they die, the games are over and I've got to find a new CHUMP to take their place. Hey baby, I'd rather keep playing with them; destroy them a little at a time. No, I do my damnedest not to kill you since I want you to live—miserable, wretchedly, horribly!

One way I get my jollies is from being the world's greatest collector. Didn't know that, did you Pal? Got a warehouse the size of Africa! I happily take things away from you that rightfully belong to you. These are things that you have worked hard for, earned, and deserve. I laugh all the time; I rob you of them and store them so I can enjoy my thievery when things get a little dull.

See, there's John's RESPECT over there; and Mary's MORALITY. That's what's left of Frank's HONOR, look at this, what a blast I had ripping away Helen's INTEGRITY, and did I ever have a ball taking away young Bob's ENTHUSIASM.

How I savor fondling these trophies from my past and present robberies. Hey, get a load of all those jobs over there, how sweet it was grabbing them, and how about that pile of previously good marriages? Had a ball destroying them. Down there in that pit is where I keep active people's SELF-ESTEEM. There's Don's FREEDOM (laughed like heck when they put him in the slammer). This pile of rubble makes me just shiver with ecstasy, don't you recognize it? It used to be people's CREDIBILITY. And here sweetheart is my most prized stolen possession. Yep that big steel cage is full of thousands of broken people, what a fantastic sight all of them stumbling around! Know what I stole from them? THEMSELVES. Certainly one of my award-winning traits is to steal away YOU! I have absolutely perfected my techniques for causing the process of self-abandonment. What I excel most at is taking you away from YOU!

I'm also the unequaled master at converting things; early on I convert you into a procrastinator thus letting you build up unnecessary tension, and stress. I adore converting warm, caring people into self-centered, omnipotent jackasses, and bright, intelligent people into bumbling, fourteen carat idiots. I am the absolute Champion of Deception! I get one heck of a bang doing my Muhammed Ali "ROPA-DOPA" routine on you. I make believe you've got me whipped (that, CHUMP is called complacency) and when you let your guard down (start missing meetings) I beat the heck out of you again! How I applaud you and cheer you on each time you get into the fight ring with me again—Hurry, you fool! Love it when you keep coming at me with your right fist cocked; your big punch that you're going to flatten me with. What a laugh! Of course I make sure you don't get wise to the fact that I'm cutting your face to ribbons with my jabs. I let you ignore the blood running down your face from the cuts I've inflicted over your eyes that blind you even further.

I go from grinning, to smirking, to belly-laughing as you stumble around throwing powder puff punches that achieve nothing except to further tire, frustrate, and anger you. Eventually I get quite bored by it all and deck you, and you, you fool, expect me to go to a neutral corner. Hey stupid, I know no honor; I abide by no rules; I am the dirtiest of the street fighters, and I thoroughly, totally, fully enjoy your suffering. How I relish the sight of you, a person of honor, struggling to get to your feet. I stand right next to you and as you get to your knees, I kick you right in the head before you can get to your feet again; (Maybe now you'll understand why relapses are so devastating). I am extremely proficient at map-making. Didn't know that either did you cupcake? I gleefully talk you into using and following MY map!

Oh, to entice you I write on it destinations such as High, Partying, Excitement, etc., etc., etc. In truth they all lead but to one place: And it's not Heaven! You can be very sure, CHUMP, I will do everything possible to camouflage that from you until you have journeyed quite a long and destructive distance with me. How I thrill when I witness clinicians providing their clients with "Tools" to overcome me, and then you meet up with me on the front lines threatening me with your garden trowel. Hey hero don't you see I have a tank and twenty crack ground troops? I will annihilate you, you poor simpleton!

This is a war, not a garden party you are involved in and, something else you apparently don't realize—I do not engage in this war alone! Only a fool would do that (like you do stupid). I, the super strategist, enlist the aid of my allies. The Dealers, the Casinos, Business Deals, Horses? My hired hit men! Your so-called "friends" are actually my "assassins." Mess around with them and they will take you out of play, time after time, after time. I convince you that your hoopla pals in the gin mills and OTB parlors are your true-blue buddies. I sure as hell, make sure you don't listen to the propaganda spoken by the people who care about you—perish the thought! I love to puff you up and feed into that big fat egotistical head of yours, the lie that you are in control—and incredibly you fall for that outright malarkey over, and over, and over again.

Hey gigolo, hey pompous, the moment that you place one bet, CHUMP, one drink, CHUMP, one line CHUMP, one joint, CHUMP, you are a walking time bomb and you're gonna go boom! Heaven forbid you should ever look at your lousy track record for if you ever did it would become exceedingly clear what a swollen-headed prominent, superb ignoramus I am making out of you! Dear me, that does sound a bit sarcastic now doesn't it? Well, you can bet your tush I meant it to be!

Hey c'mon, I always give you what you ask me to—numb out your trouble! You don't really expect me to tell you about the consequences do you? Hey brother, hey sister, what do you expect of me? Surely not to tell you that with each relapse the price is getting a hell of a lot steeper. That the IOU's are piling up and that each time I numb out what is bothering you, I also automatically numb out your access to your intelligence, your logic, and your upbringing. When you are overcome with remorse, guilt, shame, and anxiety, then you poor fool I tell you my favorite lie. The lie that I can fix all that stuff too so you fall for it and drink or gamble some more and the whirlpool of your addiction now progresses ever faster and deeper.

Beginning to get the picture honeybunch? I'm not exactly Mr. Nice Guy or Ms. Friendly! I'll bet you didn't realize that I sit in on every group therapy session, every one-to-one counseling session every AA/NA/GA or GAMANON meeting. How I love the "counselor-pleaser" type, the "clam-upper." I could just kiss the "I don't give a damner," and the "liar" sends chills up and down my spine as I'll be able to grind their faces into the dirt in short order with very little effort needed on my part.

FINAL TIDBITS: I convince you, you are only hurting yourself—and then relish every tortured moment that you dish out to those who love you. I whisper deliciously destructive lies into your ear in a most convincing manner. Lies like "they'll never fire you," and of course I go into ecstasy when I witness the shame for you and your family. It gives me goose bumps when I convince you you'll never be arrested as your future grinds to a halt when you see the flashing lights of a cop's car at your home, or the Feds at the front door! I howl with delight when your bookie or loan shark calls in his bets and you don't have a dime to your name! Just break an arm or slam that hand! Well, Sweetie Pies, I've told you some of my secrets; told you some of my strategies, shared some of my attack plans. Of course, I'm banking on many of you not listening to what I've told you, or thinking it was hogwash and dribble. I intend to capitalize on that and convert you into a CHUMP again—CHUMP!

So long for now, you gorgeous active person you! Of course we shall meet again—and again! I'm looking forward to that! And for those of you in early recovery, Au revoir---certainly not so long, you're doing real good kids!

I AM YOUR DISEASE
(THE MANY FACES OF ADDICTION)

DRUGS

We have turned our backs on people suffering from the disease of addiction, with our cavalier attitude that "only bad people do drugs."

The stories that follow, by caring, loving parents and siblings, will show you just how wrong our collective thinking was.

GOOD KIDS DO DRUGS TOO!
YOURS MAY BE ONE OF THEM...

SCOTT GRAEME MCGINNIS, RN

JULY 29, 1971 – DECEMBER 1, 2002

(AGE 31)

ACCIDENTAL MULTIPLE DRUG TOXICITY

"MOM, NOBODY WAKES UP ONE DAY AND DECIDES TO BE AN ADDICT."

"Sherry, answer the phone." Those four, very ordinary words, spoken to me by my husband, were the beginning of what would become our nightmarish descent into an existence that we had long feared might happen, but never really believed it would be so.

It was 1:15 a.m., Monday morning, December 2, 2002. Why does it seem that THE CALL always comes when you're in bed sleeping? I know that bad news arrives at any time of the day or night but when the phone rings during the day we tend to assume it's nothing bad, maybe a friend calling or, at worst, a telephone solicitor. However, when the phone rings late at night or in the wee, small hours of the morning, you know it has to be bad. Nobody is calling you at that time to tell you that you've won the lottery or have just been promoted. No, your gut tells you that it's bad news.

I answered the phone and it was our local police department calling from their cell phone. They were standing outside our front door. They either didn't knock or they did and we didn't hear them.

So they called. I picked up the phone to hear a detective asking me to go to my front door.

I threw my robe on over my pajamas and flung myself down the hallway to the front door as quickly as I could, all the while my heart beating so rapidly in my chest, I thought it would explode. I didn't know what was wrong but I knew something was very, very wrong. My husband had to make a trip to the bathroom first so I was the one who greeted the two detectives.

Their calm, indifferent manner didn't portend the absolute gravity of the visit. They asked me matter-of-factly if my son's name was Scott and was he born on July 29th, 1971. I answered in the affirmative, still not knowing exactly what was going on.

I assumed my son had been in some sort of trouble. Being a drug-addicted person, he had done things that were totally out of character from his early growing up years. I thought the police were going to tell me that he had been arrested. (Boy, what a relief that would have been; if only they were here to tell me he was in jail).

It's ironic how our goals for our children evolve as they evolve into teenagers. There was a time when the thought of him going to jail would have infuriated and humiliated me but after a few run-ins with the police, you begin to face reality. Your child is in trouble. He's been in trouble before. He's a teen, he'll grow out of this; after all he comes from a loving home with two loving parents, an older brother who was a good role model and doting grandparents. Punishment will be meted out once again though, with loss of privileges, and all that that entails.

But punishment means little to a drug-addicted person. It's worth whatever punishment they're given so long as they know that soon they will be off restriction and back on the streets again looking for their next high.

So it was that I was standing outside my front door, listening to the detectives and thinking back over all the years that we'd been living our lives in quiet desperation, trying to fix our broken son.

The detectives had now gone from questioning me to filling me in on the events of the previous night. Actually it was just 3 ½ hours previous. According to the detective, Scott had been at a local bar with two "friends" when he suddenly complained that he didn't feel well. Apparently he gave one of the men his car keys, saying that he was too sick to drive. The three of them allegedly got into Scott's car with Scott sitting in the front passenger seat. According to the detectives, Scott then slumped over in the seat and wasn't breathing. One of the young men allegedly tried doing CPR on him and thought that he had gotten him breathing again.

I stood at my front door listening to the detective relate this story to me, all the while not comprehending the enormity of the situation. Not even when the detective told me that the men had taken him to the hospital (why didn't they call 911?) but "he didn't make it."

Didn't make what? My mind refused to think logically. I was still thinking that my son was in jail. I stood there in the warm December air that is so typical of the weather in Florida, and waiting to be told what jail he was in. The detective, now realizing that I wasn't grasping the situation, finally had to say the words that no parent ever wants to hear and I'm sure that she was dreading having to relate to me..." He passed away at 10:30."

"NO!!!!!!!!!!!!!!!!!!!" I wailed. Over and over and over, "NO! NO! NO!" My screams pierced the stillness of the night and brought my husband running. With total panic in his voice, he asked me what was wrong.

SCOTT'S DEAD!!!!!!!!!!! "OH NO! NO! NO!" My husband yelled in his loud, booming voice. "NO!!!" It's almost, as if we scream NO! loudly, and long enough, the situation will reverse and all will be well again.

We were not prepared for this. What parent is? Even though our handsome, wonderful son had suffered from the disease of addiction for 14 years, and had battled it with every fiber of his being, we still were not prepared for the reality of the inevitable end. We lived those last 14 years worrying constantly and hoping that every parent's worst nightmare would not happen to us. You know how it goes...these things happen to other people!

We did not take Scott's addiction lying down. We had tried to help. We had called two police departments and given them the names and numbers of dealers. My husband offered to take the police to one of the homes and show them where the dealers lived. Nobody took him up on the offer. Nobody cared…just another drug addict.

Scott had been in and out of rehabs. He TRIED. He desperately tried to beat the disease. He hated himself for being addicted. He hated that he could not control the enormous appetite for the drug. He was so disciplined in every other aspect of his life.

Scott always took great care of his body. He ate a very healthy diet, he exercised, he ran, he worked out with weights. He was a surfer. He exercised his mind too. He was an avid reader and writer, even being paid for something he had written. He was an extremely talented musician.

When Scott was 16, he had his own band, Tantrum. They were good! They were very good! Practice was at our house and it was always filled with teen-age girls who were crazy over him.

Crack cocaine was just coming into prominence in the mid to late eighties in Florida and I would have long talks with both of my sons, imploring them to never do drugs. I explained how even the first hit of cocaine can kill some people. We never lied to our children. We gave them forthright, honest information about the dangers of hard drugs. Both of our sons assured us they would not even try cocaine.

On Scott's 17th birthday, one of his older band mates laid out a line of cocaine for him as his birthday present. Scott knew he shouldn't do it. He also was 17, and teens tend to think they're invincible. As he would later explain to me, "Mom, you said it could kill me and it didn't so then I didn't believe you."

Scott was immediately addicted! It was no time before he graduated to the crack form of cocaine. He loved it! Couldn't get enough of it! He later told me that he and his friends would spend their days planning how they were going to make (or get) enough money to supply them with all the crack they wanted for the rest of their lives.

Drugs made Scott feel "normal," he told me. He imagined this was how other people felt, the normal people. Scott, like so many addicted people, had very little self-esteem.

I AM YOUR DISEASE

Scott was no dummy. He had a very high IQ of 150. Even though he was failing all of his classes because his efforts were all aimed at scoring more crack, he made straight A's on his report card for the last six weeks that he was in high school. He just wanted to show people that he was not stupid. He certainly wasn't, but he just didn't care about anything other than feeding his insatiable appetite for crack (later heroin and "meth" would be added to his favorites).

There will always be people who say that nobody forced the cocaine on him. True! Probably nobody forced the cigarette on the person who went on to develop lung cancer. Probably nobody forced the sugary cookies on the person who went on to develop diabetes. We have to stop blaming and hating the person. We can hate the disease but first we have to have an understanding of ADDICTION.

Research is showing that there is indeed an addiction gene. Unfortunately as of right now there is only one way of knowing whether or not you have the gene. But it's like closing the barn door after the horse has gotten out. It's too late!

Prior to moving to Florida, our sons were brought up in our home state of New Jersey and then when they were 4, and 3, we moved to the country in North Carolina. There they played in the woods, built forts and did things that normal country boys do. My husband and I devoted our time to them. When the boys joined the Cub Scouts, I became a Den Mother and my husband became a Webelos leader and then for three years he was the Cubmaster.

My husband and our two sons became certified SCUBA divers. We took nice vacations in Tennessee. My husband took them camping and hiking. We did everything together as a family. We ate all of our family meals together at the dining room table, discussing, listening, laughing, arguing…but we were together. Our children were loved and adored. For several years they attended a private school. We tried to always give them the very best without spoiling them.

Weekends at our house were always filled with our sons and their friends playing. I would make them all pizza at night and my husband would make them breakfast in the morning. Our house was filled with love and raucous boyish laughter.

I am so glad that we had these wonderful years because they give me solace. These are the memories that I draw on to sustain me when the deeper, darker ones creep into my mind to torture me; the What Ifs, and the I Should Haves, and the Why Didn't I's and the Why, Why, Why is my baby gone?

The absolute joy that we once experienced, is gone from our lives now. Our happiness is now on a different plateau, never reaching the highs of before. Yes, we have learned how to smile again and even to laugh. We still take great pride and joy in our other son, Dale, but nothing will ever be the same.

Scott was an EMT. He then became a Paramedic and then an RN. He accomplished all of this while suffering from the disease of Addiction. He was what they call a functioning addict. His goal was to be a physician. He certainly had the brains for it and the bedside manner. He could charm the birds out of the trees.

Scott was compassionate to the point where he could not bear to see a stray or injured animal. Most of our animals have been brought home by Scott. "Mom," he would say, " you should see this cat. He's the most beautiful cat I've ever seen and he's being abused and mistreated. Can I bring him home?" Of course, I would relent and then in he would walk with the most ordinary looking cat! But they were all beautiful to him.

From the beginning of Scott's life, he marched to the beat of his own drum. For some reason he lacked self-esteem. He was handsome with huge, brown eyes, a great physique, an inquisitive mind, a drop dead gorgeous smile, a way above average intellect, and girls and women of every age just adoring him. He was one of the most compassionate, caring people I've ever known in my life. He knew we loved him unconditionally. Still, he had no self-esteem.

What some people took for a bit of arrogance was Scott's way of trying to compensate for lack of self-esteem. Lack of self-esteem seems to be a big factor in the lives of drug addicted people. I don't believe they lose their self-esteem by becoming addicted to drugs. I believe they become addicted to drugs because they don't have self-esteem to begin with. The addiction just compounds the condition.

Scott had his own home, filled with 4 cats and his beloved dog. Fortunately his cats have a loving home, living with Scott's girlfriend and we took his wonderful dog.

We had Scott's memorial service at one of his favorite surfing spots, and we brought his dog, Kazak, with us. Kazak was quiet and still during the entire service. All of the mourners walked to the water's edge and threw flowers into the ocean. Scott's friend paddled out into the waves on the surfboard that we had bought for Scott as his Christmas present that year. Sadly, he never knew about it or got to use it.

Kazak never took her eyes off of Scott's friend on his surfboard. As his friend began to scatter his ashes, suddenly Kazak emitted the most mournful, sorrowful howl that we had ever heard and have not heard since. She knew! Her best buddy was gone, and she knew it.

A few nights before Scott died, he came over to our house. He was sick. Drug sick. He was lying on the couch with his head in my lap as I stroked his head and hair. He then reached his arm up around my neck and said, "I love you mom." We're the kind of family that always says I love you and means it.

I wish I could say that was the last time I talked to my son, but it wasn't. The next night, he called to say that he had lost yet another nursing job, all due to his addiction. We had an argument and Scott knew I was very upset.

His dad and I decided to finally give Tough Love a chance. After all, nothing that we had tried had worked so far. When Scott called and left a message on our answering machine the next morning, we didn't return his call. He had said that he would make it on his own. We didn't call him the next day either. That was a Sunday, December 1, 2002. That night he OD'd.

Never again will I pick up the phone and hear him saying, "What are youuuuuuuuuuu doing?" Then we would talk, sometimes for hours. He would tell everyone that I was his best friend. I still have a note that he wrote when he was young…" My mom is the best mom in the whole world."

His brother is now an only child again, who will have no one after his father and I pass on. He doesn't have a brother anymore to share the family stories with, to share his experiences with. He does not deserve this fate. Addiction has spread its ugly tentacles and grabbed his life too, denying him the love and companionship of his brother.

Our hearts try to heal, and it seems as if a scab starts to form. Then suddenly out of nowhere something will trigger a memory or feeling so profound that the scab rips off and we must begin to try to heal again.

Scott was 31 years, 4 months, and 2 days old when he passed away. So young! He had a whole lifetime ahead of him. Scott lived and loved passionately. He didn't do anything by halves. Skydiving! Surfing in Australia! Bungee jumping!

As I write this, with tears streaming down my face, I have one consolation. Scott knew how much he was loved! Other people have told us that he knew we loved him and how thankful he was for that. At least our boy went to his death knowing that he took our love with him.

The official autopsy report says that he died of accidental multiple drug toxicity but I will always wonder if he didn't die of a broken heart. He would wake up every morning depressed because of the mess that he had made out of his life. Yet he would never count the many wonderful things that he had accomplished, what a terrific Paramedic he was, what a kind and compassionate nurse he was, what a loving, caring human being he was, and what a wonderful son he was.

Our lives as we knew them, will never be the same. People ask me how am I doing? I know what they want me to say. "Oh, just fine thank you."

Well I've been a lot finer I can tell you that. Not a day goes by that I don't mourn the loss of our son.

There is a huge nursing shortage in the country and every time I see an ad on TV for a nurse, I cry. Every time I get mail in his name offering him a job, I cry. If an ambulance passes by, my heart sinks, not only for the unfortunate person inside the ambulance, but for my son who is no longer here to administer comfort and help to that person.

Drug-addicted people must do all they can to avoid "triggers," those nasty little things that pop into their head and scream to them to do more drugs. They can avoid certain triggers by dodging people that they used to do drugs with or they can avoid going to certain parts of town or watching drug-themed movies, or any one of a number of things.

But how does a parent avoid these triggers? Every time we turn around there is another reminder of our child, of our loss. One second you're doing fine and the next, a person walks by you wearing the same scent that your child wore, or similar clothing, or walking with a similar gait and suddenly your world collapses again. There seems to be no escaping it, so we try to devise ways to get around it. We slowly try learning how to live again, how to find meaning to life, how to sustain our relationships with those who love us. We put on The Mask, and smile wanly, not for our benefit but so as not to make the other person feel uncomfortable. It's strange…we are in great pain yet we try to spare others our pain.

Looking back on Scott's life, I am filled with tremendous joy and pride in who he was, his accomplishments, his kindness, his goodness, his generosity. If he had ten cents, he would give you five. If he had steak for dinner, his beloved dog had steak. He couldn't stand for anyone to be angry with him, especially me, and he was always the first one to make up with anyone after a fight. Scott had no problem saying, "I'm sorry, I was wrong."

I wish that I could just focus on all the good things, but I am tortured by memories of his sadness, his low self-esteem, his disease, the times he told me how many times he woke up in the morning wishing that he was dead. I think of him alone in his house with just his cats and dog for company, wanting to do the right thing but being pulled down into the bowels of hell by the drugs.

Scott never kept anything to himself and he shared stories of the good times and the bad times with me. He knew there was nothing that he couldn't talk to me about, nothing that he couldn't confide in me.

He had the best luck in the world and conversely, the worst luck in the world. He strove to be the best at whatever he did and he succeeded. He graduated first in his class from EMT school. He was an outstanding paramedic and the best nurse, full of compassion and caring for his patients.

Unfortunately, he was also the best drug addict in the world! Whatever he did, he was going to be top-notch.

Whenever Scott would land yet another really good job, his dad and I would worry. We knew he would lose the job, because Scott would always shoot himself in the foot. He never felt that he deserved anything good that came his way.

He wanted desperately to succeed and to enjoy the admiration of those he loved, and who loved him, yet the Addiction Monster always made sure that he threw it all away.

When people ask me how many children I have, I always respond with "Two. One lives nearby and one lives in my heart." I will always be the mother of two children. Nothing, not even the monster of addiction can take that away from me.

I will miss and love Scott every minute of every day until I take my last breath. I know of no crueler fate than to outlive your child.

Scott didn't deserve his fate. He made a wrong choice at a very young, impressionable age and once that choice was made, there was no turning back. No tap backs, no second chances. He was born with the Addiction Gene and it determined the course of his life…and death.

For 14 years our energies were consumed with trying to help Scott. No matter how many children you have, if one child is sick you try to help that child. You do everything you can to heal your sick child. You hope that your other child, or children, will understand what you're going through and will understand the need to be there for that child, even if it means putting your other child's/children's needs aside for awhile.

Scott was our baby. How I wish he could have lived to have a wife and baby of his own. He would have made one hell of a dad. He enjoyed kids; maybe because he, himself, was just a big kid.

I've learned so much about addiction and the addiction gene since Scott's death. How I wish with all my heart that I had really and truly understood what he was going through at the time. The times when he would tell me, "Mom, I'm an addict. I will have to fight this for the rest of my life."

I would say, "No, Scott. You aren't an addict. You can beat this."

I realize now that I was in great denial. I didn't want to believe that my son was an addict. It's one of the ugliest words in our language. How could such an intelligent, kind, loving, caring person have such an affliction? Because he was born with the addiction gene, didn't know it, and made a mistake. Who, amongst us, has not made a mistake? His mistake cost him his life and left ours in tatters.

I recently came across his horoscope and, although I don't personally believe in horoscopes, I was amazed at how accurately this described my youngest son. Read on...

Leo Traits:" Powerful, creative, arrogant, intolerant, warm-hearted, opinionated.

"There are no shrinking violets in the kingdom of the Leo. His roar can be heard from a mile away. He is self-assured, confident and he always stands out in a crowd. He has a natural knack as an entertainer – He is highly theatrical and dramatic. He is exuberant and magnetic, and people love to bask in his sunlight. While his confidence is often mistaken for arrogance and an overbearing attitude, nobody can deny the fact that he is open-hearted, humane and genuine in everything that he does. Because of his bold nature, he tends to detest a life that is mundane.

Leos feel most natural and productive in a leadership position.

Leos are very generous and easily forgive those who hurt them. They always mean well, but sometimes their good intentions translate into being overbearing and trying to push their opinions on others without letting their own voice be heard. His ego becomes wounded easily, but it is effectively masked by his sense of bravado.

If there's a position at the top, it's likely you'll find a Leo inhabiting it, but as a Leo, he probably expects to achieve it right away rather than having to work at it. He'd rather give the orders than receive them.

There's something beautiful in his simplicity – he is

uncomplicated and unabashed in his power and confidence. All the world is a stage for him, and as long as he doesn't try to constantly hog the limelight, his bright personality will continue to shine in the lives of those who surround him."

That was my son to a T!

I relive the words spoken to me by the police detective over and over and over, every day of my life… "He passed away at 10:30." "He passed away at 10:30." Why do I torture myself with those words reverberating in my mind constantly? Is it because I'm trying to accept it? If I keep saying it will it finally sink in? Yes, I know my son is dead. What a horrible word! Dead! Oh, the finality of it! But do I accept it? Apparently not. So I repeat the detective's words until I am almost physically sick.

The rational part of me does accept it to some degree but the emotional part of me has not made that transition yet. I'm working on it. I've been told that it is not fair to the living to dwell on the dead. This is true. I have another wonderful son, our first-born. The one who made us parents for the first time. I have a loving husband and am lucky enough to still have my dad and many wonderful friends so I try very hard to stay in the land of the living although my heart is not always here.

We try to keep Scott's memory alive. We donated a nursing scholarship in his name, and we have given to many animal charities in his name. Scott may be gone from our lives but his legacy of kindness and goodness will continue as long as we're alive.

No man is an island. What we do in our life has a ripple effect that spreads out to those who know and love us.

To young people who may be reading this I would say please make your ripples gentle and kind so that you may leave a legacy of love and pride, not hurt and despair. Do whatever you can to avoid negative peer pressure, avoid drugs at all costs! Respect yourself and your body and mind. Don't convince yourself that you're cool because you do drugs. Drugs are definitely not cool! They make you a fool.

Be a leader! Not a follower! Don't be afraid to stand up for yourself and your beliefs. Maybe if you refuse drugs, that first drink of alcohol, that first cigarette, that first joint, maybe your friends will follow suit.

If they ridicule you for saying " no" then they really aren't your friends. Choose your friends wisely. They will serve you well in the years to come.

Childhood is just a brief blip on the radar screen of your life. You can survive it and go on to lead a happy, fulfilling and challenging life. If you stay away from drugs, believe me, one day you will look back and be so glad that you did. You will have a life!!

You can't get Hugs if you're dead from Drugs!

My message to parents is to love your children and let them know it! Show it! It doesn't mean that this will protect you from what we've been through but at least, should the same fate befall your family you'll have some peace knowing that your children felt loved and cherished!

Scott's story as told by his loving mom and best friend, Sheryl Letzgus McGinnis, Palm Bay, Florida.

"I loved the boy with the utmost love of which my soul is capable of and he is taken from me - yet in the agony of my spirit in surrendering such a treasure, I feel a thousand times richer than if I had never possessed it." Letter of William Wordsworth on the death of his son, in 1812.

Scott's website: www.geocities.com/scottmcginnis31/index.html

SHERYL LETZGUS MCGINNIS WITH HEIKO GANZER

A poem written for Scott by Mom

FOREVER 31

Forever 31,
Is what you'll always be
For that's how old you were
When you left so suddenly.

I know you didn't want to leave
Your dreams so full of hope
Now we are left to cry and grieve
And somehow try to cope.

I'll never forget your loving ways
And that smile! And those eyes so brown
They will live with me for all my days
Lifting me up when I am down.

Had I known when you were born
The pain your death would bring
Would I have borne you anyway?
I would not have changed a thing.

I'm just so glad we had this time
And so sad that we had to part
But you'll live forever, oh son of mine
Deep within my heart.

I AM YOUR DISEASE

A LETTER TO SCOTT

Hey Scotty-Boy,

Your dad and I and Popeye and Dale miss you and talk about you all the time. You will never, ever be forgotten during our lifetime. Your dad cries for you and it makes me so sad.

The sadness of your passing overwhelms me but the joy of having had you for a son lifts me up. I am so sorry for all of the sadness that you endured in your short life all because of one brief mistake that started the whole chain of events.

I wish I could have really understood what you were going through. You tried to tell me but I wouldn't listen. My heart hurt too much to listen to your pain. I wanted to take your pain from you but I didn't know how.

As much as I want you back Scott, to see you again, and to hug and kiss you again and to wrap my arms around you and laugh with you, and be teased by you, if you were still addicted, then as a loving mom, I couldn't ask for you to come back to me. Not if it meant you were still suffering.

The only thing I know now is that you are not suffering anymore. That is the only consolation I have. Will we ever see each other again? I don't know. I wish I could believe that we will. I suppose I will find out in my time...or not.

But if there is another realm, another time and place and you are listening to me, just know that you are so loved and missed and that we carry you in our hearts and thoughts always.

Love, your mom and best friend

KEITH TEDESCO

OCTOBER 14, 1978 – JUNE 9, 1997

(AGE 18)

ACCIDENTAL POLYDRUG TOXICITY

" MY NINE DAYS OF HELL"

It has been over nine years since the death of my son, Keith. Still a part of me has not dealt with the fact that my son died. How could he die from a drug overdose? We did what parents are supposed to do to raise happy, drug-free children.

He was smart, handsome, happy, athletic, and popular. This list goes on and on yet it still happened, he OD'd! If there was one message I could give to every parent in America it would be...Never say "Not MY child!"

Keith was the oldest of my four sons. He was born in October of 1978. We lived in a big city and decided before he started school to move to a small town. My husband and I thought our children would be safe from crime, drugs and everything else that comes with living in a big city. We now know we were so wrong. There is no safe place in this country to raise children.

Drugs are everywhere and are killing our loved ones daily. Still some believe this only happens to the bad kids, the kids who have divorced parents, the latch key kids, the poor kids. It's the parents' fault they didn't raise their children right. What fools they are.

To many I may sound angry or in denial. I have been through every emotion there is and today I feel I carry a bit of all of them within me. I know one thing---the person I once was died with my son. My family is forever changed and not one of us feels secure about anything in this life.

It was June 1, 1997, a Sunday. A bad thunderstorm was over central Florida while Keith's dad drove around looking for Keith and a 16-year-old friend. It was raining so hard he had to come home. Driving was too dangerous. A friend of mine who was the mom of the 16-year-old was sitting in my house with me in a panic. Her son had never, not come home without asking.

Things were different for me. Keith was 18 and in the last two years of his life he tried just about every drug out there. His dad worked out of town and it was very stressful raising four boys of such different ages. My youngest was just turning four.

Keith was the one son I wasn't worried about. He never gave me any problems. He loved sports and from the time he was six years old he wanted to play on a team. He started with baseball. Our family went to every practice, every game. For six years he played on the same team and when he was twelve they came in second in the state of Florida. How proud he was of the dozens of trophies he had and the fact he was also on all the All-Star Teams.

Keith was loved by his teachers and had many friends. They would always tell me how respectful he was. His coaches called him their Quiet One. Keith was always so shy and never felt he fit in. Even with several friends and as he reached his teen years with several girls chasing him he still had no confidence.

I remember him telling me a few weeks before he died, "Mom, I feel like everyone is waiting for me to leave before the party starts." Meaning no one really wanted him around. To this day I don't know why he felt like this.

In high school he wanted to try out for football. He ended up playing and is featured in his school yearbook when he was a freshman. He was very good at sports and loved playing. He also was on the weight lifting team and was number one in his weight class. He was always busy with sports or his studies, staying on the A/B honor roll.

Although he was shy he was also such a daredevil. It was like he had no fear and if someone was to try something new it would be Keith. He started dating a girl when he was sixteen who was so opposite of him. She smoked, drank and did everything Keith always said was stupid.

He always wanted to help people. He was going to get her to stop all she was doing. This didn't happen. Within no time, besides never smoking a cigarette, he started trying alcohol. Soon it was pot and from there quickly went from Rohypnol - " roofies," to ecstasy to cocaine and his last high he was ever to try...heroin.

Keith changed so much in those two years I hardly knew or understood my son anymore. He got in minor trouble with the Police, and went through the court system. He was put in a Juvenile Detention for two weeks and sent for a drug evaluation. They told me they wished all the kids there were like Keith. All he did was drink a little beer and smoke a little pot on occasion. They had kids there addicted to crack and heroin that were in so much trouble.

I thought it was just a stage he was going through and would soon stop and he would go on to live a happy life. It never happened.

I grew up in a city and time where almost everyone of my childhood friends got into drugs heavily. Only a few of them survived that life. Living this myself, I talked to Keith about every drug. We would stay up nights talking about the drugs that were around teenagers of the 1990's.

He admitted to me he had tried all of them except heroin and said he didn't like any one drug enough to use all the time. I really believed him, forgetting how well addicts can deceive the people they love most.

Back to that Sunday, his dad was coming home from out of town every other weekend. The week previously a letter came in the mail for Keith from the State Attorney's office. Even though he was 18, I opened it. He lived in my home and I knew something was wrong.

On May 1, he had been arrested for possession of crack at 2 a.m., in a well-known crack town. I was totally caught off guard, shocked and in a panic. How in the world could my son, who I saw everyday, be doing crack and I had no idea! I called his dad and told him we had a serious problem and needed to help Keith right away.

I was working part time, three nights a week back then and Friday night was a night I worked. My hours were from 6 to 9 and in those three hours things happened that would become my worst nightmare.

Keith called me at work and he was crying. He said, " Dad and I got in an argument and he said I could not live in our home and be doing drugs. He's right Mom. I am a bad example for my brothers and I really screwed up. Dad is really mad."

Such a sick feeling came over me and I asked him if he had a place to spend the weekend. I would talk to his dad and he could come home Monday and we would figure out what to do. In my mind my husband told him to leave in anger and would change his mind.

Saturday Keith's brother who is 2 1/2 years younger let Keith in his bedroom window to get a change of clothes. He had taken nothing with him. He also called home that day and I answered. He asked if dad was home and I said yes. He said, "Okay mom, I love you." Little did I know I would never hear his voice again.

The rain finally stopped on that Sunday, June 1, 1997. I got a call through to Keith and his friend's boss at 9 a.m. They both work at his restaurant and that was the last place they were. His boss told me he THOUGHT he knew where they were and would have Keith call me. This happened while my husband was out looking for them.

The next call came in at 2:45 that afternoon. The caller ID was from his boss's house. It was a new girl he had been dating about two weeks who I had only met a few times. Her words were..." You need to get to the hospital right away. Keith OD'd on heroin."

The sound, scream, whatever it was that came out of me was so horrible everyone jumped up and our dog hid under the table shaking.

My husband flew out the door, got in his truck and drove to the hospital. My friend and I were so shook up we couldn't drive so I had to call my sister-in-law to drive us. Her son was home in bed and had sneaked into her house around 11 a.m.

That was the longest drive I ever took. We didn't know if he was dead or alive. Keith was strong and healthy, he would be okay, we would bring him home and get him help is what I was trying to tell myself. Yet I had a feeling of pure dread and fear but really had no idea what I was about to go through.

I'll never forget the look on his dad's face when we arrived at the hospital. I knew it was bad. He hadn't seen Keith yet and they kept saying we could see him as soon as they were done with tests. They were doing a CAT scan.

I was so distraught I started to panic and felt like I was going to faint and was begging them to let me see my son. They finally took us back to the ER and there lay my beautiful son with his hair sun-bleached and his skin so tan from being at the beach surfing. Tubes were down his throat, up his nose, machines everywhere and his body was shaking uncontrollably.

People were all around him doing different things to him. "What in the hell is going on?" I thought as I started screaming. "KEITH!!! KEITH IT'S OKAY, MOM'S HERE!" My husband crying his heart out looking at him.

We were taken to a room where we were told he was in full respiratory arrest when the EMTs arrived at the house that he was at. They gave him Narcon several times and it didn't work because he had died. They shocked his heart and got it to start pumping but he still wouldn't breathe so they put him on life support. We have a doctor, we were told, coming in soon to look at his CAT scan to see if he suffered brain damage but to prepare ourselves. They didn't think he would make it through the night.

Not make it through the night???? When I heard those words I felt like my life drained right out of me. Really there are no words to explain these feelings. Keith had no brain activity except for a small part of his brainstem which is all involuntary movement. He was in a coma and on life support. I was in a state of shock I guess because I really could not grasp what I was seeing.

He did live through the night. In fact he lived for nine days! I never once left that hospital and only left his room when they needed to wash him up and change the bed. I held his hand and tried making deals with God and everyone I could think of to let my son live.

Everyday he got worse as I sat there watching my son slowly die. Organ after organ failing. Family and friends coming in and out day and night. Teenagers on their knees sobbing for him. The hospital allowed everyone to see him, two at a time for 5 minutes.

I would not leave Keith. In my heart I knew he was dying and no way was he going to be alone! If love could have saved him he'd be alive today.

On June 9th the doctors told us they could only keep him on life support for so long. He had developed pneumonia and his body was starting to do what they call "posturing." He would suddenly jump up a little and the entire bed would move. I didn't understand half of what they were saying but this wasn't good. They said we needed to think about turning off life support, that there was nothing anyone could do now but pray.

How in the world do you turn off your child's life support? Yet how in the world do you watch him lie there knowing he would never live a normal life again? Just lie in a coma for as long as he lived. As hard as it was we signed the papers and had to write a letter saying Keith had said he wanted this.

At 9 p.m., on June 9th, our family gathered around Keith's bed. The machines were shut down. For ten minutes I watched in horror, screaming and jumping as I watched my son turning blue and gasping for air. At 9:10 he took his last breath along with my heart.

I relive this over and over and go through the WHYs and IFs. Until the day I die I will never understand how Keith's so-called friends watched him dying and knew he needed help yet waited until it was too late to call 911. I'll never understand how such a kind, smart, loved young man with his whole life ahead of him could lose everything including his life so fast.

But I do understand that this country is in dire need of drug education, rehabs and more research done on addiction. I do understand that your children can die from a drug overdose. And I finally do understand that this can happen to anyone, any family.

Keith's story as told by his loving mom, Pam Tedesco, Oviedo, Florida

"It has been said, " time heals all wounds". I do not agree. The wounds remain. In time, the mind, (protecting its sanity), covers them with scar tissue and the pain lessens. But, it is never gone." ~Rose Fitzgerald Kennedy

http://www.geocities.com/keithtedesco97/index.html

JASON ANTHONY BARGANIER

OCTOBER 21ST, 1974 - MARCH 1ST, 1998

(AGE 24)

LSD

"ONCE UPON A CHILD"

My son Jason struggled with the disease of addiction for five years. Every day I wondered if this would be the day Jason died. I thought he could be murdered like his life-long best friend, Joey. Or he could overdose on drugs or die in an accident because he was high. I imagined almost every possible cause of death that could result from his drug use.

It was Joey's murder that sealed Jason's fate. I knew when Joey died that Jason wouldn't live long. I prayed I was wrong but something inside me knew Jason was destined to die. I kept telling myself if I could keep Jason alive until he was 30, he could make it. I thought if he made it to thirty he would grow up, fall in love, have a family, and leave the dark underworld of drugs far behind him. But still there was that part of me that wondered how and when Jason would die.

Joey's murder devastated Jason. He was wild with grief and anger. He was filled with guilt. He believed that if he had stayed home that night instead of going out of town to a "rave," he would have been there to stop Joey's murder. He blamed himself for the loss of Joey's life.

Joey was the kindest, gentlest person I had ever known. He had the face of a cherub. He had a smile so beautiful and perfect that it made you smile too. Jason had grown up with Joey since the fourth grade. They were closer than if they had been brothers. They told each other everything. They dated sisters. They were never apart. If you saw one the other was close by...but not on that terrible night.

Four "friends" were responsible for the murder of Joey. They came in the wee hours of the morning, on August 1st, 1995. After an argument over some LSD the boys had sold them, they shot Joey in the back of the head execution style. They had planned on killing Jason that night too not knowing that he had made a last minute decision to go to that Rave in Nashville. Joey was only 18 years old when he died.

I was completely unaware that the boys had gotten involved with LSD. They had begun selling large quantities. They found they could make so much money selling LSD that they quit their jobs and sold drugs fulltime.

It was after Joey's murder that Jason sat me down and told me the whole story. The boy who was responsible for planning Joey's murder had been someone they had taken in off the streets and given a home. He had lied about his background and the boys felt sorry for him. Soon their money began disappearing and eventually they kicked him out. When he wanted to buy some LSD that day the boys decided to get even and rip him off like he had done them. The boys sold Mick fake LSD. Mick's revenge he had so long waited for had become reality. He had gotten revenge as he said he would since the day the boys kicked him out of their home. Our precious Joey was dead, and Jason's life was destroyed.

After several days the killers were arrested. The trigger "man" was a 16 year old boy! Mick was smart enough to get a teenager to pull the trigger thinking he wouldn't do much time. He was wrong and Jerome was tried as an adult on second degree murder. Mick and one other boy were charged and convicted of voluntary manslaughter. The fourth boy's parents sent their son into hiding. I can't imagine a parent doing such a thing. One parent's child is dead, due partly to their son. Instead of making him do the right thing and serve a couple of years in prison they sent him on the run.

As far as I know Daniel has never been captured. The boy who planned the murder only served a couple of years in jail. The trigger man was sentenced to 15 years but got out in seven. His family and friends targeted Joey's handicapped elderly grandfather with threats and harassment. They vandalized Joey's grandfather's home. They swore they would kill him if Jerome went to jail. The police did absolutely nothing about it.

At the hearing to decide whether Jerome would be charged as an adult, I stood up after the hearing was through and walked up front and stood there facing the kid who shot Joey. I told him to remember my face because I sure as hell was going to remember his. The judge ordered me removed from the courtroom and the bailiff dragged me away.

Outside of the courtroom I asked the homicide detective why the murderer was only being charged with second-degree murder when it was a premeditated homicide. The detective told me the boys all claimed it was an accident. They said they only went there to scare him. They claimed that Joey tried to run and when they went to chase him the gun accidentally discharged. I said that was bull crap. They went in the middle of the night, they wore black gloves, they brought a gun and they shot him in the back of the head. The detective looked and me and said, " Lady, I don't give a damn. It's just another murder and I have a two foot stack of them on my desk. I don't give a damn!" And he was right. No one but the people who loved Joey gave a damn.

During a parole hearing Jerome's mother had the nerve to beg Joey's mom to ask the parole board to let Jerome go free on parole. She said his life was being ruined. She never once thought about Joey's life. Not once did she think about the family and friends whose lives were shattered. Joey's mom replied, " At least your son is alive."

After Joey's murder I did everything I could to keep Jason safe. I got him an apartment upstairs in midtown and I rented the one below him so I could keep an eye on him. I paid his rent, utilities, bought his food, and clothes. I worried about his safety. I worried about all the other kids who crashed at the apartment every day and night. There were many scary episodes in the next five years. Who would ever have believed this was how my family's lives were forever going to be changed?

There were drug arrests, fights, guns, children dying. There was fear. There was danger. There was never a moment of peace since Joey's death. There were FBI agents who kicked in doors. FBI who harassed Jason trying to get him to turn in other people for crimes they thought Jason knew about.

I remember the agents telling me one day that I needed to convince my son to cooperate and testify against a Laotian gang member who the FBI believed was responsible for a murder. I told them Jason did not know anything about the murder, and I would never tell Jason to put his life in danger by talking to them.

Jason told them over and over again that he didn't know anything about the murder but the FBI made Jason's life pure hell. In a couple of years the murder was solved and the Laotian gang member had had nothing to do with it. The FBI was wrong. For the rest of his life Jason had to call the FBI and tell them if he moved or changed jobs or they threatened to harass him and make his life hell.

The years slowly passed. Jason spiraled deeper out of control with his addictions. He had gone from pot smoking and occasionally taking LSD to using cocaine, ecstasy, crystal "meth" and other hallucinogens. The chronic drug use had begun to affect his reasoning.

His thinking became distorted and illogical. He took stupid risks. He got involved with all the wrong people. At times he became paranoid and frightened. Most of the time his logic and the way he was living made no sense to me at all. But still I didn't know the extent of the drug use. I thought he was just tall and skinny. I thought he just had a bad complexion because he was unlucky and had inherited his dad's traits. I had no idea that his poor physical health was due to chronic drug abuse.

One day I had gone upstairs to talk to Jason but he wasn't home. I asked the usual motley crew gathered at the apartment where my son could be. Finally they told me that he had been arrested the night before. I immediately called the jail to find out what the charges were and how to get him out of jail. They informed me he had been arrested for possession of LSD with intent to sell. I went to the jail and asked to see my son. After a long wait in a nasty room full of people who looked like they belonged in jail too, I was allowed to see Jason.

They led me into a room with glass walls and a chair. There my son came walking into the room with his eyes cast down at the floor. That was usual for Jason. He couldn't look me in the eye when he was in trouble. This was definitely trouble.

I asked him what happened and he told me that he had bought the LSD and was taking it to a friend's house. After he left their house he made it to a block from the apartment when he was surrounded by cop cars. They ordered him out of the car and down on the ground. They put guns to his head. They asked him if he had any weapons or drugs on him. Jason told them he had LSD in his back pocket. They handcuffed him, threw him in the back of a patrol car, and took him to jail.

Jason never knew it but the friend he had delivered the LSD to was the person who set him up to get busted in order to get out of trouble himself. It would have broken Jason's heart to learn one of his best friends had done that to him. I just sat there staring at my son. Jason told me he was so sorry and he was scared. I told him I would bail him out and I left to go see the bail bondsman.

Once Jason was released we went straight to a lawyer. We told him the situation and he told us how much money he wanted to represent my son. I, along with several of his friends, scraped up the money for the bond and a retainer for the lawyer. That began the two years of court dates and a chain of different lawyers. Eventually, the charges were dropped when Jason's latest lawyer demanded the evidence be tested.

To everyone's shock and surprise the evidence came back as blank sheets of paper. There was no LSD and Jason was finally free of the threat of 8 years in prison he had agreed to in exchange for a guilty plea. Now he feared people would think he was a narc and had turned others in to get out of trouble himself. Jason never once in his life told on a friend. His loyalty was unparalleled. He would rather take the blame for something than tell on a friend.

The drug world is full of danger, backstabbing, and the ever-present risk of death. Several years later many cops were arrested for stealing drugs and guns from the evidence room. It wasn't a surprise to me and I guess it finally vindicated Jason in the eyes of his peers.

As soon as Jason was bonded out of jail I told him I had had it with all this crap. I told him he was going to college, and he was turning his life around if it was the last thing I ever accomplished. We made an appointment at the college and we both decided that it would be a great thing for Jason.

Jason was so brilliant and had a very high IQ. School had always been a breeze for Jason. His friends would always tell me how he slept through class all week and then still managed to ace his tests on Fridays. Jason started college, got a job at a parcel delivery service working nights, and eventually got a job as a student teacher at the college he attended.

Things seemed to be going great for Jason. I was so proud of him. He was breezing through school. But soon the pressure of working two jobs and attending school got to be too much. Jason began using cocaine to stay awake so he could work his night job and attend school.

One day he came to me and told me he was in trouble. Jason told me that he had become addicted to cocaine and he couldn't stop using. I held him in my arms and cried. I begged him over and over again, "Please don't die Jason. I don't want you to die!"

Jason said, "I won't die mom. I promise but I need help." We stood there in the dining room in the dark hugging and crying. I asked him what could I do to help him and he told me he needed to go into treatment. I promised him we would find help the next day. We said good night with the promise that in the morning we would find the best place in town for him to receive treatment.

The next morning I called my boss and explained everything to him. He gave me a referral to a drug and alcohol center in town. I called them and was referred to a recovery center. I made an appointment for that afternoon. I called Jason and told him I would be picking him up and we would go together.

We arrived at the recovery center and were told to be seated. We sat there in dead silence. Jason was shaking and so was I. Finally a man came out and introduced himself as a counselor there and said he would be doing the evaluation. He took Jason into a little office and closed the door. They talked for what seemed like hours, then emerged from the room.

The man told me that Jason was eligible for treatment but we would have to see the financial office about signing a contract to pay for the long-term treatment which would last about 22 months. Even though Jason was an adult they made me sign the contract guaranteeing payment.

My son was killing himself and I would sign anything to get him into treatment. They took my son right there on the spot. No time to back out or have a change of heart. He looked so scared. I hugged him and told him everything would be okay. I told him I had faith in him that he could do this. Inside, it was the last thing I was sure of--- for this son of mine was a rebel and a radical and he would be a tough nut to crack.

Following anyone's rules was impossible for Jason. I said a prayer that this would be his saving grace. I had chosen this recovery center because they offered long term residential treatment that required family participation. I knew that Jason and I had a love/hate relationship. I wanted that mended. I wanted to get through all the layers of bull crap life had thrown our way.

Jason's dad was never a father to him. This hurt him emotionally as much as Joey's murder had. Since he was six years old and asked me for the first time who his father was, Jason had been begging his dad to be in his life. He wanted a relationship with his father so very much. Mom being the only one in his life, left me the center of his anger and resentment. I always told Jason it wasn't his fault that his dad refused to be a part of his life. I told him that his father was just trying to hurt me and get back at me.

I never bad-mouthed his dad to him when he was a child. I knew he would grow up and one day see for himself, who loved him and who was always there for him. It's ironic how a child longs for the parent who has deserted them and directs their anger at the only parent who has been there and loved them. I was not a perfect mom by any means.

I had Jason when I was only seventeen and still a kid myself. His father and I split up before he was born. I was sixteen when I married him and became pregnant within a few months of our marriage. Here I didn't even know how to drive a car and I was married, pregnant, and getting a divorce. Life was always a struggle. There was never enough money. Nothing about our lives was stable or secure.

Jason stayed in rehab seven months. The rules there were rigid. Many made no sense at all. It was about as close to prison as one could get and not be behind bars. It took Jason a long time to drop the attitude and submit to the rules. After a couple of months of being stuck in what they referred to as stage one, which meant no privileges, that you could only wear pajamas, and house slippers, Jason finally decided that he would act like he was making progress for no other reason than to get out of confinement.

Finally he could wear his own clothes. I was finally able to visit him. I had been going to the rehab every weekend to attend the parent therapy sessions. Then after parent therapy we would attend group with all the addicts. We all sat in a circle and participated in group. Up until then I had to leave after group while other parents got to visit with their child for an hour. I was also required to attend Alanon meetings every Saturday. Now that Jason was in phase two I was finally allowed to visit with him.

It wasn't much of a visit. We were monitored by counselors who made sure that we didn't discuss things about the outside world, or pass on any notes or messages from girlfriends or friends in general. All we could do was play cards or dominos. It was so rigid and I was so proud of Jason for sticking it out. I never thought he would stay in treatment.

Then after seven months I received a telephone call from his counselor. He informed me that Jason had gotten in an argument with another patient. He told me that Jason used a racial slur and was thrown out of treatment for it. He couldn't tell me where my son was or if he was safe. No one even bothered to call me; they just threw my son out to die. His counselor, Ron, had been off that weekend and when he returned Jason was gone. Ron tried to get Jason back into rehab by making an appeal but the Board refused to allow him to return. I couldn't believe a rehab would throw kids out for name calling when their lives were at risk. To think addicts would be perfectly behaved was insane.

Jason was ashamed of being kicked out of rehab. He had begged and pleaded with them not to kick him out. The truth was that the other boy had called Jason a racial slur first so Jason returned the favor. The other boy who was there because he had been arrested and told it was rehab or jail, got in no trouble at all. He was a hateful, uncooperative biracial kid who had a big chip on his shoulder. He broke rule after rule and started fights with everyone but because he was there through the courts, which meant the center was getting paid a lot more money through the county, they weren't about to throw him out.

My son didn't have a prejudiced bone in his body. Everyone who knew Jason knew that and his counselor told me that Jason had said in therapy that he felt like he had more in common with his black friends because we had been poor and struggled for so many years. We had lived in so many mixed neighborhoods and Jason didn't see color. He just saw friends.

Finally after a week of worrying to death Jason came over to the house. He told me everything that happened. I was just grateful that he was alive and safe. He had drug dealers looking for him because he still owed them money when he went into rehab. It wasn't safe for Jason on the streets due to the dealers and the risk of relapsing. He told me the first people he saw offered him drugs right on the spot even though they knew he had just spent seven long hard months in rehab!

I was worried about where he would stay. In rehab they made him promise he would not ask me to enable him in any way or ask for a place to live. I offered but he said no, he was going to try and make it on his own. He started back to college, moved in with two girl roommates, and went back to work at the parcel shipping company.

Since getting out of rehab Jason had not asked me for money. He kept his word and supported himself and was doing great. He was so healthy and handsome. He looked like a completely different person. He had gone from skin and bones to a six foot two, two hundred pound handsome young man. His complexion cleared up, his eyes were bright and he was focused. He had cut his very long hair off which I never expected him to ever do. For the first time since Joey's murder I began to believe that Jason was going to make it.

He was not going to die. He was only a few weeks from college graduation, had already been offered a job up north with a major corporation, and his future was looking very bright. It had been 16 months since Jason had gotten out of rehab. For the first time we both had hope.

We went to New Orleans together. I knew Jason would love the place. I had been going to Mardi Gras every year and promised him we would return in February together and he would attend his first Mardi Gras. It was a hot, humid Fourth of July in New Orleans but it didn't stop us from walking, shopping, and eating. It was a wonderful trip. We went on a canoe trip to the Ozarks. My coworkers and I had planned a trip and Jason came with me. We were the only ones who didn't turn over our canoe! We had so much fun. We camped out, went trout fishing, played on inner tubes in the rapids, and cooked out at night. We went to see the musical Stomp when it came to town. We had healed our relationship and it was the best it had ever been. He finally knew how much I loved him. We had become best friends again. We had made it through the drugs, the legal battles, the confrontations, rehab, and we were enjoying life together. I was so proud of Jason.

For Mother's Day which was a couple of weeks after he got out of rehab, Jason wrote me a beautiful letter. He couldn't afford a gift but the letter was the most precious gift I could ever receive from him:

"Mom,

I am writing this letter to tell you how much I love you and how much I am grateful for all that you have done for me. I have made a lot of bad choices in my life---dropping out of school, people I hung out with, selling drugs, and so on. But you were always there for me and you never put me down for what I had done. I have lost lots of loved ones in my life also. But, again, you were there for me. No matter how much trouble or pain I was in, you were always there for me. I know I don't show it enough, but I love you and I am the most blessed son in the world to have you for my mother. I know at treatment and your meetings they told you that the things you did for me were enabling me to kill myself, but you were the only reason I lived though all those times. I hope our relationship gets better every day. But even if it does not change, I am happy for the one that we have. I have already had a lifetime of bad events happen so hopefully I am coming upon the good ones and I hope that we can share them together as a family should. Thank you from the bottom of my heart, and I love you.

Happy Mother's Day,

Jason

Things continued to go well. Jason was close to graduation. Life had become peaceful and happy. I wasn't thinking about Jason's death anymore. I think for the first time in his life he thought he would make it too!

February came around and it was time for Mardi Gras. Jason called me to say that he would not be able to take the trip with me as we had been planning. His wisdom teeth had become impacted and he would have to use his vacation to have oral surgery. I was so disappointed but we said we can always go next year. Jason had the surgery and used his vacation to recuperate.

Then on a Saturday afternoon the next week I got a call from Jason. He said he needed to talk to me. I told him I had planned to go fishing with friends but I would wait for him. He said he would come on over. We hung up the phone and for the first time I began to worry. Jason had not called to ask me for anything since he left rehab. A feeling of dread came over me and I was anxious as I waited for him to arrive.

When Jason got there we went back into my bedroom and I sat on the bed. Jason stood there looking down at the floor. A sure sign that this wasn't going to be good! He began to speak and I learned that the dealers were after him again for the money he owed them. He said he had taken his paycheck and given it to someone to buy some pot. He had planned on selling the pot to make the money he needed to pay his debt and get the dealers off his back. Unfortunately the person he gave his money to ripped him off. He was broke and behind on his rent.

I got out my checkbook and I wrote the landlord a check for Jason's rent. I tried to be light hearted about it and told him he sucked at selling drugs. He was still looking down at the floor but a smile came to his lips. I told him to not wait until things got out of control. Come to me in the beginning. It only causes more trouble and ends up costing me more money. Jason apologized to me. I hugged him and told him I loved him. He told me he loved me too! I walked to the porch with him and sat down and watched him drive away. Then I went back inside to get my things together and go fishing. It was now two in the afternoon on February 28th.

Four hours later while at a friend's house my daughter called and told me that my son had just called home looking for me. Mindy said that Jason told her he had taken too much LSD and was freaking out. When she asked Jason where he was his reply was that he was in hell. After finding out I was not home to come save him like I had always done, Jason hung up the phone. From what I have been able to piece together I have some idea of the last few hours of his life.

Jason had left my apartment and gone home. He had gotten some LSD the day before from a friend and everyone was supposed to come over that night. Jason's best friends were coming from out of town. He was looking forward to a party that night. I guess he thought he would get a head start and took the LSD around four that afternoon. I didn't know Jason was using again.

Jason was at his apartment and there were others present when he first took the LSD but eventually everyone left. His friends from out of town had told him they would be there by 5 p.m., but they had not arrived. Jason was having a very bad LSD trip with nightmare hallucinations and was alone with no one to help him and unable to reach me.

I headed out for Jason's apartment as soon as I hung up talking to my daughter but I was 45 minutes away from him and wasn't sure where he was even calling from but took a chance that he was at his apartment. I called from my cell phone and asked my daughter to check caller ID to get the number of the phone he used to call me. By now I was almost there.

I called and a girl answered the phone. I told her I was Jason's mother and I asked to speak to Jason. She started crying and said "Sandy, something terrible has happened here."

I screamed, "What happened? Where is Jason?" The girl told me Jason had jumped out a window. I screamed out that I was almost there and hung up the phone.

I was flying as fast as I could to get to Jason. I was finding it hard to remember the back streets and concentrate on the drive. My fear was mounting every moment and somehow I knew that this was the day I had been dreading for the last 5 years. I called my daughter and told her to get to Jason's right away. I asked her to call a couple of friends first because I couldn't handle this alone.

When I arrived at the apartment building I jumped out of the car and started towards the back stairs of the building. There was a young woman standing outside with a little girl holding her hand. As I began up the stairs I heard her say to her little girl that she had to wait for Jason's mom. I told her I was Jason's mom and she told me the ambulance had taken Jason to a hospital trauma center downtown. I hopped in my car and headed for the hospital.

I arrived at the hospital and ran to the security officer sitting at the desk in the Emergency Room and asked for my son. I was told to wait in a small waiting room. I entered the room and a girl came up to me crying. It was the roommate who Jason had told me was in love with him. I had never met either of his two roommates. We put our arms around each other and began to cry.

In a few moments the hospital chaplain came in and told me the seriousness of Jason's condition. He had extensive head trauma, and was bleeding internally, the chaplain gently told me. He needed to be stabilized before he could be taken into surgery to stop the internal bleeding. The chaplain said he would be back when there was more news.

My daughter arrived at the hospital and stayed a little while with me. I sent her on home when my friends arrived. I was like a zombie. I have never been so afraid in my whole life. I knew in the back of my mind that Jason was not going to survive. I tried to tell myself that he might be okay but my heart knew better and there was little hope.

The chaplain returned and got down on his knees and took my hand. He told me that they had stabilized Jason and he had been taken to surgery to stop the internal bleeding but that the doctor feared that Jason may be brain dead due to the injuries to his skull.

"Oh, dear God! No, no, no!" I fell to my knees and looked toward Heaven as I begged God for my son's life. I cried and pleaded with God to not take Jason away from me. "Please God" I asked, and slumped to my knees on the floor, "Please don't take my baby!" The chaplain helped me back up and to a chair. When he left he promised to return when Jason was out of surgery and that they should know more then.

I asked my friends to take me outside so I could smoke a cigarette. It was February but it had been a beautiful warm day and as dusk came upon us I reached for a cigarette to light with my shaking hands and stood there silent with my three friends in tow.

When I finished my cigarette we walked back inside and were met by the chaplain in the hall. He told me the doctor wanted to speak to me and led us down a hall to a door where the doctor stood. The doctor told me that Jason had a ruptured spleen and that had been the source of the internal bleeding which they were able to repair. He went on to say that Jason had a broken shoulder, his lungs were crushed, and then the doctor casually told me that my son's skull was "shattered like an egg dropped on concrete".

My friends were standing with me when I received the news. One fainted, and another slid down the wall and fell to the floor. I just stood there staring at the doctor and shaking my head in understanding as we spoke.

He explained that a test would be required to determine brain death but informed me that the law required a wait for a certain number of hours before the test could be administered. The doctor told me the tests would be performed in the morning. I shook my head okay and asked to see my son. The doctor said when they got him to a bed they would take me to see him.

We headed back towards the waiting room in silence. One of my friends had to be wheeled away to have stitches above his right eye from hitting the ground when he fainted. Later he would tell me that it was not so much what the doctor had said that made him faint but that it was the look on my face as the doctor explained Jason's condition.

When they came to get me so I could see Jason I asked my friend to come with me. I was led down a hall with curtained off beds all up and down the hall. We were in the NICU wing. I was led to a bed where I saw my son lying there lifeless. His head was so swollen and his right side of his forehead and eye were bruised deep purple and yellow. Jason had tubes and wires all over him. He was hooked up to a machine doing his breathing for him. I just stood there and stared down at him lying there so broken and bruised. Blood was running from his nose and he was completely lifeless.

I was in shock. I stood there staring at my only son. I really can't tell you what I did next. I remember telling him I loved him and asking him to not leave me. But I knew he was already gone. I just stood there staring at him and caressing his cheek. The nurses led me away after a few minutes.

I went back out to my friends and we were led to the NICU waiting room to face the long night that lay ahead. It would be hours and hours of waiting.

My friends fell asleep on the little couches and chairs in the waiting room. I sat up all night just staring into space and praying. I could never describe how it felt to be alone and sitting in a room waiting to hear whether my son would live or die. The hours ticked away so very slowly.

I sat there until 6 a.m. and then I started to make phone calls. I called my son's father and told him about Jason's accident. I called some close friends and told them the sad news. Jason's friends began arriving at the hospital in the morning and soon the waiting room was full of his friends.

My best friend Laurie arrived and took over the thinking for me and remained at my side until everything was over and done. My little sister arrived with her husband. I had to call my mother in Texas and tell her. I knew it would destroy her. My mom had lost two sons herself and now she was losing her grandson as well. As it happened, my oldest brother was visiting my mom in Dallas and he answered the phone so I told him the news and he said he would break it to her.

The hours passed and friends arrived and I led them back in small groups to see Jason. I kept asking when the test would be done to determine if there was brain activity. The morning crept by. There was still no word from the doctors.

I called my mom thinking that she had been told by now about Jason but when she answered she was upbeat and I knew by the sound of her voice that my brother Rick had not told her yet. I broke the news to her and she began to cry. She begged me not to remove Jason from life support if they determined brain death. She asked me to wait until she could get here. I told her I would call her back when I got the report from the doctors.

The hours of waiting were taking their toll on me. I began to get upset and demanding that the test be administered right away. The nurses told me the doctor had been paged but had not returned the page or arrived at the hospital. I waited and finally at some point around noon or so the test was performed.

As I sat in a small room, the doctor came in and broke the news to my family and me. Jason showed no brain activity and was declared clinically dead. Only the machines were keeping my son alive. The doctor looked at my friend Laurie and asked her if I understood what I was being told. She assured him that I did.

Next the organ donor team approached me about donating Jason's organs for transplants. I could not bring myself to allow them to cut up my child and leave him alone to die. When they told me he would have to be kept on life support and then would be taken into surgery to harvest the organs (as they put it) I simply could not let that happen. I told them I wanted my baby to die in my arms. Not alone, left for dead in an operating room while everyone rushed around to save someone else's life completely unaware that my child had just died. I would not let him die alone. They kept on asking me over and over again until I got upset and told them to leave me alone. They finally left me to my grief.

I went out to the waiting room and called my mother again to tell her that we would be removing Jason from life support in a little while. She begged me to wait and was crying and pleading with me to wait until she could get to Memphis so she could see him and say goodbye. I told her I had made my decision to let him go because it was only keeping him from entering Heaven. I had to let him go. I did not want her to see Jason in the condition he was in. I didn't want that to be her last memories of her grandson.

I felt I was making the right choice. As I sit writing this story I know I made the right choice for the memories of Jason and the way he looked haunt me everyday. I spared her from those memories and nightmares.

"Where is the damn doctor and why is it taking so long to carry out my wishes?" The nurses explained that they were waiting for an anesthesiologist to arrive because he was the only one allowed by law to discontinue the life support and shut everything down.

Finally, twenty-two hours after his fall I climbed into my son's hospital bed and lay my head on his chest with my arms around him. I placed my ear over his heart so I could listen to the heartbeat. Family and his closest friends surrounded us as the machines were turned off. There was complete silence with the exception of soft sobs that could be heard as people fought back their tears in silence and struggled to maintain composure.

When I was pregnant with Jason, the doctor placed a stethoscope on my tummy. "Would you like to hear your baby's heartbeat?" he asked. I heard the first heartbeats of my child that day. Now, twenty-three years later I lay in a hospital bed with him and once again I listened for his heartbeats. Only this time they were the last…

It was like a clock winding down, gradually decreasing and becoming slower. I don't recall how long it took for Jason's heart to stop beating.

My sister says it was about ten minutes. Seemed like seconds to me and I remember trying to adjust my ear against his chest to find the heartbeat again but there were no more beats. No more life. No more Jason. He was gone. He had silently slipped away surrounded by those who loved him.

My only son was gone. I was led away in shock and grief as my only son was left behind. The orderly would come and my son would be covered with a white sheet. They would put a toe tag on him and he would be taken away to the morgue. My son would be in the morgue until the coroner performed an autopsy to determine cause of death. Just like on the television shows. Then the hearse would come from the funeral home to claim his body and he would be cremated. Ashes to ashes, dust to dust.

Jason Anthony Barganier died at the young age of 23 only weeks away from college graduation. He never got to grow up, marry, and have his own children, and grandchildren. He never found the happiness he had longed for and his dreams would never come true. I would never see him turn into a man with a family. I would never get to hug him or kiss him again.

All I have left is a story to tell about a young man who was handsome, brilliant, and who is so dearly missed by all who knew him. I have memories of a child a little on the shy side with a beautiful smile, blonde hair, and beautiful blue-gray eyes. Memories are all I have left of Jason.

I lost part of my life that day and there is a hole in my heart that will never mend or ever be filled again with the love of a son who needed me. A brave son who fought hard to beat the disease of addiction but in the end could not find the strength to overcome his demons.

It has been eight years now since I lost my son Jason. I still cry every day. I suffer from post-traumatic stress. I have flashbacks several times a day. I see him lying in that hospital bed broken and crushed, blood running from his nose. I hear the doctor's words over and over again…"his skull is shattered like an egg dropped on concrete," shattered, shattered, and shattered. I see him lying in that coffin so cold and his skin so gray. The bruises still there, his head still swollen.

He wasn't supposed to die before me. Children aren't supposed to die before their parents. Nothing my son did in life was so unworthy that he deserved such a terrible death.

I remember those days. I think about all the kids I loved and how much I miss them. My home was always full of the unwanted kids. They all knew they were welcome in our home. They all knew they could trust me. They all knew I loved them and Jason loved them. There were five boys that were always in my home. Five boys who ate my food, trashed my house, worried me sick sometimes, got into more trouble then anyone else could but I loved them all. Jason, Joey, Josh were the original three and along the way came Kai and Woody.

Recently Josh passed away. I was devastated again! Once again I collapsed on the floor crying and asking God why. Josh had always called me mom and I called him my son. Like the boy in rehab who had called Jason a racial slur and got him kicked out, Josh was biracial. Josh's birth mother was a heroin addict and he was born addicted. He was adopted by a wonderful woman who loved him and was gracious enough to share him with me.

Josh always struggled and things didn't come easy for him due to his birth mother's heroin addiction. Josh had trouble concentrating on things. It was hard for him to learn but you would never know it because he was so smart. He wrote the most beautiful poetry. He was a gifted artist as well. The girls were all crazy about Josh just as they had been over Jason. Josh was so beautiful. He had the most beautiful eyes I had ever seen and a voice that when he spoke sounded like a song. It was hard for Josh to make friends but from the day he met Jason in high school they became brothers. Then Jason introduced him to Joey and they formed the same brotherly bond. My three boys...all gone now.

After Jason's death Josh turned his life around. He found out one year after Jason died that he had contracted HIV. We were devastated but we never lost hope and knew that with medications he could live a happy, healthy long life.

I remember he came to me and sat me down and told me that he had HIV. He talked about wanting to just take an overdose and die. I told him he was like a son to me and that he was all I had left and I couldn't bear to lose him too! I loved him too much and if he would just take the medications he would live a long time. Eventually Josh accepted his disease. He moved to California where his mom had been moved. It was more important for him to be with his mom and even more important for him to have access to the best HIV treatment facilities in the world.

Through the years he was the only one who stayed in contact with me. He would come and visit and I always hated it when he had to go back home. Josh would get depressed from time to time and stop taking his medicines. Each time he stopped he would get sick. His immune system wasn't strong enough to fight colds and the flu. He would end up in the hospital and when he got better he would start taking his meds again. That went off and on for the last seven years. Many times he talked about just wanting to be with his "brothers" Jason and Joey in Heaven.

Josh got pneumonia and passed away on March 25th, 2006. I had not known he was in the hospital. He didn't remember my phone number or where his mom might find it at his townhouse so he told her to just go to Jason's web site at www.angelsofaddiction.com and leave a message for me in the guestbook. He told her to just say, "Mom, your third son is on his way to Heaven." His mom told him she would not write that because she wasn't going to let him give up. He had to fight to live and he would get better and be around many more years.

I was devastated that I did not get the chance to talk to him and tell him how much I loved him before he died. If only I had known a couple of days earlier I could have called him. My life now is just one big "If only."

As soon as I found out about Josh, I tried to find Kai to tell him that Josh had passed away. Kai had moved to Florida with his dad. He came to town and stayed with me before he headed to Florida. He had been living in Detroit. He spent the night and we went to the movies. We talked about Jason, his death, and how much they loved each other. Kai promised me when he got to Florida that he would call me and give me his phone number and address but I never heard from him again. The only thing I knew to do was get on my computer and do an internet search for him. I typed in a search for him by his name. Two results came up. I clicked on one and it was some kind of a newsletter and it had the heading of Memorials! I said "no, that can't be. I know Kai is an unusual name but this can't be right." Then I opened the second result and in a blog there was an entry asking everyone to keep this family in their prayers because they had just lost their son Kai.

"Oh my God! No, this can't be." In the course of fifteen minutes I had just found out that my Josh had passed away. Then in trying to find Kai to tell him about Josh's passing I find out that Kai had passed away five months earlier!

Joey died at the age of eighteen. Jason died at the age of twenty-three. Kai died at the age of 30. Josh was the oldest. He died at the age of thirty-three.

They will all live forever in my heart. I still don't understand how four out of five boys that I loved have passed away. I know that they are all together again but their passing has left this world a cold and lonely place for those of us who loved them.

There is little sympathy for addicts who lose their lives. There is little sympathy for parents whose children die from this disease. Our children were football players, nurses, cheerleaders, scholars, artists, musicians, and teachers. They were the kid next door! Addiction does not discriminate.

The treatment for substance abuse is substandard and too costly. Only the wealthy have access to the best facilities. Many low cost rehabs won't take a person until they have their first overdose! That is horrendous and unacceptable.

The people who ran the drug and alcohol center and recovery center were a husband and wife team. When Jason died I went to the media and an investigation was done by a local news magazine. What they uncovered was scandalous. Improper use of funds just to mention one thing was found to have taken place at the drug and alcohol center and their state funding was revoked. They did not pay payroll taxes and a federal tax lien was levied against them. Both directors eventually resigned their positions. I had a meeting with the new director of the rehab and he assured me that no more patients would be thrown out of treatment as in the past.

I founded an online support group in memory of my son Jason. Angels of Addiction has reached out to other parents who have lost a child to substance abuse all across this country and overseas. While we wish that no parent ever needs to belong to our support group it has been a blessing to us. We had nowhere to turn. There was no one who understood the pain and devastation our children's disease and deaths have cast upon us. There were places for widows, and widowers, for parents who lost a child to miscarriage, disease, or drunk drivers but nowhere for us to turn. No one cared because they believed our children had done it to themselves but their children didn't deserve to die.

The parents who have joined forces to write this book and tell our children's stories do so for one reason. To make sure that our children did not live and die in vain. If this book saves one person's child, then our children did not live and die in vain. It is too late for our children. It doesn't have to be too late for you or your child.

Educate yourselves about the disease of addiction. Pay attention to the changes in behavior you see in your child. The only bad choice our children were guilty of was self-medicating their pain and depression. Most of all, love your children. Always tell them and show them you love them. Don't be afraid to ask questions, monitor their friends, and talk with their teachers.

You never want to be writing a book like this I can assure you. Reach out to your children and to the children in this world who don't have anyone who cares about what becomes of them. The life you save could be your child's.

Jason's story as told by his loving mom, Sandy LaCagnina, Memphis, TN

"Grief is not a sign of weakness or lack of faith. It is the price of love." – Author unknown

http://www.geocities.com/dyingtogethigh/jasonbarganier

MIKE DIGIANTOMMASO

August 21, 1980 – May 15, 2004

(Age 23)

COCAINE/HEROIN

"MY SON'S JOURNEY TOWARDS DESTRUCTION"

When I think of the word "addiction" I think homeless, poverty, alcohol and abuse. When I was forced to learn about addiction, I learned and understood what the true meaning of addiction meant. It was not what I originally imagined.

Addiction is defined as a chronic, incurable, yet treatable disease. It begins with experimentation, abuse and insidiously becomes addiction. The disease of addiction does not discriminate. It can attack the young, old, male, female, rich or poor. The disease of addiction knows no boundaries. Drug addiction is in epidemic proportions with so many young lives lost. The faces of Addiction are faces now new to society.

My son Michael was born on August 21, 1980. He had an older brother and loving parents. Mike was a fun loving, sensitive and compassionate child.

When Michael turned 15, the early stages of experimentation were beginning. His addiction began with alcohol and marijuana. As ignorant as I was to this behavior, I assumed he was going through a teenage stage. Michael graduated from high school. His next step in preparation towards a healthy life was to enter college. Mike was a year younger than most of his peers. He hung around with a group of good kids.

As Mike pursued his education at Plymouth State College, I began to notice that he was not traveling the typical course of a student in a college environment. The drinking continued, as did the use of marijuana. The more serious behavioral change was a fight with another student, resulting in Mike having a fractured jaw requiring surgery. This and other incidents led to a one year suspension from college. Michael returned home now to look for a job. Without any skills or education, he worked as a roofer. He would recite the phrase, "I'm a roofer" with little pride. He began to make money and spend it as fast as he could make it. Purchasing things like, a truck, a motorcycle, a dirt bike, a cell phone to mention a few.

The creditors were now beginning to call. The bills were piling up. Now he was borrowing and stealing money to support his addiction, which I was still oblivious to. Owing customers was becoming Mike's way of life. Borrowing money, asking me to co-sign loans and an endless need for more money. I still couldn't comprehend this erratic behavior. I continued to bail Michael out of risky situations, still unaware of his cocaine and OxyContin addiction.

My sons would tell me that "OxyContin" was everywhere and " everyone was using them." But, my sons, in my mind of denial, were not part of this new face of addiction. This is a powerful protection called denial: The inability to deal with and accept the obvious. Michael's brother also continued struggling with his addiction to multiple drugs. But, not my Michael. This just couldn't happen to my other son. My inner self wondered about Michael, yet my denial continued to protect me.

It was late in 2003. After lending/giving Mike money totaling over $10,000, his brother finally made me face reality and told me that Michael was addicted to cocaine and heroin. My denial was beginning to come to a reality of fear and disbelief. My job now came to a sudden halt with the hopes that I could save my son. Michael's life of rehab, recovery and relapse began to take its toll. Yet, eventually he agreed to enter a long term inpatient rehab. He was sober, well groomed, his voice was clear, his eyes sparkled, he was going to be OK. My hopes were high, this was going to save his life. Yet, once again Michael walked out of the rehab.

By March of 2004, both of my sons were hospitalized with hepatitis A. Their weight was dropping, their skin and eyes were yellow and Mike was now clearly very depressed. Discharged from the hospital, this disease once again consumed the lives of my sons.

By April of 2004, Michael began Naltrexone therapy as Paul struggled to regain his life through NA meetings and continuing his education as an electrician. Naltrexone is an opiate blocker, yet other drugs can be consumed by an addict. As Mike continued his Naltrexone therapy, I was once again elated. My son Michael was slowly coming back to what he once was. The "old" Mike we all knew and loved so much. His personality began to flourish, his old friends were back, he was smiling. He loved his life once again. The little white pill was working. It was a miracle. Finally hope!

It was May, 2004, Mother's Day. Three days later Michael called at work to apologize for not coming by, he had overslept due to late hours at work. "I will see you tomorrow." Did I notice a slight slur to his words? No, I didn't. Did I?

On May 15, 2004, Paul and Michael were to go to work together. Mike not ready, Paul decided to leave without him. Having second thoughts he decided to go back and check Mike's room. On this day Paul was fifteen days into recovery, still frail and vulnerable to his disease.

It was 7:30 a.m., on a sunny Saturday morning. The phone rang. "Mom? It's Mike, it's bad."

"Call 911, I'll be right there, don't worry he'll be fine." I arrived at their apartment within minutes. Police, fire engines and paramedics were on scene. Thank God they arrived on time. Michael would be OK. I ran to the third floor of the apartment they shared, ran in Mike's room...and heard an earth shattering scream come from my mouth. He was cold, very cold, like ice. His eyes were closed, like he was asleep. His upper body and face were purple, he was cold. As I held my youngest son's cold lifeless body in my arms, I saw his cell phone near his right hand, it was open. Was he trying to call me? Oh God, no, God no, please take me and let Mike live.

He was dead. My son was really dead. Words once incomprehensible to me. My world, now shattered, came to a complete and sudden halt. Michael died from a cocaine/heroin overdose at the age of 23.

It is now two years since the death of my son. Life is different now. I speak about the prevention, dangers and education of substance abuse to high school students. I have spoken in public forums, rehabs, churches, and was invited to a small radio station to speak. I take continuing education courses to educate myself about this horrendous disease that claimed the life of my son and threatened the life of my other son. I am a member of three support groups and I will continue my journey to change the *stigma* of addiction to the *disease* of addiction. Pray for better resources and more bed availability, better and longer treatment with vigorous after care. Each day I open my eyes to the memories of my son Michael.

In 2005, the "Michael DiGiantommaso Memorial Scholarship" became a reality thanks to donations and support from all of Mike's friends and family. May Michael's memory live on forever.

Mike's story told by his loving mom, Carol DiGiantommaso, Everett, MA.

"When you are dead, your sister's tears will dry as time goes on, your widow's tears will cease in another's arms, but your mother will mourn you until she dies." —Arabian proverb

http://www.geocities.com/dyingtoghigh/mikedigiantommaso

I AM YOUR DISEASE

"JUST FOR FUN"

A LETTER WRITTEN ABOUT MIKE DIGIANTOMMASO BY HIS BROTHER, PAUL

Mike D's spirit will last forever in the hearts of those who knew him. Mike had one of those infectious personalities and was always the first to push his needs aside to address yours. I envied that about him. He grew up in North Reading, Massachusetts and was a rather talented athlete.

He had the ability to push himself to his limit and achieve beyond expectations. He had a passion for football and wrestling and excelled in both. The thing about Mike was that he loved people and people loved him back. Some people have a couple of friends, some have a few. Then there was Mike who had just too many. It's hard to not buddy up with someone who is always smiling and joking, then on the flip side he was always there for those who needed him in a crisis.

I can honestly say Mike had not a mean bone about him. He had many a girlfriend in his day. I recall girls calling him all day and into the night. The thing about Mike, he was always faithful in any relationship. Besides, he was too honest and would have gotten caught. He wasn't good at carrying a lie. His morals were strong and his confidence high and a lot of that had to do with the structure he was raised in.

When I think about Mike's personality, I think easy going, happy, generous, and in a lot of ways fearless. See, now that's the one that got him in trouble. He always maintained that leadership, " I'll do it first" type mentality. It was visible in all areas of his life. But, the thing is that he carried that into his drug experimentation. I say experimenting because that's what it was-just for fun. It started with weed and alcohol. It was acceptable and everyone seemed to be doing it. That went on through the majority of his teens and it really didn't seem to be much of a problem to anybody witnessing it.

He went to college at Plymouth State and made even more friends. The parties got bigger and that was when the progression began.

Progression is one of the many symptoms of the disease of addiction. So Mike went to parties and stepped it up a notch. Instead of just drinking he decided to try cocaine. At that time he had no idea of the hell which he had decided to take on, the instant in which he decided to merely try it-just for fun. After trying cocaine again on a later day, he started buying it. After buying it a few times, he started selling it. This is the progression to which I am referring, but, it doesn't end there.

Now Mike maintained this lifestyle and outwardly his life seemed ok. He didn't establish a dependency and would always recite that phrase…" just for fun." As time went on, another level in his addiction was reached. OxyContin was everywhere, and everyone seemed to be doing it. It was a great thing to do on the weekends. After trying it a few times, he began to buy them on a more frequent basis. Eventually he would sell them to maintain the dependency he had now developed.

It is my experience and my belief that every time a person ingests a drug for other than medical purposes they give up a small piece of their soul. Drugs tend to make sick people well and well people sick. At this stage in Mike's story he was about half the person he started his life journey as. He would only smile half as much, had probably half the amount of friends, and began settling for half the life he really deserved. The sad part about this story is that it only got worse.

He was soon to encounter the greatest battle of his life. Mike was thrown out of college and was thrown directly into life's realities. He had to find a job and pay some bills. One of the biggest bills being his habit. He wasn't alone though. Many people were using OC's including myself. It became a way of life, getting and using. Endless efforts put into acquiring that little green pill because without it, there was a withdrawal---a mental and physical hell. Soon enough the pills were much too expensive ranging from $60.00-$90.00 each. Multiply that by two or three a day. That is a sickness for sure.

Heroin was around and available for a much more affordable price, not to mention the potency was much higher. Life was really starting to get hard for Mike now. That " just for fun" mantra was long gone. Mike's spirit was broken. His decisions went from bad to really bad.

His new friends were addicts as well because water seeks its own level. Intravenous using, once unacceptable to Mike, started to look like a good thing. He eventually tried it and with that, opened the gates to hell.

He found himself in rehabs and institutions over and over. The problem was bigger than he was and the control was out of his reach. His defiance was strong and as bad as his life was he would never surrender to the help he so desperately needed.

His bottom was low and his life was an unmanageable mess. Mikey was changed into something which he never expected. He found himself in the grips of addiction and never found his way out. Drug use and addiction guarantee three things inevitably: Jails, institutions and death. I was fortunate to have only experienced two. Mike was not so fortunate and died from active addiction. He left behind an indescribable pain to those who loved him.

Mike died May 15, 2004 at 23 years old. His life was just beginning. This travesty was unnecessary but it is my understanding that God takes the good ones first, for he was the best. His spirit is strong just like his personality. We wait for the day we will meet again.

Your brother

LANG JACKSON HITCHCOCK

June 19, 1972 – August 30, 2002

(Age 30)

ACCIDENTAL DRUG OVERDOSE

"I DON'T NEED THERAPY, GOD WILL GET ME THROUGH THIS"

Lang was born in 1972. By 1990, he was " experimenting" with drugs. He started out with marijuana and just occasionally. The effects were subtle and I was not aware of his use. He was in high school. Very, very gradually his grades started to fall and he was becoming less tied to the apron strings than before---but I knew he would not do drugs---because we had talked endlessly and he assured me he would never do drugs.

Over the next decade, Lang graduated---to more drugs, different drugs. By this time he had been in treatment many, many times. He was a familiar face at the local psychiatric hospital. He would enter the hospital and be the model patient. He would detox, get started in a program only to abandon it. He always said he could get over it with my help and with the help of God.

By the late 1990s or early 2000s, I started to miss things from my house, first a VCR. Then my daughter saw the TV going out the back window of my house (Lang's room). I started hiding everything. I rented a safe deposit box where I took everything that I valued. I hid my few pieces of jewelry in my coat pockets in the closet. It worked for awhile. Then, I started locking my bedroom door.

Lang began having short visits from people. They would stop by and they never stayed long. I questioned that but he always had such good answers.

One time he told me he needed $40 to get a guy off his back. He said he owed the guy money and the guy had threatened to hurt his sister and/or me if he did not pay him and he had no money. Well, he was so convincing I gave him the $40. Do you know that $40 is what Oxy was going for on the streets? Neither did I. I had given him money to buy a fix.

I took him to a friend's house to pick up something he had left (it was a drug deal I am sure). Drug addicts become so adept in telling their stories, they are convincing. I was always telling myself " be on guard." " Don't believe him." But it never worked. He could sell anything.

Lang worked off and on at different jobs---every job he left because of drugs. He either quit or was laid off because of failure to show up for work. He was bipolar and one day he would go to work and really, really work. The next day he did not care whether he went to work or not, was just so down that he could not handle it.

He started going to the Emergency Room for various aches and pains, anxiety attacks, etc. I told the doctors there " look at his record, he is drug seeking." But they just ignored it. They gave him what he wanted. After many, many, many visits to the local ER, he moved to the next county and started there, then still to the next county.

One time I had a call from the local police, that Lang's car had been found. It had been involved in an accident. I was trying to figure out what that was all about. Lang never mentioned being involved in an accident. He was at home without his car. He had a good story about where it was and why. Lang had " traded" his car for---yes--- drugs! The person he traded it to had been involved in an accident and just abandoned the car. That was the end of his car and the last one he ever had. From then on, I drove him every place- to work and back every single day. He did not always stay at work, but I drove him and often called to see if he was going to be there after work.

Not wanting Lang to have much money left over from his paychecks, I always got to him first, collected my money for " rent and groceries" . It was just my way of preventing him from having extra money for drugs. It worked for a time.

By 2002, I knew I could not have Lang living in my house any longer. He was stealing everything. I had to hide my car keys, everything. I had taken him to look for a place to live. I was even willing to rent a place for him, but the only thing I could afford were those places where obviously only addicts lived and then there was the transportation issue.

I had held myself together for 13 years. I could not do it any more. While I was in the hospital, my car was stolen. Yes, by Lang. He left it someplace (I guess) for drugs. Then, he had it towed back to my house! It was wrecked, it had been torn apart, windows broken out, well things that addicts do to cars when they are looking for things. Everything of value had been taken out of the car.

I decided it was time to get an injunction against Lang. The injunction papers were served on Lang on his 30th birthday while he was in the psychiatric hospital. That still hurts me so bad when I think of it.

I never saw Lang again after that. He was found dead in a wooded area of Palm Bay, Florida about 2-3 miles from my house about three months later. His " friends" had watched him overdose at a party one night, had moved him to a bed and waited for him to die. After he was dead, one of the friends borrowed his mom's van. They took Lang's body to a wooded area and dumped it. Did you know that is *just* a misdemeanor? His body was found the next morning by a couple taking a morning walk.

Another victory for the monster known as drug abuse. Lang was a good person, a genuinely good person, who was overcome by drugs! I have so many memories of his life, the good, the bad---about an equal number of years of each. I am trying to concentrate on the good ones.

I have had people ask me " what can you do?" I cannot say I would do anything differently. You cannot fight drug abuse. You can talk, love, encourage, stand by them, get them treatment but you cannot do it for them.

Lang's story as told by his loving mom, Maxine Hitchcock, Palm Bay, FL

" In the end, the drugs win."

Lang's Website:

http://www.geocities.com/dyingtogethigh/langhitchcock.html

MICHAEL MURPHY

NOVEMBER 12, 1971 – MAY 28, 2004

(Age 32)

METHADONE/XANAX

"MY SON'S DEADLY CHOICE"

One day I heard the words that made me collapse and burst into tears. The words that I was told will remain in my head forever. They found my son in a motel room and he was dead.

It was May 28, 2004, and I was at work at the nursing home. The charge nurse came and asked me to follow her up to the lobby. I said to myself, " Oh, no what did I do wrong? Am I in some sort of trouble for something?" When I got to the lobby, my husband was there. I took one look at his face and said " What is wrong?" He just had this look on his face that I will never ever forget. He said, " They found Michael dead this morning in a motel room in Florida." I said " Oh, my God," over and over. I was in shock and crying, like a wounded animal. The poor residents in the nursing home just kept staring at me and wondering what was wrong.

I left with my husband to go home. I just kept gagging and crying all the way home and thought for sure that my husband was going to have to let me out of the truck, so that I could get physically sick.

Arriving home, my son-in-law called me from Texas and I could hear my daughter screaming and crying in the background. Her little brother was dead.

He had been on a bus to go visit her when he died.

My son had called me in April asking for money so that he could go visit my daughter in Texas, as work was slow for him in Florida. I sent him the money, but he did not go. I wish that he would have, because he probably would still be alive. So, then he called my daughter and she bought him a bus ticket! I am sure that he did not call and ask me for money again because he was feeling guilty for not going the first time when I had sent him the money. I think to this day, that my daughter feels like it was her fault that Michael died because she is the one who bought him the bus ticket. But, she cannot ever think that way, because Michael made bad choices that day, that were to end his life.

November 12, 1971, was the day that I was blessed with twin sons, Michael and Steven. They were a complete surprise, as I did not know that I was having twins. I was looking forward to raising my boys. But, my joy was short lived. I got up one morning and found my baby Steven gone. He died from SIDS (crib death). I was so afraid to take care of Michael after that, terrified that something was going to happen to him also. I suppose that I was over protective of him after losing the baby and wanted to protect Michael forever, but that was not to be. I couldn't protect him in the end.

Michael was so sweet when he was young. He rushed to get up for school every morning. He loved school. He never gave me any trouble at all. I was so proud of him. But, as he got older, things changed. He started skipping school, his grades dropped. I found out that he was smoking pot. What happened to my sweet little boy? Was it perhaps peer pressure? Running around with the wrong kind of kids?

We had him admitted to a rehab center, but that was short lived. He ran away one day from the center. Only, because they would not let him smoke. The center said that there was nothing they could do. They said that they could not force him to stay there. My only hope was that my son would try and realize that he had to get his life on the right track again. While my son was still living at home, I did notice that he had this thing for pills. Sleeping pills, pain pills and whatever.

He used to scare me and I used to hide all the pills because I was always afraid that he was going to take too many. He did not use any common sense when taking the pills. If the pills did not work right away, like he thought they should have, he would take more, and more. So, I had no choice but to hide them from him. I think that my son probably thought that he was invincible and an overdose could not happen to him, only other people.

Michael got into some trouble with the police. Nothing major, just petty things. I do not remember what happened one night, but I do know that he was out all night, thinking that the law was after him. He was hiding out all that night. So, being the protective mom that I was, I took him to a bus station and he was on his way to Florida to stay with his dad. I thought that if he could start over somewhere else, things would get better for him.

He lived with his dad for awhile and then he went to Tennessee where he met Trina and they got married and had a child. I thought that things were going right for him finally. Michael and his wife had separated shortly after my husband and I were there in Tennessee to visit with them for a week. The week that we were there visiting, I noticed nothing wrong. Michael was working and taking care of his family. Later, I found out from his wife, that Michael had a serious problem with pills. He was buying OxyContin from the neighbors and had a drinking problem.

I also found out later from his dad that Michael would take a whole handful of OxyContin at one time without blinking an eye, and had been seeing a doctor in Florida who was giving him illegal prescriptions. I wish with all my heart that my son had confided in me and told me about his pill addiction. But I am sure that he was probably ashamed and did not want his mom to know. But, maybe I could have brought him home and gotten him help. That is a big why, because I realize that the addict has to want help. Maybe Michael did not think that he had that big of a problem.

I now will tell you about the choice that my son made that day that ended his life. While on the bus to Florida, he met a guy around his age. They decided to get off the bus at Tallahassee, Florida. Maybe to party? This guy that my son met had money. He got them a motel room. While at the motel, they met this woman who was there to turn herself in on a previous drug charge. This guy with my son, bought drugs from her. It was Methadone. The doctor explained to me that my son probably went to sleep, lapsed into a coma, then died. He also had a small amount of Xanax in his system. The two pills together caused a toxic effect to his system and shut everything down. That is what killed him. No alcohol was found in his system.

The woman who sold the drugs, is now in prison on the other drug charge. I wish with all my heart that I could meet her face to face or write her a letter and tell her that what she did has put me in the pits of Hell and anguish for the rest of my days. Not that she would care, because drug dealers have no morals or heart, when it comes to another person's life.

The day my son died on May 28th, is the birthday of my other living son. Now can you imagine how my son feels on his birthday, knowing that is the day that his little brother died? I do not know if he will ever celebrate that day again for as long as he lives. Why things like this happen, I will never understand.

It goes through my mind all the time, wondering if my son knew that he was going to die, his last breath, his last heartbeat and it kills me. My son did not deserve to die like he did. He was nice looking, smart, had a kind heart and everyone who knew him loved him. He had his whole life ahead of him. Cut short by the demon of addiction. He was our son, our brother, our father and our friend and we will miss him forever.

I am sure that if my son could talk to me, he would say "Mom, the pain and torment that I went through, I hid so well, out of my love for you. As you search for answers and ask all the whys, look up to the Heavens way past the deep blue sky, and remember that you and I had a love for each other that death cannot take away. We will love each other for always. Now I am free at last mom, from this demon called addiction."

"I love you so much and will miss you until my last breath here on earth and we can once more be together forever." Mom

"I WILL ALWAYS LIGHT CANDLES IN MEMORY OF MY SON MICHAEL & WHEN

I GO TO BLOW THEM OUT I WILL TAKE THE FLAME OF IT INTO MY HEART AND

REMEMBER THE LOVE OF HIM.

HIS GREATEST GIFT TO ME WAS HIS LIFE, HIS PRESENCE, AND HIS LOVE.

HE IS NOW TRODDING ON STREETS OF GOLD.

I LOVE YOU MICHAEL" - MOM

Michael's story as told by his loving mom, Barbara Dawson, Van Wert, OH

"Death leaves a heartache no one can heal, love leaves a memory no one can steal." ~From a headstone in Ireland

http://www.geocities.com/dyingtogethigh/michaelmurphy

JEFFREY SCOTT G.

October 28, 1980 - July 18, 2004

(Age 23)

HEROIN

"I HAVE HURT AND SHAMED MYSELF ON NUMEROUS OCCASIONS ALTHOUGH MY ACTIONS SHALL NOT DICTATE MY ETERNITY."

I am a single parent of 3 sons. They could call or visit their dad anytime but the everyday problems were mine. Jeff was my middle son. He was very bright but did not do well in school because a lot of the tasks were senseless to him and he wouldn't do them for that reason. I guess he was a different learner. He passed all the tests with flying colors but his grades did not reflect that. The public school teachers were not very helpful but he got by.

Jeff was very hard on himself and tried to do what was expected but the older he got the more difficulty he had trying to understand why. He chose friends who also rebelled against conformity although he was a deep thinker and he didn't understand them either, but at least they accepted him.

In his late teens I became aware of his rebellious behavior and how it would lead him to trouble but I never suspected drugs. I knew very little about the behaviors associated with this lifestyle and it never entered my mind that such a thing was about to slap me in the face.

One day my older son came to me and said he heard from some acquaintances that Jeff was using Heroin and that his so-called friends were helping him find the peace he was so desperately yearning for. He said "Mom---If YOU don't do something, Jeff will die." No more hiding from the nasty reality. Jeff needed so much and I knew nothing about where to start. We went through a few counselors, legal battles, rehab, and emotional confrontations. I watched him suffer through withdrawals. He wanted so much to be BETTER and each time he said it, I believed this would be the last time because I knew he hated where he was and how it was destroying his life and his relationship with the people who loved him. Of course you know the saga continued.

We found a drug counselor who was wonderful. She really understood his life and helped me so I could love him without the unrealistic expectations I had. He didn't mind talking to her because she didn't make him feel like a loser. She was able to reach his intelligent mind and separate that from his illogical actions.

He was also seeing a psychiatrist who diagnosed him with chronic major depression and severe social anxiety. He put Jeff on some mega doses of medication. I had a very hard time understanding the logic of the psychiatrist who seemed to view me as an enabler. I felt in my heart that I would do whatever it took for Jeff to be better but it had to make sense to me and to Jeff. Some of this doctor's ideas were bizarre. At least we had the support of his psychologist.

Jeff tried to commit suicide by overdosing on Ativan. He was on a vent for awhile. He got drunk and burned his finger with a lighter to see how much pain he could tolerate. He ended up on a burn unit with a skin graft and IV antibiotics. His arms were all scarred from self-cutting. His emotional pain was so great that physical pain helped to release it.

Through all this I saw my baby boy suffering and I felt helpless and alone. If one has never loved someone with this disease their solution was obvious---Kick Him Out! I could not do that because he was sick. I'm so thankful for that now. I always said to him " Jeff, I do not understand you but I love you." His reply was " WHY" ? Just kick me out so I can lie down in the woods and die.

He was clean---off Heroin for 2 years. He had a job and a car. He enrolled in college. He wanted to major in philosophy. (Good job prospects there.)

His brother was getting married in May, of 2004, and Jeff didn't want to go to the wedding. He was afraid he would be judged. He decided to go and he was so proud of himself. He didn't get TOO drunk. He socialized and didn't make a fool of himself. He got through it. He actually had Fun.

In July an old " friend" who had moved out of the area came to visit. He and Jeff decided to take a ride to see another friend. They made a stop along the way and on Sunday, July 18, 2004, I found Jeff dead in his room---all alone---crumpled in a corner.

I do not wish for any family to have to deal with addiction and I'm really not sure how I got through it, but my love for Jeff kept me going. He hated himself and his life. He hated what this was doing to his family. I tried to understand how this all happened from beginning to end. I have no answers.

The coroner called me after the autopsy and said my other two sons should be checked for coronary artery disease. Jeff, at 23, had a 90% blockage in one of his major coronary arteries. My oldest son who was just married got checked and they found no blockage but they did find an incidental finding of thyroid cancer! He had no symptoms. He was 24 at the time. He underwent a thyroidectomy and a course of radioactive Iodine treatment.

Just before the treatment they found out they were expecting a baby. I believe this was Jeff's gift to his brother. And the baby---my 1st grandchild---was my gift from heaven. Jeff taught me so much and I am honored that I was chosen to be his Mother, although I often felt unworthy and incapable of such a task. Thank You Jeff...I miss you so much but I know it was too hard for you to stay...My comfort is in your PEACE...I Love You with all my heart...Mom

SHERYL LETZGUS MCGINNIS WITH HEIKO GANZER

Jeff's story as told by his loving mom, Brigitte G., Tobyhanna, PA

"We all live by a system of ultimate judgments. If you expect this to be only about punishment, then you are wrong."

SAMANTHA SANDLER

JULY 28, 1982 – DECEMBER 16, 2005

(AGE 23)

HEROIN

"MY BEAUTIFUL DAUGHTER AND FRIEND"

The best day of my life was July 28, 1982, the day my beloved angel child Samantha was born. She was everything any mother would want, a dream baby, beautiful, easy, cuddly. After two brothers and two sons I was thrilled for a daughter. I nursed her for two years, just holding her and looking into her eyes---all the hopes and dreams!

She excelled at everything she did. She would always say "I did it for you mom. I want to make you proud!" A prouder mother I couldn't have been. She attended the Masters school grades 1-8, a small Christian school with good values. She loved horses, and became the Hartford County Jr. horseback riding champion. She graduated with the award for the best all around student in the school. She went on to Miss Porter's School in Farmington, CT. It is probably the most prestigious girls' school in the country. Jackie Kennedy went there.

Samantha graduated at the top of her class, president of the student council and disciplinary committee. We were thrilled when she got into Brown University. Her older brother Josh, was at Bowdoin

College, Zach was at Wesleyan University.

Always being an overachiever, Samantha became stressed at Brown. She wouldn't settle for any grade but an A. She would do papers over and over until she got an A. She started having panic attacks. On Oct. 19, 2002, she called me sobbing that she was having a breakdown and would kill herself if I didn't come and get her. I drove immediately to her dorm, slept and held her sobbing all night, then brought her home. She felt like a failure even though we assured her we were still proud of her and wanted her to be happy.

She became very depressed and finally, not knowing what to do, I brought her to an institute in Hartford, CT, a mental health facility where she stayed for two weeks. They kept her drugged most of the time, and diagnosed her as bipolar. She came home with lots of medication for depression, but it didn't seem to help. They kept changing medications because she kept having bad reactions, especially to Paxil, and terrible mood swings. They told me to keep her as stress-free as I could, so we decided to not send her back that semester.

While she was at the Institute she was housed in a coed adult floor because she was over 18. It was there that she met and befriended a heroin addict dropout, Raz. She was feeling like a failure and in a down moment he convinced her to try heroin. She was addicted immediately. The lying and stealing started. Heroin took my daughter from me.

I brought her to treatment programs but my insurance would only pay for outpatient. The director of the program, begged as well as Sam herself, for Connecticare to pay for inpatient but they kept refusing stating that she hadn't done enough outpatient first. She refused us paying out of pocket. My husband and I joined Families Anonymous so that we could learn how to help her.

I took her car and money. I drove her everywhere, watched her constantly. We were going to lick this together. If she had a craving, she would call me. She promised! She started having accidents and lost her license but Raz delivered drugs to my house.

I lived in Hell worrying about her, watching her sleep. I checked her over and over to make sure she was breathing at night. I even videotaped her high so she could see what it did to her. Her two older brothers and two younger sisters were getting very angry because she took so much of my time and energy. I was terrified to leave her alone. She convinced me that she could lick this and I was there to help her every step of the way. She had never, not been able to conquer anything she tried in her life. She was strong. She loved school and all she wanted was to go back.

She went to Umass for awhile but relapsed and overdosed and had to be taken to the hospital by ambulance. The doctor said she almost died, but she said she had learned her lesson and would never touch it again.

Finally she found Hampshire College in Amherst, Mass., a small $45,000 liberal arts college in a country setting. She said she could never find drugs there. In May she borrowed another student's car and drove to buy drugs, got arrested, had a hypodermic needle and cocaine in her possession, and ended up on probation. She said she absolutely learned her lesson and would never do it again! She promised over and over! I believed her.

She seemed to be back on course finally. She spent most of the summer of 2005, in China, going to school and working in an orphanage. She loved children and was getting her degree so she could work with troubled teens. She wrote me this email in June, 2005, while she was in China.

"MOMMY, sorry it's taken awhile. I have so much to tell you. I can't thank you enough for enabling and allowing me to take this trip; it is the single most healthy and life-enriching experience I have ever had. I wake up every day exhilarated, with energy and a natural high that is more sensational than anything that could ever come from a dirty powder.

I have been slowly learning to speak the language, going to festivals, exploring the city, meeting and spending time with the locals, and more. I get up early and am active all day. I bought a rescue cat named Shao mao at the market and it follows me everywhere and sleeps in my arms (it already has a home when I leave) and I am buying a Vespa for very cheap (that a friend will buy from me when I leave) today so I can drive through the cities and see as much as I can. Tomorrow I am going with a few students picked to visit an ancient village and temple, and then to a traditional Chinese wedding. I feel no anxiety, cravings, or inhibitions, etc. This place makes me want to make the most of each moment and embrace all this diverse world has to offer me in my lifetime. Hope all is well. Send all my love. Hope you're feeling better. I can't apologize enough for what transpired right before my departure. I hope you will soon see I am no longer the same person. I am looking to see if I can stay a few weeks longer. dzai jen, love always, Sammy.

The day after she came home she relapsed again. She got herself back in a program at Rushford. I drove her everyday. We talked, I pleaded, I begged. I was terrified. She finally admitted she was an addict. I took her and her boyfriend to NA and AA meetings which she hated. She said it was easy to get drugs there and it didn't help. FA is a 12 step program so I learned that I could not control her life so I had to trust she made the right decisions.

She came home for Thanksgiving and all was wonderful, she seemed better than ever, and determined to lick this problem. She was getting all A's in her classes and even filmed a movie using her sisters for a class. It was brilliant!

She also found a doctor who could prescribe an opiate blocker. We got the blood work on Thanksgiving break and picked up the prescription before I took her back to school.

I was concerned as she told me the day before Thanksgiving that she had had an abortion. When I drove her back to school I talked to her boyfriend, Jimmie, and told him about the drug blocker and that because of the abortion she would be emotionally fragile and to be very careful as I worried about a relapse.

He could call me any time day or night. I felt good because it was only two weeks before she came home for Christmas vacation. I sighed with relief. I talked to her several times and everything seemed to be going well. She assured me over and over that she was doing well.

I AM YOUR DISEASE

I decided to plan a Christmas party for all my friends as I hadn't done it in years. I had been too stressed. I decorated the house and tree, and my guests were to arrive on Dec. 16, 2005, at 7 pm. It was almost 6:30 p.m., when the doorbell rang. I opened the door and three policemen came in. They asked me if Samantha Sandler was my daughter and did she go to Hampshire College? When I said yes, they proceeded to tell me that her BODY had been found by her roommate at 9 a.m., that morning, deceased in her bed at the dorm of an apparent heroin overdose.

Apparently Jimmie had borrowed his parents' car and drove her the night before to buy drugs in West Hartford. He said she just wanted to do it one last time and to celebrate the end of the semester. She had decided to wait and start the blocker drug during Christmas break. He proceeded to bring her back to the dorm. A passerby student helped him get her to her room on the second floor as she was not able to walk or talk. Tuck said she just moaned. Tuck, the passerby, tried to convince Jimmie to call the EMT on campus or bring her to the hospital. Jimmie was very adamant about knowing how to take care of Sam and finally Tuck, who had never met either one of them before, reluctantly left. Evidently so did Jimmie. He left to return his parents' car.

When he returned the next morning it was too late. He called 911. Paramedics came. They tried CPR but nothing. She was taken to the medical examiner at 9 a.m., and I was never contacted by the school or police until 6:30 that night. My family's nightmare began.

Police treated the case so cold and uncaring. My family, her brothers, Josh 28 years old, Zach 27, and sisters Sloane 19 and Sierra 13, and father were devastated. The funeral, the numbness, disbelief, shock, pain, writing an obituary for your child. Calling her brother, Zach, who was living in France, to come home. No investigation, no blame. She was a drug addict and the police were not going to waste one minute of their time on this case. Nobody cared. Their attitude was she chose the drugs and paid the price. No one was wasting a minute on her case. Case closed!

December 16, 2005, was the worst day of my life, the day I lost my beloved angel, my best friend, Samantha. I will love and miss her every moment of every day until I die. My beautiful baby, Sammy.

I was a nurse, school and sexual assault counselor, PTO president, Girl Scout leader, and I was there everyday for my children. Being a good mother was my full time job. I drove them to school everyday and picked them up. I was always there for them, to talk and help them with any problems they had. They were our lives.

My husband and I have been together thirty-three years. He is a Princeton, Harvard Law graduate. We were at every swim meet, Lacrosse game, school play, profusely read to them, and patched every scraped knee ourselves. We had family vacations, lots of pets and lived in a beautiful home in a lovely neighborhood. They all did community service. Nothing was more important than being a good parent.

I know there are no guarantees, but in my wildest dreams NEVER, EVER did I think this could happen to us. I would have bet my life. Impossible! Not us! The truth we all now know is it can happen to anyone. Addiction will rip your heart out. No discrimination here. It's an epidemic---in every school, public or private.

It's five dollars for a bag of heroin. It can kill the first time you use it. It's taking our beautiful, brilliant children, our future. It's Satan. It is HELL on earth! IT CAN HAPPEN TO ANYONE! It leaves shattered families and breaks hearts. IT KILLS anyone that gets in its way. Every day another parent will endure the excruciating pain of a knock on the door or phone call informing them that their child's body is in the morgue. You will never be the same, raped of innocence and forever wondering " how could this happen to me?" It can happen to anyone!

We loved Samantha more than life itself, as she did us, and we said it constantly. We would have died for her if we could have. Samantha was 23 years old when we lost her. If she only knew when she took that first snort or used that first syringe, the torment and pain she would put her family and friends through, she would NEVER have chosen to use. She, as well as us and countless others, became victims.

I AM YOUR DISEASE

Samantha's story as told by her loving mom, Sharon Sandler, Bloomfield, CT

"I never knew, when you lost your child, what you were going through. I wasn't there, I stayed away. I just deserted you. I didn't know the words to say. I didn't know the things to do. I think your pain so frightened me, I didn't know how to comfort you. And then one day my child died. You were the first one there. You quietly stayed by my side, listened, and held me as I cried. You didn't leave, you didn't go. The lesson learned is ...Now I know!"   Author unknown

JAMES BYRON KEATON

FEBRUARY 14, 1974 – MAY 22, 1999
(AGE 25)

COCAINE

"RELAX MOM. IT AIN'T THAT BAD. YOU WORRY TOO MUCH."

Jim was born Feb. 14 1974, in Yuma Arizona. I was married but I was a single mom. Jim's dad had decided early on that he wasn't ready to be a dad so he left us. He was in the Marines so it was an easy out for him.

After his dad left, I moved back to Ohio to be with my family. I was scared to be a single mom but I did it. Jim was a good kid. I had no trouble with him, he was a mama's boy & I loved it.

In 1977 I became pregnant with twins. Boy what a surprise for me & Jim. Now he not only had one sibling, he had two to do deal with, but he adjusted well & was a pretty good big brother.

The twins' dad was around more often than not, but we made no plans to get married, so I carried on as a single mom. Jim loved school & sports & he had so many friends. The phone rang off the wall, kids filled the house & yard all the time, we had sleep-overs & cookouts. I think they all had a pretty good childhood.

He loved kids, he would get on the floor with my grandson Cody

& play for hours with him. I ran a daycare so he did a lot of playing and the kids loved it.

Sports was his passion especially football, he played from the time he could catch a ball. He really got good at it in Middle school. He received Player of the Week awards often. In high school he excelled in football and academics. He knew if he didn't do well in classes he wouldn't play football. He played defensive tackle & fullback & was on special teams.

Jim worked out all the time, didn't drink or smoke. His grandpa would always tell him to keep his grades up, because he didn't want him to be a mill hunky like he was. So Jim did. He was the type who didn't have to work hard for his grades. He was a smart kid. Jim was a mama's boy & he would tell you so. He was never far from home. His college was only 45 minutes away from home so he was home often.

When he got hurt his first year of college playing football he had to quit school & get a job. He was a homebody who never went out much, maybe a date once in awhile. He always went to the girls' house or they came to mine, and most of the time the guys hung out at the house too.

When he did leave the house I always knew where he was. He would call & let me know his plans. Then he moved into my garage apartment. It was just a one room or one car garage, no bathroom facilities & no kitchen so he was in the house all the time, he & his Rottweiler, Zeus. Boy what a pair. Every time Jim had to come in the house so did Zeus. When I was in the kitchen fixing supper or anything, Jim was sitting on the cupboard with Zeus right at his feet wondering what was to eat & when it would be done. They are two very large things in my very small kitchen. If I wasn't stepping, or should I say tripping, over one, I'd trip over the other. Believe it or not I loved it. I miss that. I'd get whatever was cooking done & they would head to the dining room to eat, both of them. We would watch football, his favorite team being the Dallas Cowboys, and he'd jump up & down & scream at the refs. He was something else!

He would pull up out front in his little car, a two-seater with Zeus in the other seat. He said he had to go to a buddy's house and did I need anything while he was gone. He had to take the other seat out for Zeus 'cuz he was so big. They always had a good time too. One day he asked me to go for a ride with him. I get in the car and he takes off and I'm rocking all over the place 'cuz he forgot to bolt the seat down after Zeus got out. He'd just laugh & tell me to hang on.

We'd end up going out to eat, and then I would be up in my room watching TV & he would come up & tell me he needed " parental advice" and we'd talk until the wee hours of the morning about any & everything that was important to him, knowing we both had to get up for work the next day. On Mother's Day or any day actually he would bring me flowers (most of the time from other peoples' yards) or sometimes just dandelions. I loved it! He always made me feel special.

Several months before he died he decided he wanted to meet his dad. We lived in Ohio & his dad lived in Arizona. I told him it was his decision. He told me he didn't know whether he was gonna hit him or hug him. Well he didn't do either but he did say that they did a lot of talking. He didn't get all the answers he wanted but he was glad he had met him.

On the way home from Arizona he & his buddy got pulled over by the police for a cracked windshield & a seatbelt violation. I guess the police did a random search & found drugs in the car & not just a small amount. They were arrested. Jim called me & told me where he was and I flipped. He said he would explain everything when he got home. I don't remember all the details but it had to do with money.

When he went to court he had heavy fines & had to report to a probation officer every week for a year. I guess there was no jail time because it was his first offense.

I asked him if he was doing drugs, he told me he was but he wasn't hooked, that he didn't do it very often. What was I supposed to do? I never saw him high. He was the same with me all the time. I saw no signs, or did I and chose not to do anything because I trusted him? I asked his brother and sister and they told me he was getting high, so I confronted him again. He told me to relax, that I worried too much and that he was fine. I told him if he had drugs in or around the house they had to go, he assured me there were none. He was a grown man and you can't tell a grown man what to do so I believed him; well the fact that there were no drugs in the house anyway.

It was a few weeks, maybe a month after that, that his sister came in the house one evening & told me she hadn't seen Jim all day & he wouldn't answer his door, it was locked, and the music was up really loud which wasn't like Jim to have the music really loud. So I went to check it out. I told my daughter to get me a knife and we'd pry the lock, that maybe he had taken Zeus for a walk.

I pried the lock and the minute I stepped inside I knew he was gone. He looked like he was just sleeping. He'd been gone about 5 hours, or so the coroner said. Everything else after that was just a blur. That's it, no rehabs, no fights, no jail time. Just gone. The next several days after that were hard, making funeral arrangements. I never had to do this so I was clueless.

I cremated Jim (his wishes). He still lives with me. Like I said, he was never far from home. There were so many people at the funeral, I didn't know 90% of them but Jim did. Everyone who came up to me he had obviously made an impression on. I was impressed and proud.

Jim was a good guy, with good looks, and charm. He was kind, loving and compassionate.

Jim was my best friend & my right arm. It's very hard still to deal with him being gone. He took the wrong path for awhile but before he could turn back he paid the ultimate price.

Jim's story as told by his loving mom and best friend, Margie Keaton, Steubenville, OH

" Remember how I laughed, remember how I loved. Use me as the reason you embrace life, not the reason you don't."

Please visit Jim's website:

http://www.geocities.com/myjimsspot/jimsspot.html

I AM YOUR DISEASE

A poem written for Jim by his loving mom, Margie.

That Night
I Looked into your beautiful face that night,
I found you in your room.
I remembered all the special ways,
you'd brighten up my gloom.
I think about you all the time,
and why you had to leave.
I'll never ever hold you again,
and that I can't believe.
I sit back and remember things,
when you would come to my room to talk.
If only I would have said more to you,
I wouldn't have had to pry your lock.
I looked into your beautiful face that night,
I found you in your room.
The hardest thing I ever did,
was when they made me leave you so soon.
I love you & I miss you,
I want you to come back.
I know that that's not possible,
when God takes something from you,
He doesn't give it back.
You must have been very special.

SHERYL LETZGUS MCGINNIS WITH HEIKO GANZER

A LETTER TO JIM

Jim,

Why are you gone? Why did you do the things you did? I can't remember your laugh, your smile, your smell or that twinkle in your eyes. Where did you go? We stopped playing, and talking.

I wish I knew then what I know now. People would tell me things, I would ask you, but you told me to relax, that I worried too much, so I didn't believe them. I believed in you. I wish I would have listened to them. Maybe you wouldn't be where you're at today wherever that is.

You promised me you were ok. I didn't see the signs. You should have talked to me. Was I so blind to the things you did that I didn't see you hurting inside? Were you calling out to me for help and I just didn't hear or did I see and choose to do nothing?

You always said I worried too much. Maybe I didn't worry enough. Maybe if I had said more, or worried more, you'd still be here with me. I'd like to believe I did everything I could but I don't. I've failed you miserably and I can't even tell you how sorry I am. I'll never forgive myself and I'll never know if you'll forgive me. I didn't mean to let you down.

I love you and I miss you with every part of my being. Maybe some day you'll find it in your heart to forgive me and we can talk and play again.

I love you,

Mom

KATIE KEVLOCK

July 8, 1986 – June 29, 2003
(Age 16)

HEROIN

"THIS IS BIGGER THAN ME, MOM. IT'S A MONSTER I CAN'T CONTROL."

Grief is a uniquely personal experience – different for each person, even those grieving the death of the same individual. We shouldn't judge anyone's manner of grieving.

The bottom line is that it hurts. I'd always heard that losing a child was the worst thing that could happen to a person. Little did I know that I would learn this truth, first-hand.

I'd been called to the ER by John, my ex-husband, because our daughter, Katie, had been taken there by ambulance. I'd expected an overdose because we'd been struggling to get her inpatient care for her heroin addiction.

Arriving at the hospital, I'd expected her to be admitted for her "qualifying" first overdose for inpatient care. I was puzzled, however, when I was escorted to a closed-door room.

The moment that door opened and I saw John sitting there with a priest, my heart froze. Surely, the situation was grave.

But, that moment lasted only a nano second before John stood up and uttered the words that are indelibly etched into my mind for all eternity: "We lost her."

I have relived this scene over and over again so many times. It just keeps playing back in my mind. It won't go away. And I hear those words, " We lost her" , over and over and over again.

They also asked me if I wanted to see Katie. I said no, I did not want to remember her like this. But before leaving, they asked me again, saying that they didn't want me to regret my decision. I changed my mind.

Katie was the very first dead person I had ever seen, other than at a funeral parlor. They look a lot different in the casket - all stiff, and hard, and made up. Kind of like a mannequin. Not real at all.

But there she was. Dead. Cold. Gray. She looked just like my Katie, except that the life was gone from her and, with that, so was the "color" of her life. A dead person looks gray. They just have no color whatsoever.

Katie still had the tubes coming out of her nose and mouth and she looked like my baby girl, but she was gone. Her body was still there, but what had really made her my Katie, her life, her spirit, was gone.

I asked the nurse to lower the bed rail so I could get close to her. I touched her. She was so cold. I kissed her on the cheek and the neck as I often had in life, and then climbed up for one last hug. Katie, my beloved, only daughter, was gone. Forever.

It took quite a while to get used to the back door not slamming, Katie not bopping in, the phone not ringing, etc.

For months, I think I was in a state of total shock and disbelief. The reality of it took forever to sink in. Like I was living in some kind of cloud of unreality. For the longest time, it was kind of like she was still here, even though she wasn't. Accepting that she wasn't took so long.

How could I believe or accept that my beautiful and beloved 16-year-old daughter was dead and gone? It just "did not compute."

In fact, I often have dreams, which include Katie still being with me in the flesh, even though I know she's dead. And I keep wondering how she can still be with me, when she's dead. For example, I'll dream that she's sitting in my kitchen, and I know she goes to school every day, but I don't get any report cards, because, she is officially and legally dead. Yet, she is still here with me, just like always. And, I think, well, this isn't so bad. Even though she's dead, it's as if she isn't. Not much different at all, really. Totally illogical.

There is usually no big event or anything associated with these dreams, just the fact that Katie is there with me, during the normal routines of life. Yet, in these dreams, I am puzzled as to how that can be. And, we have family get-togethers, go out in public and the neighborhood together, and, no one else is the least bit phased by Katie's presence, despite the fact that everyone knows she is dead.

These dreams are frequent and recurring. My "take" on it is that I still can't really accept that she is gone. However, someone who interprets dreams for a living, recently told me that persistent, recurring dreams such as this are actually the dead person contacting us, telling us they are OK. She said that Katie has been communicating with me, and, now that I know that, and that she's alright, I won't have the dream again.

Initially, and for a long time thereafter, I also had extreme and intense anger at the " system" that had essentially "blocked" us from getting timely and appropriate treatment for Katie. Yet, in a sense, that anger had kind of kept me going. It seems that the more my anger and anguish subsided, the more my other difficulties increased. With the passage of time, I became more and more troubled about the hows and the whys of my baby girl ever even getting involved in drugs in the first place. To this day, that is still so hard for me to comprehend.

Katie's home life certainly wasn't perfect, but, nowadays, what child's is? How many truly happy, intact families do you know? Yet, there are millions of kids out there with really bad childhoods, who DO NOT succumb to drugs. Why? Why my little girl? What could have been SO bad, as to turn her to drugs?

Yet, the fact that it did happen, brings out all kinds of parental guilt. I found myself thinking about times that perhaps, in the busy struggle of daily life, I may not have paid enough attention to her.

Wishing that there were some way that I could go back in time and "re-do" my life. I had always told her that I loved her, and I had always hugged her and kissed her. But, perhaps... I don't know. I'm sure that this is probably a fairly normal reaction in a situation like this.

I just keep going over and over in my mind, every possible thing that I might have done differently, that might have produced a different result. God! If only I could be given a chance to "turn back the hands of time" and give it another shot. These kinds of thoughts cause me tremendous mental turmoil and anguish.

In general, I have to say I believe that today's dual income families, with both parents working, cause many parents to be over-stressed by the daily struggle to survive. The "fall-out" of this situation is that most kids today do not have the luxury of doting, stay-at-home moms. I think the German government, which actually PAYS moms to stay at home with their children until they are of school age, is "onto" something.

Anyhow, the more time that passed the harder and harder it became for me to stay focused, maintain any kind of organization, and to be motivated to do anything.

Tasks that would otherwise seem insignificant became increasingly difficult. A prime example would be paying a bill by mail; a nearly insurmountable undertaking for me. First, I've got to write the check. Then, I've got to address an envelope. Next, I've got to put the appropriate postage on the envelope. Finally, I've got to find a mailbox to put it in.

I know this sounds totally crazy. No big deal, right? But, to me, it is an enormous and complex, multi-step chore. Overwhelming.

By June of 2005, I realized I could no longer perform the duties of my job. Everything in life just seems to have gotten more and more difficult. During my last quarter of teaching, I had failed to post my interim progress report grades. This was a major failure for me. Throughout my entire life, I had always been an extremely conscientious person. This was NOT me!

The bottom line is that I am always sad and heartbroken, no matter how I look on the outside. Sure, I can smile, laugh, joke, look like I'm having a good time, but, the reality of it is that I am always heartbroken on the inside. It never goes away.

Since Katie's death, I have been hospitalized three times for suicidal ideation and depression. During my last hospitalization, I learned that trauma, even emotional trauma, does cause real changes in one's brain and its functioning. In a way that was a bit comforting. At least I know that these difficulties I am having are not without real basis.

I've also thoroughly researched all possible methods of readily-available suicide, only to learn that it is really not that easy to do. The thing that prevents me from attempting it is fear of failure. Fear of winding up physically disabled, or more significantly mentally disabled than I already am, instead of dead. A fate worse than death in my opinion.

A major effect of the death of a child may be the desire of the parent to die a premature death, in order to join that child. That is definitely where my heart has been ever since I lost Katie.

What I learned from my suicide research is that a heroin overdose is really a pretty good way to die. Only trouble is, I'd be terrified to go into the neighborhoods I'd need to go into to get heroin. How the hell did my beautiful, little baby girl do that? How could she have been so fearless?

I also would not want to risk getting arrested or having to first become a heroin addict. No way would I want to first have to endure the HELL of heroin addiction. Poor Katie. And all the others that drugs have claimed. By the time these kids realize that the drugs have their "hooks" in them, they must feel so trapped in a hopeless and terrifying hell.

I've really tried to find other things to make my life meaningful. I built a beautiful backyard paradise and also started a brand new hobby: Boating. Yes, these things are really nice, and very enjoyable. And, I had thought and hoped that they might change my outlook on life, might make me want to go on living. But, as nice as they are, they really aren't enough.

I miss Katie so much, I can't stand it. I long to talk to her about things. Share experiences, hopes, and dreams, babysit for her children. Help guide her into adulthood. I want to hug her, kiss her. I think about her all the time. The little daily " reminders" are constant. Things as simple as something I used to buy for her, all of the friends' houses I used to drop her off at over the years, TV commercials for a million different things, spiders, yellow VW Beetles, hair care products, nail salons, places we used to go, all the different playing fields where I watched her play sports. This list could go on forever and ever. I couldn't begin to name every little thing that makes me think of my Katie on a DAILY basis. Many times a day, actually.

I've often heard other parents who've lost children tell me that they are having a bad day because it is the anniversary of their child's death, or, it is their child's birthday, or, it is a holiday. I don't have those experiences. I just don't have any special days that are worse than others, because, in my personal grief experience, every day is bad. All of those "special" days don't really stand out for me, because the pain is constant and unrelenting.

There are many times when I lay down at night and as soon as my head hits the pillow, I see visions of Katie, and I just can't fall asleep.

There are also times when I wake up in the morning with pain in my chest, moaning in agony, thinking about Katie. I seem to go through life with a "heaviness" that I just can't explain. It drags me down all the time.

Yes, I take anti-depressants, yes, I see a counselor, and, yes, I try to drink enough beer to just make the pain go away. But nothing seems to work. It is just always there.

It is nearly impossible for me to go grocery shopping, cook, wash dishes, do laundry, change my sheets, take a shower, change my clothes, clean my house. All of these things are really basic activities of daily living and really should not be all that difficult. Yet, to me, they are. All require focus, concentration and motivation---things that are seriously lacking in me now. I consistently put them off until there is no other available option, as in no more clothes to wear, nothing left to eat, no more clean dishes in the house, etc., etc.

I also lose things. Constantly. Important things, too. It drives me nuts. Another serious problem is forgetfulness. My memory doesn't seem to work right. I frequently forget important things, like taking medication. For example, I decide to take some aspirin for a headache. But then I'll find myself sometime later, wondering if I ever took that aspirin or not. I don't know. I can't remember if I did or I didn't. This type of occurrence happens frequently and, like losing things all the time, it drives me crazy.

So, if you're a kid thinking of picking up your first drink or first joint, I hope you will seriously think about how totally the death of my little girl has destroyed all that is left of my life. And, by the way, do you know that before you make that decision, there is no way to know ahead of time, whether or not you'll get addicted? But, if you do have the genetic background, once you've made that first choice, it could already be too late. Please don't risk it!

In the course of talking to many addicts and their families, none of them wanted or expected this to happen to them. It just seemed like "the thing to do" at the time, because their " so-called" friends were doing it. They never thought that they would become addicted and have their lives totally devoted to the pursuit of their next high, leaving their lives and the lives of their families in total ruins.

One of the "symptoms" of adolescence and young adulthood is invincibility and immortality---nothing bad will ever happen to you. But, guess what? Bad things DO happen! And, they happen to GOOD people! I tell you this from my heart, because Katie was truly a good person. Her heart was good. She was loving and compassionate. But, the drugs did not care about that. They took her. hey took her away from me and everybody else in our family who loved her and who now dearly miss her.

The suffering that your drug addiction could inflict on your entire family---not only parents, but also siblings, grandparents, aunts, uncles, nieces, nephews, etc., is beyond your ability to imagine.

If you really must experiment with these deadly substances, at least wait until your brain is fully matured. That doesn't happen until about the age of 25. Give yourself half a fighting chance in this life before you risk this dreadful, lifelong sickness.

It is devastating for a parent to lose a child for any reason because it is just not the " natural order" of things. The English language does not even have a word for a parent who's lost a child. We've got widows, widowers, and orphans, but there IS NO WORD for a parent who has lost a child. Probably because it is just too horrible.

But, a parent who loses a child to drugs has an added burden. There is the issue of shame, the issue of it being the child's " choice," and the tremendous burden of introspection and regret upon the parents who wonder what they did wrong.

All of this heaped on top of having lost a beloved child. Oh, the pain. It is just so constant, so hard to bear and endure. There are so many daily reminders. So many dreams. So many regrets. I would not wish this on anyone. Trust me; it is a life of pure hell. Hell on earth. From a grieving parent's point of view, it is a fate WORSE than death. I know, because I would rather be dead than be living through this.

Katie's story as told by her loving mom, Sue Shields, Bucks County, PA

"The only cure for grief is action" - George Henry Lewes

For more information on addiction please log on to the following sites:

www.beat-the-drum.org

www.faces-of-addiction.com

I AM YOUR DISEASE

A GIRL NAMED KATIE

(by Mark Banchi)

Thirty-four years of teaching means thousands of days and thousands of faces that drift in and out of memory. Some students make indelible impressions. We'll encounter them years later and recognize them right away. Others fade into a kind of blur, and it takes real concentration and a few questions to recall their presence in our lives.

Memory is a tricky thing. We tend to remember moments and forget entire months. From hours of conversation and volumes of written work, we'll remember a phrase, a line or some brief anecdote. A lifetime of encounters is overshadowed by just a few succinct recollections.

With those individuals with whom we have more limited contact, it is often a feature or personality trait that brands itself upon our memory. With Katie Kevlock it was her smile. Once you saw that little grin you knew that you had encountered a unique spirit. There was something mischievous about that smile. It was the smile of a little girl who was more adult than her years might have indicated. Some would call her adventuresome; others might say she was a risk taker. Whatever the case, Katie wrestled with many of the same demons all adolescents encounter. She won lots of battles, but lost some too. In the end, she lost the most important battle, and we lost her.

What she left us were her words, some photographs and souvenirs. What we remember is personal to each of us, but to me she left an indelible image. It's the image of a little girl standing at her locker and smiling. Smiling an unforgettable smile, mischievous and determined, innocent and experienced.

Oh, there's one other thing. It's a battle that rages on and ensnares other young men and women. It's a battle against addiction, an insidious war that claims too many of our children and snuffs out too many smiles. And so we continue on buoyed by a memory and cheered by a little girl's grin, determined to do something to make this world just a little safer for the Katies of every generation. We simply can't afford to lose another smile like hers.

JOSHUA JOSEPH

JUNE 23, 1981 – OCTOBER 6, 2003
(AGE 22)

COCAINE/VALIUM

"A LIFE TOO FAST"

I can still feel the hug he gave me two hours before he overdosed. I had gone to see him to congratulate him for being clean a whole year.

Four hours later I got a call from my ex-wife, where he was living due to proximity to his job. (He had stayed with me for almost the entire year he was clean. I gave him random drug tests constantly). My ex-wife was calling to tell me that Josh was being taken to the hospital, that she had kicked his door down and found him not breathing. Her boyfriend performed CPR until the paramedics came and they got him breathing again.

In the hospital, they told me that they thought there was brain damage because they weren't sure how long he had had no air but they were trying to stabilize him. A nurse took me aside and told me she felt that if he lived he would be a vegetable.

I signed a DNR order. The next morning brought the shift change of doctors. A young doctor looked at Josh and begged me to pull the DNR order. She said he is so young and to give her a chance. I said OK and all of a sudden five doctors started doing everything they could.

After two hours she came over to me and said that she could not do anything and I told her to reinstate the DNR. But because we had pulled the order, now they had to get the legal department involved and many more forms had to be filled out.

While all of this was going on his heart started to slow down and I held him as he passed on. My little boy was dead.

At his funeral there were over a thousand people, and one hundred-fifty cars. The director said he had never seen anything like it. If he only knew how many people were there to help him and who loved him.

I found out where the drugs came from and first went to the police...nothing. Then to the narcotics squad...nothing. Finally somebody knew someone in the squad and his friends offered to do a sting. Guess what? Nothing! They could not care less. I gave them names and places and they did nothing. I guess it is more important to write out parking tickets.

To this day, the man who sold him the drugs is on the street selling to others and the police do not care. I am not angry with the pusher. He did not force my son to use drugs again. I am angry with my son and the police.

The anger against my son is different. I am not angry for the disease that he had, just that he didn't listen to his counselor or continue going to the NA meetings that he had started.

I run a foundation in his honor. So far we have bought a room in a half-way house and have given away a scholarship to a child that has changed the course of her life. She was an addict in high school and is now in nursing school. The scholarship is non-grade related. I promised the high school at least nine more scholarships (one a year), and hopefully as the money comes in, I will do even more in his memory.

Josh's story told by his loving dad, Paul Joseph, Port Washington, NY

"For such a big guy there was never a more kinder or gentler soul"

I AM YOUR DISEASE

"He was the sweetest, most gentle big guy I've ever known and he will be in my heart forever"

Please visit Josh's website at www.joshjoseph.com

SHERYL LETZGUS MCGINNIS WITH HEIKO GANZER

A POEM BY JOSHUA JOSEPH – APRIL, 2002

As I sit and think about my life
It makes me want to grab that knife

These drugs have brought me to my low,
Places I thought I would never go

It was those feelings I tried to hide
That made me feel I had no inside.

I thought one bag was all I would need
But all I did was plant a seed

Then it went to nine or ten
Brought me right to hell's den

I knew a meeting was all I needed
But now my plan was much defeated

Now that I am on my death bed,
I wish I would have listened to what my sponsor said.

As I start my life over again
Eating healthy, go back to the gym

I AM YOUR DISEASE

No more trips to New York
No more trips to county court

I put on ten pounds in the last two months
Stopped smoking all those blunts.

I haven't called in sick to work
If only those voices still didn't lurk

But I'm stronger than them, I know I am
I'm going to stay clean, I know I can.

I got my complexion back again
And every night I pick up a pen

To write about the day that passed
With these meetings I know that this will last.

Oh my God what did I do?
Now it's back to rehab #22

I missed that meeting just one day
Now look at the price I have to pay

I lost my family, friends, and soul
And now my life has no control

SHERYL LETZGUS MCGINNIS WITH HEIKO GANZER

Now I'm starting from Day one
Thank God I had put down that gun

When I said this is gonna be the end
And I wasn't even my own friend

I know there are good things in life
Happiness, friendship, and even a wife

But drugs always cut me short
And now I'm back at county court

The judge gave me twenty-five to life
I think I will go grab that knife

Because I don't want to rot in jail
Now instead I will rot in hell

As I look down from up above
And see all these people full of love

All the decisions that I regret
Too much loss of self-respect

This shit is real whether white, black, purple or blue
So don't ever think it can't happen to you

I AM YOUR DISEASE

I thought I was smarter, I thought I was cool
But now look who is really the fool

I had so much potential and there it went
I had not a dollar not even a cent

Now it's too late to tell this to you
Who knew I would die, nobody knew

I send to y'all from up above
With all my heart, soul and love.

JOHNNY PAUL KING

JANUARY 18, 1966 – MARCH 17, 2000

(Age 34)

COCAINE/ALCOHOL

"MY PRECIOUS JOHNNY ANGEL"

My beloved son Johnny had a substance abuse problem. He fought it long and hard but lost his battle with these demons at 10:56 p.m., on Friday, March 17, 2000.

My life and my family's life as we knew it was over! I never knew it was possible for a heart to feel such agony and yet continue to beat!

I had many emotions about Johnny's addiction; helplessness, fear, and failure.

I spent many a sleepless night sitting up with Johnny or lying awake, worrying about him. One thing I never felt was shame or embarrassment about my son. He was caught in the grips of his own personal hell.

I miss my son more every day.

Please, if you or someone you love has a substance abuse problem get HELP!

SHERYL LETZGUS MCGINNIS WITH HEIKO GANZER

A LETTER TO MY SWEET JOHNNY, FROM MAMA

My sweet Johnny Angel. Nothing is the same without you. I can still see you out in the back cutting the grass. You would get to the back porch and blow the horn for someone to bring you another beer. Boy, you really loved your beer.

I remember the farmers using the irrigation out back in their fields. You would go to the bottom of our back yard and stand under the irrigation. It watered a good part of our back yard.

Remember when you cut the limbs off the pine trees? They were never cut after that. Everyone had left out there but me. Seemed all I could do was cry.

I look back on all the good times we had. We went through some rough times but I try to think of the good ones.

I think at first what I missed the most was your phone call every day. I still hear your voice on the phone. It was Thursday night. The last thing you said to me was "I love you mama. See you in the morning."

But that didn't happen. The next thing was that awful phone call.

Granny said she remembers how she would take you a biscuit and sausage every morning. If you weren't there she would give it to someone else. She still talks about that.

I know you are in a better place and you are free of all the pain, but it sure is lonely here without you.

I just keep asking "Why, Johnny, why?"

I hope you know how much you were, and still are, loved. I hope now you are at peace and can rest.

I know you are great friends with all the other angels.

I can't believe you are 40 years old now. What do you think of that?

I see you everywhere baby. You are always with me. I love you my precious Johnny angel.

I AM YOUR DISEASE

Mama.

You are my Precious Baby,
I love you with all my heart,
But sadly the time has come,
And we must part.

So now I lay you down to sleep,
I give you back to God
For Him to keep.

Rest peacefully in the arms of Jesus, My Angel.

Love always, Mama

Johnny's story as told by his loving mom, Grace King, Albany, GA

"THE MOMENT MY WORLD CRASHED" BY JOHNNY'S SISTER, DEBBIE

Johnny is the youngest of 4 kids…the baby and he began drinking at about 14 years of age. By 16 he was up to marijuana and by 19 on cocaine. At 23 he was arrested during a drug sting. My husband was working under cover narcotics at the time and the only reason he was not on this maneuver was he was at home recuperating from serious injuries he sustained in a drug bust a few weeks prior to this. When he and I went to get Johnny out of jail, he asked him, "how do you think I would have felt going home to tell my wife, your sister, that I had just put her baby brother in jail?"

All Johnny could say was, "I know, I am sorry."

The deal had been made that if we got Johnny out of jail he would go to rehab and he did for 30 days. Deep down I think it was a relief to him and he was eager to go.

While there he talked constantly about never wanting "that monkey on my back again" . Johnny managed to stay away from cocaine for the next 10 years but did continue to drink his beer daily and use marijuana as often as he could. He often cursed drugs and hated what they had done to his life. I cannot count the times Johnny told me "I am nothing but a dope head, that's all I have ever been and all I will ever be."

He would threaten my oldest son, Jason, that he had better never find out he was using any kind of drugs because he knew the damage they could and would do, he knew how hard it was to leave them alone once they had you in their grip.

Johnny was very much a mama's boy and at 34 years old although he had been in some long-term relationships he had never married or had children. He called mama every single day, even if she was out of town on vacation, he talked to her.

He tried moving out on his own a few times but always ended up having to move back in with mama because of being unable to pay his rent because of alcohol and drug abuse. After Johnny started using again he would pawn things and we found many pawn tickets in his belongings...we were able to buy back, the majority were lost forever. There were times when he literally had to borrow money from loan companies just to pay his dealer James. In fact he was paying on such a loan at the time of his death.

Johnny always knew some how that he would not be here very long and he would get furious about the taxes that were taken out of his pay check each week, especially Social Security, saying he would never live long enough to collect any of it. He would never obligate himself to long-term purchases such as homes etc., because of all the interest he would be charged and not live to see it paid off.

Johnny never felt he really fit in anywhere and could be some what of a loner but was fiercely loyal to the people he considered friends. I rarely remember Johnny walking with his head held up, but more remember him pacing with his head hanging down and looking as though he had the weight of the world on his shoulders.

Watching Johnny struggle for all the years he did made me run the gamut of emotions. It was very difficult because Johnny would become someone we didn't even know, a stranger. Some times it was heartbreaking because it was like watching him commit a slow painful suicide. I felt many things, helplessness, pain, frustration and even anger but the one thing I never felt was embarrassment. Although I would get angry at times I think I was probably more angry at the disease than I was at Johnny, I always knew Johnny didn't choose this life, it chose him and he just couldn't beat it.

Most people do not understand my feelings as a sibling. I have been told that I have not lost a child, only a brother and that basically I have no right to feel the way I do. Other times people have merely humored me by allowing me to talk about Johnny and my feelings but really didn't understand why I felt them so strongly. My husband Robert has tried to support me and listen to me and has been a great comfort to me but deep down I know even he really doesn't understand the depth of my pain and so I have often felt very alone in my journey.

Johnny struggled long and hard and he finally lost his battle on March 17, 2000, at 10:56 p.m. His pain was over, ours continues.

Saturday March 4, 2000 Mama has come for a visit. We are talking about Johnny and his problems and I told her "I hate to say this, but something horrible is going to happen to Johnny."

Thursday March 9, 2000 I talked to Johnny on the computer today. We used voice chat and he thought that was just about the neatest thing he had ever seen. He sounded so good. Happy and upbeat. I tried to talk to him about going into a rehab but he insisted he didn't need to. "I'm alright," he said. " I am going to beat it this time. I don't want you down there worrying about me. I promise I am going to be alright. I love you baby."

Saturday March 11, 2000 Mama has brought Mema down for a visit today. I told her "Mama, I know you don't like me to say this but something terrible is going to happen to Johnny. He is going to end up dead in a ditch somewhere. It's not a matter of IF. It's a matter of WHEN, and I am afraid it's coming really soon."

Monday March 13, 2000 Today at work I was so nervous and agitated. I had a strong sense of foreboding. I felt as though I would scream if I couldn't get out of there! I finally just walked out!

Tuesday March 14, 2000 I had an overwhelming urge to go home to Albany. I began making plans to go the coming Friday. The closer Friday got the stronger the urge became. The weather predicted severe thunderstorms for Friday evening so I decided to wait until the next morning to leave.

Saturday March 18, 2000...2:39 A.M. The telephone rang. This was not unusual as my husband is a police officer and our phone often rings at night. I had become so accustomed to it that I could answer it in my sleep. But this was different. I don't know why. But for some reason I turned on the light and looked at the clock before answering it. A lady asked to speak to my husband. I knew it was not the police department because they always identify themselves but I did not ask who it was. I think I knew. His words were vague and I sat watching, desperately trying to read his face. Fearing the worst possible scenario, that my premonitions had indeed come true. I asked him repeatedly if someone was hurt. He nodded yes. I said "It's Johnny." He again nodded yes. I knew the answer but I asked anyway. "He is dead isn't he?" After what seemed like a lifetime...he slowly nodded...yes.

My 34 year old baby brother Johnny was killed
Friday March 17, 2000, at 10:56 p.m.

He was struck by a car while he was crossing a highway. It was ruled accidental but left many unanswered questions. I have been able to trace his footsteps until 10:00 p.m. when he left two friends, Matt and Jay's home with a third "friend," Raymond. We do know that Johnny was very upset with Raymond because he had used Johnny's video card and rented some movies that he never returned and the store was calling Johnny at work, holding him responsible. Apparently there was a disagreement between Johnny and Raymond and Johnny got out of the vehicle and began walking back to his car which he had left at Matt and Jay's. He did not make it.

According to Raymond who Johnny had once been roommates with, he had not seen Johnny in over a week and denies picking Johnny up at Matt and Jay's house. However, we know for a fact that Johnny did indeed leave with Raymond. Raymond does admit seeing Johnny lying in the road and not stopping. He has given three different versions of his story.

He went BACK to tell Matt and Jay about Johnny but no one was home. He went BACK and only one of them was there so he told him. He went BACK and told both of them. 'My question is HOW do you go BACK to somewhere you have NOT been?

Johnny was twenty miles from home. His car was approximately two miles away from the accident scene. It was a dark area and he was on the opposite side of a five-lane highway.

Raymond admits that even though he could not see Johnny's face he KNEW it was him and he had been hit by a car and KNEW he was dead. He also admitted no emergency vehicles were there at the time he saw Johnny lying in the road. He knew entirely too many details that no one else knew for him NOT to have been there.

He did not attend visitation or the funeral because according to him, he had received word that several people were out for him and "I did not want to cause a scene."

He offered to take a polygraph but never showed up. The investigating police officer said he is only guilty of being "morally wrong" not criminally.

Raymond moved out of state and we have not heard from him since. I believe with all my heart Raymond actually saw the accident happen and just drove away leaving my brother in the road.

The driver of the accident vehicle and strangers who stopped were more concerned about my brother than a "friend" of twenty-five or more years! With friends like this who needs enemies?

Since Johnny was high on alcohol and crack at the time of the accident it was ruled his fault and no charges were filed against the driver.

I AM YOUR DISEASE

UPDATE

June 25, 2001

Fifteen months and 9 days after the accident I finally spoke with the driver of the vehicle personally. He requested that I not use his name and I respect that. He was not charged with any wrongdoing and is as much of a victim of Substance Abuse as Johnny. He is another innocent person whose life and the lives of his family have been forever changed.

Full of remorse he stated over and over "I am so sorry, I never saw him, I never saw him. He came out of nowhere. My God I would have wrecked myself, I would have run my car off the road before I hit him if I had only seen him. I was just going to work, that's all I was doing. I was just trying to go to work."

A very soft-spoken man, he said he still has trouble driving on "that road" and in fact had been taking a longer route to work in order to avoid it.

He went on to say that although he no longer has nightmares about it, not a day goes by that he doesn't think about it over and over. He went on to tell me how many times when he is sitting at his desk at work, or trying to watch TV with his family "I still hear it, I hear that sound, My God that sound."

"So it's your body, you are not hurting anyone?"

Johnny's story as told by his loving sister Debbie Maloney, St. Mary's, Georgia

"Once a Broken Sparrow, now a Soaring Eagle."

Johnny's website: http://www.dying2gethigh.com

WADE MCLEOD GRUSSMEYER

April 13, 1976 – May 24, 1998
Found May 26, 1998

(Age 21)

HEROIN/COCAINE

"MY GREATEST LOSS"
Forever In My Heart, I Love You Wade - Love Mom

My life since losing Wade will never be the same. The day that he died, he took a part of me with him and he took his future, as well as a part of mine. When we lose a loved one, we must either give up ourselves or pick up the pieces and carry on because the world does not stop.

I know that I will never get over my loss, but I am adjusting to him not being here. The loss of a child is not natural, and I found the only way to describe it is to say it is "like a color you have never seen before." It is impossible to tell others how you truly feel and there are no words that come close to describe the pain that you feel.

As we grow up, we expect to lose grandparents, parents and siblings, but not our children. I know that there can never be any greater pain than the pain I feel now and will feel for the rest of my life. I think about Wade every single day, and not a day passes that I don't shed a few tears. I will forever wonder " WHY?" " Why did this happen to me and why did it happen to my son?"

Wade's death has taught me that nothing is forever and no one can take anything for granted because our lives can change in an instant. Time is a healer, but it is not an eraser. I try to focus on the happy memories and the time that Wade was with us. I will forever remember the wonderful person that he was and I will miss him forever and always.

If anyone believes that what happened to me cannot happen to them, then they are very mistaken. Addiction and mental illness can happen to rich, poor, famous, uninvolved, very involved parents. **It can happen to you just like it happened to me**.

I don't know what the answer is because I believed that my husband and I had done everything possible to protect our children. The demons of drugs still entered into our lives and it swallowed Wade up taking him from us forever.

I pray that by sharing Wade's story it may help others realize that drugs are not an answer to anything. It is only a complication to everything and will only ruin what should have been a wonderful life. I hope by sharing Wade's story people will stop and think, hopefully making the decision to never use drugs and when they come face to face with making the choice to use, they will remember Wade and what happened to him. I pray that others will make the right decision. If the story of Wade's life can save one person, then his life and mine will not have been in vain.

Wade was born on April 13th, 1976. He was a wonderful child and the kind of baby and little boy every mom would dream of having. He was easy to get along with and seemed to be a happy person with a shy and quiet personality. As a child he was never a dare devil and he was very cautious and studied everything that he would ever attempt. He didn't try anything until he was sure that he could accomplish whatever it was he was trying to do.

Wade's sister Lindsey, was 3 years younger and his brother Todd was 5 years younger. Both of the kids thought that Wade was a great big brother and worshiped him. As the three kids grew up we realized that Wade was different---he was so much more quiet and he seemed to hold everything inside. He constantly worried about what everyone thought. He never shared his emotions and learning was difficult for him. It seemed as though he didn't process the information correctly, but he never gave up. With lots of help from home and school he succeeded and graduated from high school in the middle of his class.

Wade was our oldest child which meant our whole family spent endless hours watching him perform in the many sport activities he was part of. I call those days the "happy ones". The one very positive part of Wade's life and what I believe kept him going was his participation in sports. Whatever Wade decided to play he was able to shine as the star of the game. We were, and still are very proud of him.

Sports began at age six beginning with T-Ball. As he grew up he played soccer, basketball, ran track, but his favorite sport of all was football. Beginning in the 5th grade he begged to play football, but his dad was set that he wouldn't play until he was in high school. We did agree that he could go to football summer camps, but that was it. Even though Wade wasn't happy about waiting, he accepted our decision and waited until his freshman year of high school.

Once the practices started, he played like he had been playing for years. He was a natural and the coaches were thrilled with him. The team as a whole didn't win many games, but Wade stood out as a "star".

The following year Wade played JV and once again he was outstanding. He and five other players from the JV team were invited to dress down and travel with the Varsity Team for the big game on Friday night. Wade never really got any playing time, but he was so excited about just standing there in his uniform and being part of the team.

Junior year, Wade had become a legend throughout the Three Rivers League. He had a nose for the ball and was very successful in defending as the free safety on the varsity team. I videotaped every game Wade ever played in and he always enjoyed watching the tapes over and over again.

At the end of his Junior season, Wade was awarded "All League Honors" and had been voted by his teammates and coaches as

"Defensive Player of the Year" at Milwaukie High. Deep down in my heart, I believe that year was probably the happiest I had ever seen Wade. He was a different person when he put that uniform on---he believed he was a star, and everyone else believed it too. He was a true football player on the field with that killer instinct, but off the field the sweet, big and kind-hearted naïve kid returned.

Unfortunately, Wade was very insecure and constantly questioned if he deserved all of the attention he received. We tried to be reassuring, however, somehow I really don't know if he ever truly believed us. As a parent we are always full of "what if" and "if only I had".

I believe in my heart that the turning point that led Wade in the wrong direction actually began on July 19, 1992, long before he had ever tried any kind of drug. It was a couple of years before the full effect of that day would actually hit, but it was the beginning.

Because sports were so important in Wade's life he not only was part of the high school football team, but also the basketball and baseball teams. The "what if" occurred during a baseball game. Wade had finished the school year season with the freshman baseball team, but because he had performed at such a high level, he was moved up to the JV Summer Team. Only two players had been moved up, so it was a huge honor for Wade. It meant however, that he would be with a group of kids that he really didn't know and a group that were one to two years older than him.

After school had ended, summer turned into a hectic schedule of driver's education classes, football camp, baseball practice and games as well as a speed camp. This schedule had been going at a steady pace and the following week we would be down to just baseball. Unfortunately, we didn't make it to the end.

The night of the 17th of July, which was a Friday, the team had played a ball game out of town and didn't get back until midnight. The morning of the 18th Wade needed to be down at the baseball field for the start of a two day tournament hosted by Milwaukie High School. Several of the teams had come in from out of town and were planning to camp out on the fields with the coaches.

Late in the day on the 18th, Wade insisted that his team was going to spend the night and he wanted to as well. At first I said no way, but of course I got the usual "I never get to do anything" and my husband overrode my "no" and said he could stay. We did take him home and he showered and had dinner, then at about 7:30 p.m., I took him back down to the field where the rest of the team was starting to arrive.

He had another big day of baseball the following morning, so I suggested that we pick him up about 5:00 am so he could sleep some in his own bed. A big "NO" was what I heard and he insisted we pick him up at 9:00 am. It was a long night for me.

The next morning was Sunday, July 19, and my husband went down to pick him up as Wade had requested. When he came back I could tell Wade was extremely tired, mumbling that he and his friend Kory hadn't slept because they were afraid the other kids would do something to them. He did say something about trying to call home from the dug out phone but it wouldn't go through. He kept getting a busy signal. Later I found out that in order to use that phone, "9" needed to be dialed to get an outside line. This was another "what if" because if he had been able to reach us to come and pick him up during the middle of the night, things may have been so different.

Wade went straight to bed - it was 9:00 am and he was supposed to be back at the field at 11:00 am. I didn't wake him up until 10:40 am hoping to give him as much time to sleep as possible. I should have let him sleep through and skip the game. Maybe if I had this story would have had a different ending.

We arrived at the field a little after 11:00 and the game started at 11:15. Wade was a designated hitter for the inning so he was sitting in the dugout working the scoreboard. At 11:35 a teammate came running out of the dugout yelling "Wade, Wade" and looking up at us. My husband jumped up and took one step to the end of the bleachers running into the dugout. I hesitated a minute but I needed to know what was happening. As I rounded the corner I saw Wade lying on the ground, his body shaking and he was very rigid. It took everything I had to stay on my feet - I felt like I was going to collapse. Tears were streaming down my face as I watched in terror and suddenly I heard sirens. The paramedics arrived and they did their work and then loaded Wade into the ambulance. His Dad went along with him and I gathered up Lindsey and Todd and ran for the car.

As soon as we got to the hospital I asked to see Wade. When I walked into the room he was conscious, looked very tired and seemed confused. The confusion didn't worry me as much as how tired he looked. When the doctor told me Wade didn't know what day it was or the date, I wasn't concerned because stuff like that was normal for him. The doctors weren't sure what had happened, but they said it looked like a seizure. In order to be sure, tests needed to be run and they began by taking blood and running every test possible, including drug tests, MRI, CAT scan, etc.

Before we left the hospital all the tests appeared normal. The doctors began to believe that it was a look-alike seizure, which meant that in certain instances, the body mimics a seizure but it really isn't. That is what I prayed for day and night until we got all of the results. The last test to be performed was an EEG and they couldn't do that until the following morning.

An appointment was set for 9:00 am on July 20th, which was Monday. Because the EEG was done at the hospital, results couldn't be given immediately - the tests had to be sent out to be read, and they said they would have the results later in the week. It was probably one of the longest weeks of my life.

Finally on the 24th of July our primary doctor called and very bluntly said " well it was a seizure and Wade needs to be started on medication immediately". I kept asking questions - I needed answers. His name was Dr. Bow, and I must say he was one of the worst doctors our family had ever had. I told him I wanted to talk with him and he reluctantly said we could come in at 3:00 pm. I called my husband and together we went to the appointment.

As Wayne and I entered the examination room, Dr. Bow hurried in behind us with the prescription in his hand, expecting us to take it and leave. I immediately began to ask questions - I wanted to know "why". Nothing he said made any sense to me and finally his voice raised and he shouted " you both need to come out of denial".

I was stunned. I stated that I wanted answers and if he couldn't provide them, then I wanted a referral to see a specialist. We went round and round and I think he finally realized that I wasn't leaving until I had what I wanted. The only good thing that had come out of that meeting was the referral to Dr. James, who was the best child neurologist in the city. We finally left Dr. Bow's office and I filled the prescription of Dilantin that he insisted that Wade take.

I immediately contacted Dr. James and set up the first available appointment possible. He was the very best, so we had to wait for 2 weeks before we could get in.

All of Wade's summer activities had finally come to an end, so by the time we had our appointment he appeared rested and it was hard to tell anything had happened to him. Dr. James looked over all of the information provided by both the hospital and Dr. Bow. He explained that he believed the seizure was brought on by what was called "sleep deprivation." He believed that Wade's body threshold was low for this sort of thing and it threw his body into the seizure as a reaction. He believed that it would probably not happen again and said he was not going to put him on any medication, that he wanted to wait to see if he had another one.

My heart sank. I said it was too late, Dr. Bow had already started him on Dilantin. Dr. James explained that this type of medicine cannot be stopped suddenly because that could throw Wade into another seizure. I was instructed to continue to give Wade the medication and we would wait to see what happened.

The appointment seemed positive and I felt that Wade was really going to be ok, but I continued to worry constantly about him. Deep down I was scared to death. I will forever wonder "what if" I hadn't started him on the meds, would things have been different---I will never know.

The third week of August football daily doubles started and Wade was ready to play. The season was a great one for him. At the end of football, he started basketball. The year prior, which was Wade's freshman year in basketball, he had played almost non stop.

A new coach had taken over for his sophomore year, and I believe that the new coach was scared of Wade and the possibility that he could have another seizure. Wade's playing time was limited and this upset him. He managed to finish the season and he moved on to baseball, where he had a great season as the catcher.

With baseball, the high school season starts in about March and runs through late May, then the summer league starts and that would run through the end of July.

In late June, Wade began to complain about his vision and at times he seemed very confused. He was hesitating when he would normally have had no problems. We made another appointment with Dr. James and explained what was happening. It was determined that the symptoms were side effects of the medication and a decision was made to switch Wade to a new medication called Depakote. Wade had to decrease the Dilantin down and gradually increase the Depakote and within two weeks Wade said he felt great and the side effects were gone.

The sports cycle started all over again mid August with football, which proved to be Wade's best and most successful year at any sport. This was the year that everything came together and Wade was "Mr. Everything."

When football ended, Wade was going to start basketball and wanted to be on the varsity team. He didn't want to play for the coach from the prior year, however, it appeared as though he would be playing with the JV team and he was very unhappy. It was during this time that he began to get moody, very down in his emotions and he was doing things that he had never done before.

Without talking to us, Wade made the choice to quit basketball. This was another one of the times we have thought "what if" we had not let him quit. For the first time in Wade's life, he was not involved in sports and I will forever wonder if we had made him stick it out, would his life have been different. Without structure Wade suddenly had time on his hands.

From the time he had entered high school his friends had not changed and we believed that most of them were fairly nice kids. It was during this time that Wade and his friends began to party and with the loss of sports, Wade's medical condition threw him into a very deep depression.

Looking back on everything now, I realize that Wade had been depressed ever since he had had the first seizure. He didn't want to be different from anyone and suddenly he was. Unfortunately, we did not recognize the symptoms and he chose not to confide in us about how he was really feeling emotionally.

Spring of 1994, was the time period that Wade and his friends began to use alcohol and drugs. For someone with depression, it was also a means of self-medication and I'm sure as time went by the alcohol didn't do the trick so Wade started on pot. When pot didn't work he moved on to something else, and so the chain of addiction went. I don't think Wade ever realized what he had started and he never thought that drugs would take over his life and control him.

Sports were never the same for Wade. Drugs took over and pretty soon it was impossible to be successful at anything. The medication that Wade took for the seizure condition caused him to be sleepy and lazy.

I had never had problems with Wade not attending school, but suddenly he was skipping classes and his attitude about school had changed. When I finally got the reports that he was not attending his classes, I told him I would be attending school with him daily. He knew me well enough to know that I meant business and if I said I would be attached to him at the hip then I would be. I agreed that I would give him one more chance to do what was right, but I also told him I would be calling the attendance office daily to see if he had any absences.

June, 1995, Wade graduated from high school. It was one of the happiest days of my life and we were so proud of him. The best part though, was Wade was proud of himself.

Shortly after graduation, Wade had an appointment to see Dr. James. He desperately wanted to be taken off the seizure medication and the doctor agreed that he could, but cautioned him that it would be necessary for him to get lots of rest and take care of himself.

Wade had made contact with his Uncle Bob, who owned a

commercial construction company, regarding a job. On July 10th, Wade started working and I felt like he was finally on his way. He seemed really happy and began to look towards the future.

It was also during this time that Wade met a girl by the name of Susy. He was crazy about her and they were together most of his free time. I really liked her and it was nice to see him happy because showing his emotions had always been difficult for Wade.

The job had started out temporary, but he had done a good job and was hired on as a permanent employee. Lindsey had gotten her license so the two of them had to share the car that Wade was used to having as his own.

In August, we agreed to co-sign for a truck for Wade. He picked out a brand new silver 1995 Ford Ranger with the extended cab. Now that he had his own truck, he could pretty much come and go as he pleased. That week following his purchase, he spent every evening with Susy, and sometimes he wouldn't get to bed until after 11:00 p.m., and then he was up at 6:00 a.m., for work.

Wade's body required a lot of sleep and now that he was not taking the medication for the seizure, it was even more important that he get lots of rest.

Saturday, six days after he had purchased the truck, he had to work at his construction job. It had been a hot day and when he got home about 3:30 p.m., I commented to him that I thought he should rest. Looking back on that day, his face looked the same way it had on the 19th of July, 1992, when he suffered from the first seizure. Of course he didn't listen to me and by 5:30 p.m., he was on his way to Susy's house. They didn't really have big plans, just have pizza and watch a movie.

At 7:30 pm the phone rang and a female voice was crying and kept saying over and over, " he just fell over and his whole body is shaking" . My heart sank when I realized that it was Susy and I knew that she was telling me that Wade was having another seizure--- the second one in his life. I jumped up and handed the phone to my husband. I was crying so hard myself by now, screaming "no, no." If hearts really could break, mine would have been broken into tiny pieces.

Wayne and I left immediately and drove out to Susy's house. When we arrived, Wade was awake but kind of dazed, kind of like he had been sleeping and just hadn't really woken up. We talked to him for a few minutes and then Wade and I rode back together in my car and Wayne drove Wade's truck home. When we got back Wade just wanted to go to bed.

The pills that I had hoped Wade would never have to take again were once again administered and I knew that the next day Wade would realize the full impact of what had happened. When Wade got up the following morning, his tongue was mangled. Apparently during the seizure he had bit it and it was so sore he could hardly eat. He was upset with everything and everyone, just as I had expected. He had believed all of the meds were behind him and now they were very much part of his life again. I just wish Wade had listened to the doctor and to me when we told him how important it was to get lots of rest.

Between August of 1995, and April of 1996, things seemed normal. Wade and Susy were still together and Wade was still working for the construction company. With the exception of having to get up early he seemed to like his job.

I prayed night and day that Wade was going to be ok, that he would move on to enjoy a good life. Little did I realize how much Wade's life and my life would change, and it wouldn't be for the better.

Late April, 1996, I began to notice little things that didn't seem right. At first I remember thinking I must have misunderstood what I thought I heard, or I was trying to find excuses for why Wade was becoming so hostile. I did notice that Wade and Susy had begun to argue more and more, which wasn't normal. It almost looked like Wade would start things and then as quickly as he started the arguments, he was ready to make up. Looking back on things, I think even he was confused by his own behavior and this behavior grew gradually worse.

Finally on the 28th of June, Wade announced that he and Susy had broken up and he seemed glad about it. Two weeks had passed and Wade's behavior began to grow even more strange. We believe that this period was actually Wade's first psychotic break. He was extremely paranoid and afraid that everyone was after him and out to get him. He kept insisting that he needed to leave town.

Over the next few weeks he cut himself off from all of his friends and began to isolate himself. I was scared to death and insisted that he see a doctor for help. He agreed and began to see Dr. Tim who was a psychologist. He did seem to help Wade, but mental illness cannot be treated overnight and Wade's use of drugs as a form of self medication only complicated things.

Wade was suffering from delusions and he didn't know if they were real or not real. Dr. Tim suggested Wade start taking antidepressants hoping that they would make him feel better. Gradually over time more and more medicine was added to what Wade had to take daily.

Wade was still trying to work, but his delusions were beginning to interrupt his performance at work. He was making irrational decisions about things and on several occasions, he would just walk off the job because he said he couldn't handle the pressure.

In mid September of 1996, Wade was laid off from the company and his mental health gradually declined. Because he wasn't working for the same company and had no income he was forced to go on the state health insurance. His mental health care was turned over to the county system. I learned the hard way that if I ever needed mental health services, the last place I would ever go is the county.

It wasn't until the spring, of 1998, I learned that Sam, the so called counselor that Wade was seeing was nothing more than an intern. He certainly was in way over his head trying to work with Wade, and he had no experience in helping someone with what appeared as several mental illnesses, complicated with the use of drugs.

I learned that the people who suffer from the worst mental illnesses, are being treated by individuals with no first hand knowledge or experience. The majority of the doctors who are hired to work in our county systems are ones who have just recently graduated from school, have been unsuccessful working on the outside on their own or recently retired working part time. I suddenly learned a lot about things I never thought I would have any interest in. This was a huge reality check for me and I will never forget it.

By December, 1996, Wade was having severe mood swings and he had a great deal of hostility. We walked around the house on egg shells hoping not to upset him.

On December 21, 1996, we had to call the police to come and help calm him down after he and Todd had gotten into an argument. The police talked him into going to the hospital to just talk to someone.

A few days after he was admitted to the psychiatric unit I got the biggest surprise of my life. The doctor informed me that Wade was "getting messages from the radio" and had delusions about all kinds of things.

At first I was shocked and told her I thought they had him mixed up with someone else, but then I started thinking about all the things that had happened in the spring with Wade and Susy. I realized that it was during that time that all of this had started. I realize how scared Wade must have been.

There are stigmas with both mental illness and drug addiction and I think in Wade's mind he would rather have problems with drugs than to admit that he was suffering from a mental illness.

This was Wade's first admission to the hospital for the first suicide threat, and over the next year and a half, he was admitted to the hospital six more times for suicide attempts. Over this time his attempts ranged from slitting his wrists, trying to poison himself with carbon monoxide, overdosing on two bottles of aspirin, trying to shoot himself with a gun (he had the wrong bullets), overdosing on antidepressants and threatening to jump off the Burnside Bridge.

Each hospital stay ranged in length from five to twelve days and once the hospital had him stable, they would release him. Wade was taking medication for seizures, depression, anti-psychotic meds, and meds to hide some side effects of the meds. In addition to the meds that should have been making him feel better, he was using " his drugs". If he had only realized that he had to stay away from the street drugs and concentrate on taking what the doctors had prescribed he would still be alive today.

Over time Wade's choice of drugs from the street ranged from everything between A to Z. The steps were gradual, and the usual progression of use was pot, acid, mushrooms, cocaine, "meth" and finally heroin, which he only used between five to seven times.

Wade had been diagnosed with personality disorder, delusion disorder, bi-polar disease, schizophrenia, and severe depression. With mental illness the diagnoses can change and with Wade it did depending on the doctor who was treating him. I know that Wade suffered terribly from mental illness, and I also know that his drug use only complicated things.

In January of 1997, Wade was admitted to the hospital because of an aspirin overdose. I went to Intensive Care to see him and as he laid there in a semi conscious state, I reached down to hold his hand. He looked up at me and it was like something had taken him over. He opened his eyes and said " I'm the devil's child". This was not the first time he had made this statement and it wouldn't be the last time I heard it.

After being released from Intensive Care he was moved to the psychiatric unit and stayed there for a week. When he was released he appeared stable and I heard the usual "I'm going to be ok now."

Wade's health would decline gradually and grow worse over time. His next big problem occurred in late April of 1997. Lindsey came home and found Wade in the garage with the car running and the garage door down. He had run a hose from the exhaust and pulled it up into the car window, taping it into place. Lindsey immediately opened the garage and called 911. The police arrived and saved Wade by breaking the window in the car and pulling him out, giving me 13 more months to have him in my life.

I had been at work so when I arrived home I pulled up to find police, fire and an ambulance parked in front of my house. The paramedics had Wade hooked up to oxygen and I could see all the pain from his heart in his eyes. I leaned over and grabbed his hands, whispering "Wade, we love you so much, why do you keep doing

I AM YOUR DISEASE

this?" He just looked at me with his big blue eyes.

One of the police officers helped me get ahold of the doctor at the county to find out which hospital's psychiatric unit he was to be taken to. That young policeman helped me so much that day. Not only did he save Wade by breaking the window, but he helped me emotionally and I will forever be grateful for his kindness. We still see and talk with him occasionally and he has told us how much of an impact Wade has had on his life.

After Wade's release from the hospital on May 7, 1997, he went into a religious phase. Wade began to attend a church where many young people attended. There was a young girl there that Wade had gone to high school with and they renewed their friendship. Andie had not ever done drugs and she became a very positive influence on him. He desperately wanted someone in his life and in a matter of weeks he was head over heels in love. I know Andie cared about Wade a lot, but she wasn't ready for the things Wade was talking about, which was marriage.

The first part of July, 1997, Andie told Wade she wanted to slow things down. This was Wade's excuse to gradually turn back to his old ways. His mental health began to decline and we believe it was during this time that he was first exposed to heroin.

Wade's mind in some instances was that of a child. There were times when he would leave or as he called it, he would " run away." Usually he wouldn't be gone more than about three to four days, but this time he was gone over three weeks and when he finally came home he brought back a five week old little black lab mix puppy.

She was a sweet little puppy, but I didn't want another dog and I tried desperately to find a good home, but no one would take her. As time passed I started taking care of her like she was our puppy and by September our whole family was attached to her. Wade had named her " Auto" because he said the two of them were going to live in the car.

Gradually her name was shortened to "O" nd today we call her

"Oie" (O-E). I know that God gave Oie to Wade to help ease our pain when the time came for Him to take Wade to heaven. She has been a great source of strength to my whole family and each of us calls her " the angel dog." We love her because she is a wonderful dog, but most of all we love her because she was a gift from Wade and God. Oie has helped us through this terrible and heartbreaking time in our lives.

In March of 2002, Oie was given a stuffed toy football and she carries it in her mouth everywhere she goes. At night when we get ready to go to bed, Oie has her ball as she heads up the hall to the bedrooms. The strangest thing about this ball is that football was Wade's passion before the drugs took over. When I see her carrying it around, I believe that Wade is close by and this is his way of letting us know that he is with us. I always smile when I see her and her football.

Drugs, alcohol and mental illness walk hand in hand. Suffering from one or the other is extremely difficult, but when you put the two together, existing becomes the primary goal. I have always said that if Wade would have stopped the street drugs he may have had a chance at a good life. He would have struggled some and things wouldn't have always been easy for him, but the drugs made it impossible.

On May 21, 1998, Todd was participating in the district track meet and when I got home at about 7:00 p.m., Wade was not there. At about 8:15 p.m., the phone rang and it was Wade asking if I would pick him up in downtown Milwaukie at the transit center. To this day I cannot drive down the street where I picked him up from on that day. I can still see him standing there in his black and white running suit.

A short time after we were home, I went upstairs to see if Wade was hungry and I realized he had drugs. Wade and I had a huge fight, yelling, screaming, pushing and shoving each other. He was a big kid and much stronger than me. He finally was able to get away from me and ran downstairs, locking himself in the bathroom with his "crap" as I called it.

Looking back, I should have called the police, but I tried to handle it on my own. I did call Dr. Coleman who was his doctor with the county. He told me that if I felt threatened, to call the police, but he never insisted that I call them. To be honest, I knew that Wade would never hurt me even when I knew that he wanted to. I was never afraid of him, ever.

Dr. Coleman told me that Wade couldn't stay in our home any longer and he was going to make arrangements with Sam, the counselor, to have him placed into respite the next day. I waited all day Friday for the phone call from Sam or Dr. Coleman. Finally about 1:00 p.m., I called to talk to Sam and left a message. He finally called me back and informed me that he knew nothing about what had occurred the night before. It appeared that Dr. Coleman had not said anything to Sam and it was just one more thing to add to my list that proved that Wade had fallen through the cracks once again.

At about 4:15 p.m., Sam called me back and said that Wade was going into "respite." He gave me the address and I felt that the location was not a very good one for Wade, but the county was in charge and I didn't have much choice but to go along with what they said to do.

My husband and I took Wade to the address given to us and from the very beginning I could not believe that the county was placing Wade in that location. As we drove up to the facility I realized the "respite" was a well-known "homeless shelter."

It was Friday the 22nd of May, and Wade had been approved to stay until Tuesday, May 26th. He was right in the middle of Old Town, which is where all the drug traffic is in downtown Portland. Whenever Wade would "run away" he would go downtown to this area and I could see his eyes light up as he realized that he was right where he wanted to be but this time he had a place to sleep and food to eat.

On the drive downtown, Wade seemed detached and showed absolutely no emotion. When we arrived, I went in with him to register and got some information from the people in charge. The people who worked there seemed pleasant enough, assigned him a room and told him he could go into the dining room and eat. He showed absolutely no expression.

I looked up at his face and wrapped my arms around his neck. I kissed him and hugged him tight and said "Wade, I love you so much".

He looked down at me and mumbled, "I love you too".

He turned away from me and I watched as he walked across the room to get a tray of food and slowly I started for the door. As I left the building, I knew in my heart it would be the last time I would ever see him alive. I cried all the way home, my heart felt heavy and I felt helpless. My whole life I had had a sixth sense about losing Wade and I could feel my world turning out of control. I was so afraid.

Saturday night about 10:00 p.m., on May 23rd, I tried to call Wade. I was told that because of "confidentiality law" they could give me no information but they would leave a message for him to call home. I woke up about 1:30 a.m., on Sunday the 24th of May, and couldn't go back to sleep. I remember looking out the window and staring at the huge full moon. The sky was clear of clouds and the air was extremely still. At about 2:00 a.m., a panic feeling came over me and I couldn't understand why I was feeling the way that I was. I was scared to death.

The following day which was Sunday, and again on Monday, I called the "homeless shelter" and got the same information from the lady who answered the phone. New messages were taken on both days and I was told she would make sure he got them. Finally on Tuesday, I called at 12:30 p.m., and again got the same message regarding confidentiality. I asked several questions regarding the county and if they were going to extend his stay there. She said only that she could give me no information.

I'm sure that my phone call triggered the woman to begin looking into the situation. I was so worried and began to wonder what was going to happen as the hours passed and I sat in my living room.

At about 3:15 p.m., I noticed a police car drive up and park in front of my house. Two men got out, one in a police uniform and the other in street clothes. Suddenly my doorbell rang, but my heart had been racing the moment I saw the car arrive because I knew before I ever opened the door what I would hear. One man asked if I was Michele Grussmeyer and if I had a son named Wade. My answer was yes to both questions and he then said he had some bad news for me. He said at 1:15 p.m., Wade had been found dead in his room at the "homeless shelter" and it appeared as though it was a drug overdose.

We will never know if Wade's death was accidental or his way of ending his life. My knees buckled as I fell to the floor unable to stop crying. My husband came home soon after and he took all the information down. My worst fear about Wade had come true and I didn't know if I could survive it.

All the hopes and dreams that you have for your children are suddenly gone. Something a parent never plans on doing was suddenly happening and we were planning a funeral. That day a part of me died along with Wade.

When I finally was able to gather my thoughts, I called Dr. Coleman and I will never forget his statement to me. There was a long pause and suddenly he said "I knew I should have put him in the hospital". It's too bad he hadn't been concerned about Wade on that Thursday night before his death.

Dr. Coleman had very little experience working with someone like Wade and I believe he truly didn't believe Wade would ever do anything to harm himself and didn't take anything seriously. Wade always said that the doctors didn't listen and didn't believe him when he talked to them, and today I know that he was right.

Dr. Coleman thought he had all the answers, but because of what happened to Wade, I think he learned a huge lesson. I hope he thinks about Wade daily and remembers the mistakes he made. Maybe because of what happened to Wade, his decision about treatment will be different and someone's life can be saved.

Wade's date of death is listed as May 26th, however, he actually died on May 24th, at about 2:00 a.m., which was the same time that the panic filled my body.

When we obtained his autopsy report, we learned that Wade had been dead for 2 1/2 to 3 days and his body was in a decomposing state. He had insect larvae invading his face and body and this is the vision I will live with for the rest of my life. Wade was sent to "respite" because he was in crisis.

The county had a release from Wade that I could obtain information but this was not shared with the "homeless shelter." No one called to check on him during his stay there even though they knew that he was suicidal. They failed my son. In addition to the county being negligent, the shelter was also negligent. During the time he laid dead in his room, no one checked to find out why he was not coming down to meals, why he had not gone out to smoke a cigarette, and why he had not picked up any of the messages that I had left for him.

I learned after his death that he had checked out of the building at 5:30 p.m., and checked back in at 9:45 p.m., on Saturday evening. He never checked back out of the building again. My call was time stamped at 10:00 p.m., so he never knew I had even called. Because he laid there for so long before he was found, it broke my heart and I have a vision in my mind that will remain forever.

The county health system is a bunch of people who work from 8 a.m., to 5 p.m., and they don't want to be bothered outside of that time. Wade always said " they really don't care" and you know what, they don't care.

From the time Wade was a little boy both Wayne and I worried about him. It was just a gut instinct that we both felt. Being the oldest child is always a hard job. There were areas of Wade's life that he excelled in and there were other areas that he struggled. No matter what happened in the 22 years of his life we never stopped loving him and prayed night and day that he would turn his life around.

Losing a child is the hardest and most heartbreaking thing that any person will ever experience. I learned that men and women grieve differently and just because I didn't do it the way Wayne thought I should, didn't make my way wrong. He didn't want to talk about it and I wanted to talk about it all the time.

In the beginning I cried almost non-stop and I do believe I could have filled a river. I still cry everyday, but sometimes I just tear up. In the beginning, Wayne would hide his feelings and I think he believed if he didn't mention it then it wouldn't hurt so much.

Today, four years later I think he talks about Wade much more, but when we talk about it together we both end up crying. Our marriage struggled at first, but we have come through that and we rely on each other now for support. We both believe that Wade is around us all of the time and we both believe that when Lindsey was married he was with us.

Please visit Wade's memorial website and view the pictures taken on that very special day. I now realize how important it is to have pictures taken often of your family and especially your children. You never know when your world will fall apart and those family pictures will never be complete.

Wayne always believed that if Wade would stop the street drugs his life would be ok. Today he realizes that Wade did suffer from both addiction and mental illness and he understands better what Wade was going through. Depression was the root of the problem and the flower above grew wide.

I believe that today he is sympathetic to Wade's problems, which explains why he is willing to discuss Wade, his life and his problems more openly now. Wade was our first-born child and that makes him special regardless of his problems. No matter what happened in our lives, Wade made us parents for the first time and everything that we experienced he was the first one to expose us to it. We will forever love him.

Another thing as a bereaved parent that I have learned is many people are supportive of you right after the loss, however, they believe that after just a few months you should move on. This does not happen when a child has been lost. Many of our friends were with us in the beginning, but as time went on, I believe that we became a sign of something they did not want to face. They were afraid to be around us because if it could happen to us, it could happen to them.

After time, friendships ended and for a time Wayne and I stood together, just he and I. Gradually we have added new friends to our lives and because they know what we have been through their friendship means so much more.

I want to acknowledge one friend who I work with who has become so special to me. Her name is Marianne and she has always encouraged me to talk about Wade and share his life. As a Mom she has always been able to understand where my mind was and why I did all the things that I did and am still doing. In so many ways she has been a life- line for me. Even though she never knew Wade, she wants to know everything about him.

What people don't understand is the biggest fear we have as bereaved parents is "people will forget our child." By surrounding myself with people like my friend Marianne, no one will ever forget Wade and the wonderful person that he was.

Wade was suffering from mental illness and drug addiction. Dealing with the mental issues was difficult enough, but also dealing with the "monkey on his back called addiction" made survival impossible. Wade would have always struggled in his life, but there was always hope. With the combination of the right people around him he could have had the happy life he had always dreamed of. Drugs made that impossible.

PLEASE, I pray if you are experimenting or thinking about using any type of drugs including marijuana, I beg you, turn your back on them. They will only destroy your life and maybe even cut your life short just like they did for Wade. Life is difficult enough; don't complicate it with drugs because they will eventually destroy you.

I hope that Wade's story has had an impact on your life. There are various degrees of mental illness and drug addictions, but more times than not, the two illnesses are seen together. Drugs lead to an addiction that you don't need. If you are feeling down and depressed, see your doctor and get medical help, please don't start down the path that Wade chose. That path leads nowhere. Without drugs there is always hope, but with drugs, your future is very bleak and dangerous. Don't let what happened to Wade happen to you. Remember, when you are hurting yourself, you are hurting the ones

I AM YOUR DISEASE

who love you more than you can ever know.

Wade's story spread out over a seven year period, but the worst part was the last two years of his life. It was impossible to include every detail of the pain that Wade suffered through. Please know that I am always willing to talk and share. I can be reached by email at gruss10nov@comcast.net.

I also have created a memorial website for Wade and I hope that you will visit and view the pictures of Wade and his family. He was loved so much and he is missed more than anyone can even come close to imagining.

PLEASE - if you are doing drugs - STOP - they will eventually kill you just like they killed my son. All drugs are bad. There isn't a good one out there. I hope Wade's story can be the turning point in your life if you have chosen the wrong path. Wade was a wonderful person with a huge, kind heart. He was the kind of person everyone liked. He will forever live in my heart and I will love him for the rest of my life. Drugs destroyed him. Don't let them destroy you!

Michele Grussmeyer - The names of doctors and locations have been changed to protect me, not to protect them.

Wade's story as told by his loving mom, Michele Grussmeyer, Milwaukie, OR

"If we are loved and remembered, then we live on forever in the hearts of those who love us."

Ted Menten

www.geocities.com/wade_my_son

VERNON CREAMER, JR.

JANUARY 29, 1972 – JANUARY 23, 1998

(Age 25)

GHB (gammahydroxybutyrate) " Scoop"

"IN LOVING MEMORY OF VERNON"

My beautiful son was born on January 29th 1972. His dad and I were so proud of him, as all parents are of their children. We loved watching him grow and turning into a warmhearted, loving personality. He became a great sports lover.

He played baseball until he was 16 years old, receiving many trophies for this. Then in his last two years of high school he started playing football and was very good at that also. He was one of three picked as a Top College Prospects at his school to be put on the National and State Recruiting List in the Florida Football magazine, 1990 edition.

He had so much going for him in life. Then in 1993, he had an accident and messed up his knee pretty bad. He had 3 operations on it and was supposed to have many more before all could be fixed. He was in therapy for more then a year.

In September 1997, I found out he was doing drugs. This devastated me. I couldn't believe my son was doing this. We decided to go and get him, bring him home. His dad went to pick him up.

We sat down and talked to him. All he could do at that moment was cry and tell us how sorry he was because he knew that he was not brought up this way. I started crying and told him that it didn't matter what he had done, that he was my son and that I loved him with all my heart. He told me not to cry. He never liked to see me cry.

I found out that a lot of his friends were doing drugs also. I called some of them and told them I knew what they were doing. I also told them that I would contact some of their parents to fill them in. Of course they did not want me to do that. I told them that if nothing was done, I would soon be putting my son in the cemetery. Naturally, they thought I was exaggerating, and that they would help me with Vernon. They would call me and let me know if Vernon started doing drugs again.

My husband and I did not know how to handle this. (Does any parent really know?). We had never dealt with anything like this before.

Vernon told me he would get doctors' help, and he did. In fact, his last visit to the doctor was just one week before he died. One of the things that still bothers me is why the doctor did not pick up on the fact that Vernon was still on drugs. I thought being under a doctor's care, meant that things were getting better. I was so very wrong!

I talked to Vernon on the night he passed away. I could not tell he was on drugs again. He was very upset because a good friend of his had passed away earlier that week, from a drug overdose.

I told him "See how upset you are? Now put yourself in my shoes. What if that was me finding you that way?"

He said "that's not going to happen, mama. I love you mama!" I keep hearing his words over and over again in my mind.

The next morning the police were at my door, telling me that my wonderful son was gone. Now, when it's too late, all his friends feel bad. He is gone. If I had only known he was doing drugs again...The "ifs" ...they are tearing me apart.

I have since talked to many of his friends, trying to get them to talk to their parents, to find help. When things like this happen, family and friends are left behind to suffer. Some of them have done so since then, but some are still doing drugs.

I AM YOUR DISEASE

I don't understand why our children are doing this to themselves. It is so dangerous! It ends your life before it gets started.

I have been doing a lot of research on the subject since Vernon died, something I now wish I had done before this happened. When kids do drugs, they get depressed and don't realize it. It's like a disease, and they do not for a moment realize they are in danger of dying.

This does not mean they are bad kids. It means they are in need of help.

I have been writing to a lady on the internet, who also lost her only daughter because of a drug overdose. Her name is Renee, her daughter's name is Erica, born the 16th of February 1978 and went home to our dear Lord on the 14th of January 1998.

I thought it would help to write to another parent who was going through the same thing I am. She told me it did help to talk to other bereaved parents, especially bereaved parents who lost their children the way we did, to drug overdose.

This is not socially acceptable as to say, being in a car accident. I knew exactly what she meant. At first it was so hard for me to explain to people how Vernon had died. It made me feel ashamed. This bothered me so much, because when I thought about it, why should I feel ashamed? He was my beloved son, and what others think, really does not matter.

I loved him with all of my heart and was proud of him. Even if you do know that your children may be doing things that are harmful to them, you still love them.

I wrote a letter to my family and friends, that you can find on Vernon's website - http://www.fortunecity.com/millenium/lassie/286/ Perhaps you could follow the link and read this while you are there. Here you will also find the Mother's Day card Vernon made me when he was 9 years old.

I wanted to make a Memorial Page to let everyone know how much my son was loved. Perhaps this also can help other parents with their children.

I go to Vernon's gravesite everyday, and sit there and cry. I know he is watching me from above and saying "Mama, don't cry." But it is so hard. I miss him so much.

Vernon's story as told by his loving mom, JoAnn Creamer, Southport, FL

"A Mother sees through eyes of love, and listens with her heart."

Vernon's website - http://www.fortunecity.com/millenium/lassie/286/

Vernon---by his sister Stephanie.

Everyone that knew Vernon, knew that he was a very special person. If anyone ever needed something, he would get it for them, no matter if he had it or not. Vernon lived only 25 short years, and in those 25 years he touched many people's lives. This was not supposed to happen this way, my brother and I were supposed to grow old together. He always protected me and watched over me. I know that he is still watching over me. He loved all of us very much. Saturday, we found a paper where he had written down scriptures from the Bible. Quoted was: "Philippians 4:13~ I can do all things through Christ, who strengthens me. Vernon also wrote some quotes of his own.

"Allow yourself time to change." "We are imperfect." "God never requires you to do anything that wasn't built in life to make you stronger."

"Mistakes we make we must repent to open our terminals for God to come in and change us." My brother loved the Lord. He just made a poor decision. I want this to be a learning experience for everyone.

EDWARD ANTHONY CAPPIELLO

SEPTEMBER 8, 1983 – FEBRUARY 17, 2006
(Age 22)

HEROIN/XANAX

"SO LITTLE TIME"

For 22 years, 6 months, and 9 days, I had the honor and privilege of being the mother of a truly remarkable son. Eddie is my heart, my soul and my best friend.

I was only sixteen years old when Eddie was born. Almost everyone in my life at the time tried to convince me to terminate the pregnancy, preaching everything from "you're throwing your life away" to "what do you know about caring for a baby?" I listened to what they told me and made mental notes but abortion was out of the question, not because of any strong religious beliefs or personal views on the issue, simply because I was already in love with him.

Due to my age the clinic where I went for prenatal care assigned my case to a Social Worker; a wonderful woman who gently guided me through each stage of my pregnancy. She became my main source of support from start to finish and then some. I don't believe I would have been able to do it without her. I am forever grateful.

Eddie was an absolute joy to raise from day one, an amazing baby with sparkling brown eyes and a smile that lit up his entire face. With Eddie's help, all of my fears and inhibitions regarding my abilities to be his mother quickly faded. In record time I figured out which cries were for hunger, gas, or just wanting to be held. Everyday he brought me a new wonderment, this little person was teaching me something new every single day.

As he grew and his own personality started developing, I knew in my heart he was special. He was extremely bright, (learning was effortless for him) kind, sensitive, loving and very intuitive. Even at age two he had the ability to sense if I was feeling sad. So many times just out of the blue he would give me a big hug, put his little hands on my face and say "Don't worry mommy---I love you."

Eddie's biological father and I separated in 1987, (he did the daddy thing for about a year and a half and then disappeared for the next 15 years, having no involvement in Eddie's life whatsoever).

To simply say I was petrified would be an understatement; being barely 20, no job and a toddler in tow was overwhelming but I was determined to make it work. Eddie was my driving force. Whenever I felt as though the walls were closing in all I had to do was look at him and my faith would be renewed. Eddie had no idea how many times he literally saved my life.

In the winter of 1988, I met my younger son's father and married him six months later. Ryan was born exactly one year to the day we were married. We were separated by the time Ryan was 6 months old (it wasn't until years later that I realized I only married him out of fear; fear of being a single mom, struggling to raise a child in a big city. Just wanting so much to have a family atmosphere for Eddie).

So here I was on my own again, this time with a 6-year-old and an infant. To this day I am still uncertain weather it was my stubbornness or my guilt for another failed attempt at providing stability for my children, that drove me to make my life work but make it work I did.

With the assistance of some unseen forces I was afforded the opportunity to work at home as a typist (for a man who would a few years later become my soul mate).

I moved us into a small but clean apartment in a good school district. I won't pretend and say that all was wonderful. Money was always an issue and I constantly lived with the fear that I would not be able to raise two boys on my own. Once again Eddie made my job very easy and more times than not he was able to make my doubts disappear.

He was an excellent student; he graduated elementary school with awards in almost every subject, including the United Federation Of Teachers Award, and never had any disciplinary problems in school or at home.

During the summer before Eddie was to start middle school, Mike, (my soul mate) and I decided to move in together. Because Mike and I had been a couple for about a year prior to our making this move, the transition for my boys was relatively easy. Even before we started dating Mike had become a positive source of male influence in their lives.

Eddie was so excited about going to middle school. He was looking forward to walking to and from school with his friends, going a little bit earlier in the morning to play handball before class and I suppose the extra freedom was the most exciting.

Although I shared his enthusiasm, my fears went into overdrive. I was now working outside the home and Eddie would be what was considered a " latch key kid," coming home by himself and staying alone until Mike or I got home from work.

Everyday at 3:15 my heart would jump to my throat but everyday without fail at 3:16 my phone would ring and I would hear " Hi mom, I'm home, you can breathe now." It was a running joke for the three full years.

All through middle school he hung out with the same group of kids, most of whom had known each other since elementary school. They were always together, playing roller hockey, having sleepovers, pulling harmless neighborhood pranks and just loving life.

I can honestly say that Eddie never showed any signs of being an "at risk teen." He didn't miss not even one day of school and maintained a 90+ average for three full years. He was never late for dinner nor did he ever miss a curfew.

I always considered myself a hands-on mom, I knew all of his friends and all of their moms, never missed a hockey game, attended every single parent/teachers conference, school functions, trips, etc., and was a member of the PTA.

Eddie and I had what I considered at the time a very unique mother/son relationship. I was very open with him about all the issues concerning kids his age; I was very forthcoming to him with information about drugs and their devastating effects. He was easy to talk to, participated in every conversation, shared with me what he was being taught about drugs in school and always appeared to be paying attention.

When I found out Eddie was smoking pot (he was 15), I was, to say the least, in total shock. I was beside myself with panic. I brought home pamphlets about marijuana use and how statistics had proven it to be a gateway to other more dangerous drugs but Eddie had an answer for everything I said. He debated the issue so well that I secretly started to question my own argument.

I can still very clearly hear him tell me "Come on mom, all teenagers try pot, it's their right of passage." He tried to assure me that it was only a couple of times and that he really didn't like it.

Thankfully I was not one of those moms who said "not my kid." I clearly explained to him that it was now his job to earn my trust again and until that time I would be holding the reins tighter than usual.

I admit I put Eddie on my own private pedestal but he earned every bit of my praise. I was not one of those moms who constantly bragged about my kids and I never compared them to anyone else's children.

We were not, by far, the " Leave It To Beaver" household. Mike has two children from his first marriage, Jennifer now 21 and Jonathan 18. They spent summers and Christmas breaks with us every year. Jennifer came to live with us when she was 14, and Jonathan came about a year later.

To outsiders we were considered a dysfunctional family but I always preferred to refer to us as a "mixed family." Of course we had our share of family issues, disagreements about who would shower first or what toppings we should put on pizza but there wasn't anything I would have considered out of the ordinary. For a "mixed family" there was a tremendous amount of love and mutual respect in our home. Eddie and Jen became very close; they were inseparable as were Ryan and Jonathan.

I decided to place Eddie in a private high school in the middle of his sophomore year. This was when I started to notice subtle but evident changes in his personality. He no longer cared if he didn't ace a test or pass a class. Little by little he stopped hanging out with his long time friends and began staying with a new group of kids, kids I didn't know.

He got into some minor trouble with the police and isolated himself in his room when at home. There were absolutely NO <u>physical</u> signs that he was using any drugs, meaning no red eyes or slurred speech, etc. He swore on everything sacred to him that he wasn't even smoking pot any more and so I attributed the changes to the surrounding elements and thought it best to change them.

What I found out a few years later was that Eddie hid his drug use extremely well. He made it appear as if I had made the right choice by putting him in a private school. He brought his grades up almost immediately, seemed to be back on the right track, and he continued to maintain his average and graduated in the class of 2001.

I tried desperately to persuade Eddie to go away to college. I thought it would be good for him to get away, to meet different people and experience what life had to offer outside of Brooklyn, but he vehemently refused. Every time I made an attempt at trying to convince him how intelligent he was or no matter how much I begged him not to waste his God-given gift of a remarkable mind, I was always met with the same response; " Mom! Stop. I'm not as smart as you think I am, I'm just like everybody else."

I could not comprehend (and still can't) why his self-esteem was so low. He effortlessly excelled at everything he did. He was handsome, popular and so damn funny. Making people laugh was his forte. I used to tell him he should think about being a stand-up comic.

When Eddie told me he was going to take a year off from school I just knew it was going to be a terrible mistake. We had already completed all the paperwork. He received a full academic grant to a local college but he argued that he needed a break, that he didn't want to get burnt out. Once again he debated the issue so well that he succeeded in convincing me that his points were valid.

In what seemed like the blink of an eye he went from trying marijuana as a young teenager to taking drugs like Xanax, Vicodin, ecstasy, acid, cocaine and God only knows what else. I only knew because some of his friends who were concerned, came and told me. As I said earlier, Eddie hid his drug use very well.

Every time I heard something, I confronted him. I cried. I begged him to let me help. I screamed. I tried to manipulate, bribe and anything else I could think of, but he continued to deny everything.

Sometimes he would say "All I did was have a couple of beers. People like to exaggerate. Stop worrying so much, I'm fine."

If I had a dime for every time he told me "I'm fine" I would be very wealthy. Admittedly I sometimes thought I was letting my fears overrule my senses. I shifted back and forth between bouts of depression so bad that I struggled to get out of bed in the morning to being in utter denial and pretending everything was "fine" but in my heart I knew that drugs had stolen my son's soul. My precious boy was gone. The smiles and quick wit were replaced by scowls and silence, the sparkle in his eyes clouded by poison.

There were short periods over the last three years when Eddie was clean. The first time was in 2003, and his longtime girlfriend got pregnant and moved into our home. When they told me I was frantic.

I thought "Oh my God, this is going to be too overwhelming for him, they are so young and way too immature. They can't even take care of themselves. How are they going to care for a baby?" but Eddie totally shocked me.

Although the initial few months were scary, towards the end of Michelle's pregnancy Eddie made up his mind to get clean. He did it without rehab or a 12 step program (I realized later that because he got clean on his own he didn't truly believe he was an addict). I was skeptical and tried to convince him to at least seek some private substance abuse counseling but he wanted no part of it. Some of my doubts began to dissipate as I started to see glimpses of the old Eddie, the smiles, the quick wit, and the sparkling eyes; they all came back.

Anthony was born on December 10th, 2003. Eddie was the

proudest daddy I ever saw. I was crying uncontrollably when I saw him hold his son for the first time.

On the way to the hospital the day we brought Anthony home, Eddie turned to me and said " I promise myself that I'm going to be the best father I know how to be. I will never do to my son what my father did to me." He was on top of the world and I was overcome with emotion, completely filled with an indescribable love for my son who now had a son of his own.

When Anthony was about six months old, Eddie and Michelle started having some relationship issues. They argued over everything and anything. She decided that it would be best for her to move back in with her parents. Eddie was heartbroken and I feared that he would start using again.

I tried so hard to make him understand that just because his son was not living under the same roof that didn't make him any less of a father. But he truly believed he was a failure and terribly feared losing his son.

His self-esteem was at an all time low. Within one month of Michelle's moving out he was back to getting high, even worse than before. He managed to keep his job. He took Anthony every weekend and visited with him at least three times per week but he was in bad shape.

I knew this time was going to be different, from the day Michelle moved out up until the day drugs ultimately ended his life. He seemed to be caught in a vicious cycle; he was severely depressed, suffered from anxiety and had very limited self worth. Eventually he reconciled with Michelle and they moved into their own place but he was never the same again.

Eddie only got one chance at professional drug rehabilitation. In September of 2005, with Michelle expecting their second child he signed himself into a treatment center and completed a 28 day program. This was one of the numerous times in his life that I was proud of him. He did so well, attending all the required meetings and workshops. He even participated in family day, inviting me to join him (I'll be forever grateful, it was a truly enlightening experience. I was given the opportunity on this day to view for myself how debilitating the disease of addiction really is).

It was at the center that he was diagnosed [by a doctor] with clinical depression. Upon his release he was given a thirty day supply of antidepressants and medication to help him sleep.

He started out doing all of the recommended follow-up. He went to NA meetings every night, found a home group, got a sponsor and a list of phone numbers. The only thing he refused to do was see a therapist for the depression.

No matter what I said, I couldn't make him understand that just like addiction, depression is a disease and without proper treatment it would only worsen. He tried to assure me that he had it under control, that he had learned enough in rehab to, in his words, "keep his urges in check" but I kept trying.

I made appointments with a counselor (that he always cancelled at the 11th hour). I located various outpatient substance abuse centers near his home and literally begged him on a daily basis to just try. I did everything I could short of physically dragging him out of his house.

Once again Eddie and Michelle were separated. This time it was his choice, saying that he realized she was one of his "triggers" and that he wanted to have some clean time under his belt before trying to deal with their relationship issues.

I held my breath and waited for the bomb to explode. He stayed clean for almost sixty days. This time around he started bingeing. He would use for a couple of days and then the guilt he experienced after coming down would have him so depressed that he couldn't leave his house for days at a time.

I took every opportunity afforded to me to tell him how much I loved him, that nothing he did would ever change that fact, that all I wanted was for him to be happy. I could see that he was trying so hard to do the right thing; I tried to explain that he couldn't fight the demons on his own, that he needed assistance but he told me in so many words that self-medicating was a quicker and easier fix. Seeking some kind of therapy would take too long and all he had to do was figure out how much was too much. What he refused to accept was that there is no such thing for an addict.

Eddie's daughter Amanda was born on December 28th. The night before we were to bring her home from the hospital he went on a binge and fell asleep in the hallway outside his landlord's door.

The poor elderly man called me at 7:30 in the morning saying he couldn't wake him up. It only took me ten minutes to get there but by the time I did, he was in his own bed. I woke him up, had more than a few choice words and threatened to never speak to him again if he didn't go back to rehab.

In order to shut me up so to speak, he agreed to detox. I spent an entire day getting him admitted to a local treatment center only to have him sign himself out the next morning. I didn't follow through on my threat. I was upset with him but again I made sure he heard me when I told him how much I loved him and that I would always be there for him.

A lot of people told me I should try the "tough love" approach but I could not even begin to comprehend how shutting my son out of my life would help him and I just didn't know how to do it.

Eddie was a very big part of my everyday life; we spoke to each other everyday, sometimes several times. He was the first person I spoke to everyday and the last every night. One of the things I miss the most is our early morning phone call; he would call to say " Hey Mom! What's up? Just checking in" and ask me what I had for breakfast. He knew I never ate in the morning but without fail he asked everyday and would immediately start to laugh. Eddie's laugh was a contagious one so even if I didn't find him funny, I found myself laughing anyway. We never said goodbye; each phone call ended with "I love you, see you later."

A couple of weeks into the new year, Eddie appeared to be regaining some focus in his life, he was looking forward to his tax return so he could buy himself a used car. He was spending every weekend and all the free time he had with his kids and seemed relatively happy, but I could see that he was still struggling with what now appeared to be more anxiety than depression and I was scared for him.

I recently found an entry in my journal, written on January 3rd that says "I feel despair washing over me, like I'm waiting for something terrible to happen."

I have been accused by many (including Eddie) of being paranoid or a worrywart (especially when it came to him) but if my intuition is telling me something or I have a gut feeling I usually listen. There were many times when I was wrong but there were just as many when I was right. Had I been blessed with even the slightest bit of ESP or had the ability to know what the terrible thing I was waiting for was, I would have taken my son and locked him in a room somewhere.

On Friday February 17th, Mike and I decided to take an impromptu trip to Atlantic City. We never go anywhere and hadn't been away not even for a day in a very long time.

Eddie had a cold and took off work that day to go to the doctor. I got my usual morning phone call and then spoke to him again at around 11:00 a.m. He called to tell me that he had made his doctor's appointment (which I later confirmed he did) and to tell me to have a good time. He didn't sound like he was high. He just sounded like he had a cold.

I asked him to call me to let me know what the doctor said. He told me "not to worry" and that he would call as soon as he got back. His appointment was scheduled for 2:15. When I didn't hear from him by 5:00 I tried to get in touch. He didn't answer my call or return my text message. I did get a little concerned but I reasoned that he wasn't feeling well so maybe he turned off his phone so he could get some sleep. I was positive that I would hear from him within the hour.

By the time 9:00 p.m., rolled around without a phone call, I was inwardly frantic. I sent 911 alerts and a text message saying "just call me so I know you are alive." That was the last one I sent. I didn't share with Mike what I was feeling because I knew he would say I was being paranoid and to just "leave the kid alone."

When Jennifer called me at 10:30 to ask if I heard from him and that Frankie (her boyfriend) had been trying to reach him I really started to panic. Eddie and Frankie had become fast friends and they were very close, so him not returning calls to Frank concerned me more than anything.

I told Jen that he wasn't feeling well and was probably sleeping. She asked if I wanted Frankie to go to his apartment to check. Without even thinking I very adamantly said NO! I suppose she heard the tone of my voice and didn't question me. I know she thought it was strange but my response came so automatic that I didn't even question myself.

I couldn't sleep, I tossed and turned, I conjured up every possible explanation; maybe he lost his phone, maybe the doctor put him in the hospital, maybe he was bingeing, maybe, maybe, maybe but I knew no matter what the situation was, he would find a way to reach somebody.

The first phone call I made in the morning was to Michelle. I figured if anyone had spoken to him it would be her. When she told me she hadn't spoken to him since 11:30 the previous morning (just half an hour after my last conversation with him), I literally felt my heart sink to the bottom of my chest.

My second call was to Frankie, positive that he had heard from him sometime in the middle of the night. Once again I was told no. Once again he asked if I wanted him to go check and once again my answer was no. I told him that Mike and I were already on our way home and that we would stop there first, only this time Frankie didn't listen to me.

He went over to Eddie's apartment, got the spare key from the landlord and went in. He heard the television on in the bedroom and proceeded in that direction. Frankie told me sometime later that at first glance he thought Eddie was sleeping.

He said "he looked so peaceful" but as he got closer he saw that his lips were blue and that there was some kind of fluid coming out of his nose. He called 911 and then Mike's cell phone. I knew before Mike even answered. I can't recall all the details but Mike told me I let out a scream that could be compared to that of an injured animal.

Although in my heart I knew the truth, my mind was telling me that EMT would get there, perform CPR, get him breathing and I would meet him at the hospital. I even thought about what I was going to say to him when I got there.

I was totally numb for the entire two hours drive home. I couldn't cry, I couldn't talk, I felt paralyzed. Poor Mike cried and yelled the whole way. I remember me wanting him to stop because it made it too real, for him to be crying it had to be real but I couldn't say a word.

My heart breaks for Frankie, that he had to be the one to find his best friend, but if he had listened to me and waited, it would have undoubtedly been me, by myself to find him. I can only assume that it just wasn't meant to be that way.

Shockingly the medical examiner got there before we did so I couldn't see Eddie right away. We were met by our sons, Ryan and Jonathan, and Frankie and several other family members, all of who were trying to convince me not to go into the bedroom.

I just kept repeating, "I have to." I couldn't give an explanation but I knew I had to. I patiently paced the floors waiting for the ME (Medical Examiner; (it seemed to take forever but I think it was only about 45 minutes) when he finally came out, he introduced himself and proceeded to tell me with no hesitation in a very monotone matter of fact manner that my son had died as result from a heroin overdose.

I looked him straight in the face and calmly stated "No way! There must be some mistake, my son was not a heroin user. He only took Xanax." He then proceeded to tell me that they found two empty glassine envelopes on a table beside Eddie's bed that had a familiar heroin marking on them. Based on that fact and some medical terms he used to describe Eddie's physical appearance, he was ruling the death an Accidental Overdose.

I was required to answer some questions and sign some forms. I wasn't paying too much attention. In my head, all I heard was "when the hell did Eddie start using heroin? How could I not have known? I saw him almost everyday, spoke to him several times a day, when was I going to wake up from this nightmare?"

After I signed the last form the ME asked me if I had any questions, at this point all I wanted to know was an approximate time of death (it was now around 2:15 p.m., on Saturday February 18th). His answer was that it had been over 24 hours and he would put it at sometime between 10:00 a.m., and noon the previous day. I almost fainted; this meant that Eddie overdosed sometime within the hour of our last conversation.

As soon as the ME left I went into the bedroom to see my son (he did look peaceful). After a quick scream, I sat on the bed with him, held his hand, laid my head down on this chest and quietly sobbed. I did not want to leave the room. I wanted to stay in that bed with him forever. I wanted to go where he went. I begged for God to please be merciful and take me too, that there was no possible way I could stay here without my son. I stayed with Eddie until the coroner's office came to pick him up, praying all the while that by the time they got there, they would need two body bags.

The next five days are still a blur. My home was filled with friends and family members, day and night, and the phone rang constantly. The best way I can describe myself during this time would be to say I was having an out of body experience.

I went through all the motions without having any emotions. I was involved in making all the funeral arrangements; I chose his casket and picked out his clothing, ordered the flowers and chose the prayers for the Mass cards. Eddie's wake was filled with people, most I knew but there were a lot that I didn't. My mom said to me "now you know what the president must feel like, having to shake so many hands and greet so many people." It was, to say the least, overwhelming.

The original group of friends that Eddie knew since elementary school [Mike, Billy, Franco & Jon} came to the wake every day and night, and attended the church service and the burial. The respect and love that they showed for Eddie will forever stay in my heart.

Aside from Ryan and Jonathan, his pallbearers included, Dave [one of my nephews] Joey [one of my cousins] Mark [a close family friend] Joe, Steve and Marty (Eddie's friends and co-workers). Their wanting to do this for Eddie touched me so deeply and will never be forgotten.

Mike's mother and aunt did the presentation of gifts. Ryan and Jennifer each wrote and read eulogies that were so heart breaking, there wasn't a dry eye in the church. There were over forty cars in the procession to the cemetery. I just kept thinking to myself, "Why wasn't he able to see how many people loved him?"

As I write this, it has only been a little over three months since the angels called Eddie home. I spend a minimum of 99% of my day thinking about him and praying that I'll dream of him when I sleep.

Eddie truly was my best friend; the English language seems too limited to fully express how much I miss him with words. To me, Eddie being an addict was just a fraction of who he was but in reality being an addict consumed him. The drugs robbed him of the ability to look in the mirror and see the remarkable person that not only I saw but the countless number of people whose hearts he touched.

Unlike so many other diseases that may only affect a certain group of individuals, addiction is a universal, worldwide non-discriminatory disease. It makes no difference where you live, what or whom you know or don't know. Your drug of choice makes no difference either; some people (especially teens and young adults) seem to have the misconception that if they are only taking drugs that a doctor can prescribe, i.e., Xanax, Vicodin, OxyContin, etc., they can't possibly be addicts. This misguided thinking ultimately ended my son's life. Although the Medical Examiner was certain that Eddie overdosed on heroin, had it not been for the alprazolam (Xanax) already in his system, he would have lived.

Since losing Eddie, I have been doing some research on the subject of our youth and their abuse of prescription drugs. Kids as young as 12 years old are getting their hands on this stuff. Dentists and orthopedists prescribe Vicodin to anyone who has a root canal or sprained ankle. Primary care physicians are writing scripts for Xanax for high school kids stressing out over finals.

Unless your family has been directly affected, most parents would not even think to question a doctor about the kind of medication they are giving their children. It's our nature to trust them and unfortunately most doctors don't think it's necessary to say, please monitor your child's use of this medicine, it can be ADDICTING.

I love Eddie with every fiber of my being. I would sell my soul to the devil to have one more chance at saving him but if his or any other story can save even one person and spare even one parent the unendurable anguish of losing their child to this disease, I will be comforted by the fact that at least he did not die in vain. Eddie will continue to live in my heart forever and through me his voice will be heard.

Eddie's story as told by his loving mom, Lisa Cappiello, Brooklyn, NY

"Grief is the taker of many things but it cannot steal from me the place in my heart where he will forever be."

www.virtualmemorials.com/EddieCappiello

A Mother's Son

Oh my son, you beautiful one,
who has Fulfilled my life beyond belief,
you are my heart, a reason to live,
to see you grow, to rise, to give.
   A son holds a place in the heart of a mother
   that is shared by no other.
   A bond that cannot be severed.
   A mother's son is forever.

----*Lisa Cappiello – for Eddie*

JENNIFER CAROL LEE

MAY 14, 1977 – NOVEMBER 5, 2005
(AGE 28)

HEROIN

"A BRIGHT STAR NOW"

Jennifer was a star who came to us on May 14, 1977. She was the most beautiful child with curly hair that sparkled in the sun. From grade school and all the way until high school Jennifer flew through the air as a gymnast. Her favorite event was the bars.

Once she entered high school she moved on to the Palmdale High School Marching Band flag team. She also joined the Velvet Knights Drum and Bugle Corps and traveled the country each summer for 4 years. She graduated Palmdale High School with honors and went on to receive her Bachelor's degree at Loyola Marymount University.

Jennifer was a soul with two sides. She loved her parents deeply. She loved seeing her Grandma Ellie and Grandpa Joe. She was a loyal, devoted and true friend. The love of her life was Barry and she told her mom many times how much he made her happy and that she wanted to be with him always.

Jennifer was also a rebel in conflict. She was strong willed, independent and had her own way of doing things. She drifted into a life that seemed to take ahold and not let go. She tried so hard to break away and in a sense, she did. In the last year she came as close as she could because of her love for Barry. She has now returned to the stars as that happy, content, loved soul.

Her conflict and struggles are over and she is now at peace.

Above is part of what was written at her "Celebration of Life" service that I had to plan. What mother ever thinks that their beautiful 28-year-old daughter would die from a drug overdose?

Jennifer came from a pretty typical middle class family. She was an only child, the first granddaughter and very loved and spoiled. She was extremely bright and excelled in all of her classes throughout her education.

Unfortunately the illness of addiction ran on both sides of her family. Her dad and I tried to educate her about drugs and alcohol but Jennifer started smoking marijuana and taking speed at age 15.

At 16 she was experimenting with speed and acid until she had a seizure and it scared her so much that she quit for a while. When she got her own car, she and her friends started driving to teen clubs and " rave" parties. As parents, her dad and I were not blind to her change in personality, behavior and friends.

Jennifer always felt her drug addiction was under control. When she woke up one morning to find that her roommate had died of a heroin overdose on the couch, she said "Mom, you will never have to worry about me doing that."

She spent 8 years in a methadone program trying to stay off of heroin. She also told me how terrified she was to be clean, to feel her emotions without any drug to help.

As a mother what do you say? You are desperate to help your daughter and you are terrified that something awful might happen. You try to convince her to speak to the counselors at the clinic. You pay for her to go into rehab twice. She walked out twice. I used to call her every day and jokingly say "I'm calling to make sure you are ok and alive today". She would laugh.

Jennifer and I were best friends and she would tell me everything. There were times when I really just didn't want to know. I may not have liked what she was telling me but I always made sure that I ended every conversation we had by saying "I love you". And I feel somewhat comforted because those are the last words I ever said to her and the last words she heard from me.

About 6 months before she died Jennifer started drinking. She talked herself into thinking that it would be easier to substitute alcohol for heroin and then get off of alcohol. Obviously I questioned this logic.

You watch your child (even at 28 years old, she was my child) and feel helpless. Thus began a spiral downhill. Jennifer was taking methadone, slipping in heroin once in awhile and drinking.

Her last evening was spent drinking and having that one last high on heroin. She didn't plan on dying that night; she just wanted to get high.

The next morning you get a phone call from the hospital calling about your daughter. They tell you it is very, very serious. And, you don't work at a hospital for 20 years and not know what they are saying. You ask over and over again if she is alive and all they continue to say is it is very serious.

That was the day a piece of my heart died. I have a big gaping hole and the pain is so horrible I don't know how I will get out of bed or get through the day.

You spend hours thinking about the "what ifs" and feeling guilty. "Why couldn't I save my daughter, why couldn't I help her?"

She had all of the tools: a loving family, a good education, information about drugs and its dangers but it was not enough. She had an illness that was just too hard to overcome.

The more I reach out to find support from parents like me, the more I learn just how widespread a problem drug addiction is. If telling Jennifer's story can open the eyes of just one teen to its dangers then Jennifer is still here, still that bright shining star.

Jennifer's story as told by her loving mom, Sandi McClure,
Lancaster, CA

"I lost my best friend. Even though Jennifer had a drug problem, she was a bright, loving, and happy person."

BRETT M. TOZZO

SEPTEMBER 8, 1982 – JUNE 19, 2005
(AGE 22)

OXYCONTIN/ALCOHOL/HEROIN

"THROUGH THE YEARS...WITH MY SON, BRETT, HEAVEN SENT – HEAVEN BOUND"

I remember it like it was yesterday. My six year old son, Brett, standing at the top of the six steps in our home in Westfield, N. J., and hearing his words "Don't anyone worry about me...just take care of my mom."

A few minutes before, I had the task of telling my three children that their father had died when he reached the hospital marking the end of his five year battle with a lung disease. Brett's words will forever haunt me because his love of his dad and the void left by his death would play a huge part in his journey on this earth from that day forward. If I had only known then where that path would lead him...what would I have done differently? Could I have changed his course...altered his thinking...filled the hole in his heart? I truly don't believe anyone could have but God and Brett.

Brett was a rambunctious kid right from the start. He played hard at whatever he did...throwing everything he had into his play, his work and his dedication to his family. Well liked wherever he went, he never lacked for friends or for something to do. His brother, Justin, was three years older and his sister, Christy was eight years older so he fit right in as the little brother, though, many times, creating havoc with his boundless energy and need to be the center of everyone's universe.

As a single parent, I tried to keep life as normal as was humanly possible after our loss. The boys were in Boy Scouts, soccer, baseball, CCD and I was room mother for each of them as often as I was able to. Christy was in gymnastics and life was full, hectic and settled into a new normalcy and routine. It was around this time that Brett took a marble notebook, those familiar black and white assignment ones...and started writing to me. It would be years and years before I even knew it existed...and yet it held so many clues and bittersweet insight into his mind and heart.

I made the decision to move to Florida in 1993. The bitter cold and my need to "get away" from the New Jersey memories were the motivating factors that guided me to Sarasota. I thought of the boys and their love of fishing and the year-round activities they could do.

What I did not realize was that Brett could no longer tolerate loss, (his best friend and 15 year old babysitter, P. J. died a few years after his dad) and although it was not evident on the outside, he had a hard time adjusting to a new place without the familiar faces and the deep understanding of those he left behind.

Life in Florida was new and different and the boys settled in and made friends. Brett took up BMX racing and was an excellent rider...taking the #2 Novice trophy for 13 year olds in the entire state. He lived to ride his bike and it consumed his days and he spent many hours working on the latest gadgets to make the bike go faster and he built jumps to practice his skills. I went to every practice and every race and videotaped every one. His obsession with racing came to a screeching halt when his "perfect' bike was stolen...and he decided to give up the sport entirely.

That "all or nothing" pattern surfaced again...and again as he grew into his teenage years...trying to find his place in this world. Nothing seemed to please him...nothing made him truly happy. Oh, he always had a smile for his friends and was the life of any party or gathering...but a growing sadness in his eyes haunted me...I could see through him and yet felt powerless to help him see that life was not as bleak as he imagined it to be.

He fell in love with Nicky in 7th grade and a new Brett emerged. They were so cute together, and yet had that typical love/hate relationship that is normal for that tender age. Nicky became his life...she was Italian and he was so proud of his "Sicilian" roots and he connected with her and really liked her parents. He was different...so funny and full of life and surprised me with the depth of his love and caring for her. Their love was full of turmoil as they both were trying to grow and find their way and yet there was such a deep connection between them that it was beautiful to watch them when the storms were calm.

Nicky and Brett broke up soon after they entered high school. I will never forget the torment in his eyes when he told me...how I ached for him...how I wanted to tell him it was for the best and that if meant to be, it would be. But, he wanted no such talk from anyone and certainly not his mom...he just wanted to live in the pain...and try to make sense of another loss...another ending and another reason to fear loving someone. Yet, he hid that pain from anyone who saw him...played the "I don't care" card and showed the strong, confident young man the world believed him to be. Inside, a little bit of him died...and there was nothing anyone could do to help him heal.

Life went on...there were other girlfriends, some casual, some deeper...but it all seemed superficial from the outside looking in. It was as though he went through life waiting for that hurt, for that pain to reenter his heart and he always readied himself for the inevitable.

After graduation, Brett landed a job as a personal trainer at a local gym. Although he was always quiet and introspective, he quickly earned the respect of many of the members who relied on his knowledge and calm demeanor. He readily admitted that he did not like the gym's owner and routinely felt underappreciated and undervalued.

I could see that struggle emerging again...the one that crushed his self-esteem and made him blind to his value and worth. No matter how many times I told him that the guy was a jerk...and that as long as he knew he was doing his job...to ignore him. It was a huge deal to him and he constantly looked for another job or another path to follow. He ended up being there for three years...and up and quit when the time was right.

Shortly after I moved out to the country, Brett started to drink quite heavily. I was so naive that I did not know that he had been doing quite a bit of imbibing before that...but I guess it was more noticeable because it was just the two of us. Friends would come out...and he would go out back and soon came the stumbling and incoherence that followed suit.

It was hard for me...since I had become an Officer with MADD years before and knew all the dangers of drinking, let alone drinking and driving. I tried to talk, plead, reason with him...and it would get better for a while...but only for a short while.

Soon, I started learning lessons that I never thought I would have to learn. I learned that Xanax and alcohol are a deadly combination that causes severe personality changes. Brett had an incident where he had to be Baker Acted (put in a mental hospital for 72 hours) and he was found with a number of Xanax with no prescription. He crashed his car into several mailboxes coming home at 6 a.m., after a binge of alcohol and Xanax...not because he was drunk...but because the combo made him keep falling asleep at the wheel. He called one morning at 6:30 and said "Mom....I just rolled my car" ....once again he fell asleep trying to come home.

I had a huge decision to make...and it is one I will regret for the rest of my life. I decided that since he hated living out here in the country...he should go live in town with his brother since he needed someone to share the house he rented. Brett left in January of 2003...very quietly and I wept in silence not wanting him to know how hard it was going to be for me to not see him every day and be able to monitor his progress and drinking.

His older brother, Justin, was the one with the "experimental" problems...always trying some new combination of stuff to get high on. He is brilliant, and I never really worried because in my mind, he was too smart to ever hurt himself, and Brett was a drinker...not into drugs or any of the stuff Justin used.

Wow, how deep in the sand did I have to stick my head to believe that it would not and could not happen to Brett? Yet, it really never crossed my mind that Brett would try drugs because he was so into health and his body. He started bodybuilding around 7th grade and grew to love the challenge and how it made him look and feel. He continually lectured me about what I ate and how I needed protein and that I should exercise more.

Brett and I talked almost every day. He never ended a conversation without saying "I love you" and neither did I. Our relationship was better...he seemed to be better and I worried a little less. My obsession was keeping food in his house and things to drink that did not involve alcohol. In my little mind, if there was enough Gatorade and bottled water, he would not have to spend money on liquor or beer.

I must admit I had no concept of addiction since I never touched a drug in my life and drank very little in my younger years...hating every swallow of the stuff. There was no comprehension of drinking to forget problems and float them away...it was not in my programming, I guess.

Brett told me he wanted to be a fireman in April of 2005, (he was 22) and filled out the necessary paperwork at a local school. He was very excited about it...and yet worried about how it would be paid for. I took out a Home Equity Loan and made sure to tell him not to worry about that. I was so happy that he was finding his place in this world...and started to relax just a little bit. This was what I had been hoping for for so long...him finally being enthusiastic about something...something I KNEW he would excel at! He could even still do personal training in his spare time. This was what I had been praying for!

In early May of 2005, Justin had a very bad experience with a drug I had never even heard of...it was Crystal "meth". It made him see little bugs in his room...bugs that laughed at him and then ran and hid under the rug. He took a knife and tried to kill them...seeing green goo coming out but never quite being able to kill any of them.

Brett called me very upset...and told me he was calling the police on Justin and having him Baker Acted. I screamed for him to wait for me to get there and jumped in the car and headed for their house. The police were there already...and had called an ambulance to take Justin to the hospital. I watched helplessly as they took him away...and put my head on Brett's chest and sobbed and sobbed. He patted my back...telling me it would be okay. His cool, calm and level-headed demeanor was evident. He hugged me again, as I left for the hospital to check on Justin.

About a week after that incident, which was a nightmare, Brett stopped over at his sister's house where I was babysitting my little granddaughter, Halle. As he sat there eating lunch, he dropped a bombshell that rocked my world and my sanity. He told me he had a problem, too...that he was addicted to pain killers. I stared at him in disbelief.

"Oh no, Brett," I cried..." How did that happen?" He mumbled about doing them recreationally with the girl he was living with who had just ripped his heart out.

I asked him what he was going to do about it...he "ad a plan" ...he replied. He was going to a program...he had it all figured out and was scheduled for the following Monday. I asked and asked...and he kept telling me that it was safe...and that it would work.

The next few weeks were a blur with me worrying about Justin and continually asking Brett for progress reports. The program worked just fine, according to him...he was ok...he was fine. The program did NOT work...it did not help at all...it made things worse. It made the cravings worse...blocked the ability to get high...made his life a living hell...yet he did not let on.

He made the decision to try heroin for reasons I will never comprehend. He was desperate...he wanted to start fire school...he wanted his life back. He told his brother **"How did I ever get involved with this and how am I ever going to get out?"** He could not find his way out no matter how hard he tried.

His friends knew NOTHING of his addiction to drugs or recent heroin use. He kept the secret so well hidden and showed no signs in any way, shape or form. He got up every day and went painting and his boss knew nothing. He was playing a part and slowly dying inside and filled with anguish and desperation. He hung with all his friends and to them he was the same Brett they always knew. His depression over the recent breakup was the only sign they could see and they all helped him through it as best as they could. This too shall pass...or so they all thought.

On June 18th, 2005, Brett went out with his friends. They all say he was in a good mood...until his ex walked in and upset him one more time. He decided to leave and was driven home. What transpired and what went through his mind that night can only be speculation on my part.

The next day was Father's Day...a very depressing day for him and all the letters that people had written about his dad were next to his bed because he had asked to read them. He had already taken some OxyContin and drank quite a bit...and I believe he could not get the pain out of his mind or off his heart. I can only picture him deciding to go that one step further...to make the pain blur and fade into the night...with a syringe full of heroin.

On June 19th, at approximately 3 a.m., Brett went to be with his daddy in Heaven. His strong, beautifully built body lay slumped against the bathroom wall for almost 12 hours before he was found by his brother. My call telling him to remember his daddy on Father's Day went unanswered and I imagined him just enjoying his day off...maybe even going to the beach.

His brother was at work and then came home and napped. The strange thing was that I felt sick all day...my stomach was churning and I had a dull headache. I remember at one point lying on the floor trying to figure out what was wrong with me. Still no call from Brett or Justin...but I felt so awful that I let it slip to the back of my mind.

I spoke with a friend and then went to feed the animals...and as I passed the radio...the song, "My Son" by Mark Schultz came on. I stood there crying...thinking of my nephew who had passed nine months before. Twenty minutes later, the dogs barked and there was a policeman at my door. His words were to the point...saying, " Your son, Brett, is no longer living."

I did not comprehend...What hospital? Where did he have his accident? Where is the car? He then told me that Brett was found dead at his house by his brother...and my world came crashing down around me...and I screamed.

I got to read my little marble notebook a week after his death. I read what he wrote on June 26th 1996...exactly nine years earlier.

"Dear Mom...I love you...you are the best mom in the world. I am going to New Jersey tomorrow and I will miss you. If I die...I leave my bike to Jeremy. Well, I have to go and pack...sorry I have been so lazy lately...I will try harder. I love you very much and will miss you. Love Brett XOXOXOXOXOXO (p.s. if I die...please don't be sad...because, when you are sad, amazingly...so am I)".

How well he knew me...but he can't take away that sadness. He has sent me so many signs of his new life...and with each sign I feel his presence and the peace he is trying to send me. But, it does not fill the hole...nor does it end the pain. It just makes the longing to hold him one more time stronger.

I miss his laughter...his wit and his smile. I miss his ornery side and his very calm and reasonable side. I miss my son. I go to schools and tell his story and play the DVD of his life...and watch as the kids cry along with me.

It feels like it is all part of some sick joke...our children dying because they did not know how to live with their pain, their insecurities and their hurts. God help us all and all parents, who like me, thought it would NEVER happen to my family!

Brett's story as told by his loving mom, Chris Tozzo, Sarasota, FL

"When the time of our sunset comes...it will not matter what we have accomplished...but rather the depth, strength and clarity with which we have loved one another"

Brett's website: www.bretttozzo.com

JOHN KONEWAL

OCTOBER 4, 1967 – MAY 8, 2003
(Age 35)

HEROIN

"YOU'RE IN THE ARMS OF AN ANGEL"

John was my first born. I was 17 when I had him. I didn't know how to be a mother. I wasn't sure of anything. Then I saw him and I loved him so much. Nothing else mattered because he loved me back! He became my life, my baby, my best friend.

John was very shy and I believe that's what started his addiction. He went from drinking and smoking pot, to heroin. I remember the last months of John's life. He was finally straight. I was so happy!

He had lost his brother Dennis, to heroin. He knew how our family struggled to deal with our loss. One morning my husband, John's stepfather, took me to look for John. We found him and went to breakfast. I couldn't stop crying. I hated to see him when he was sick.

He went to jail for a few months. When he got out, he went to live with his brother. He was doing so good, but he wanted to drink. I kept telling him that he couldn't. He got drunk one day and left.

We looked for him but couldn't find him. I thought he must be in a program. My son was so determined to find John that he called every police station in Philadelphia, and then he called the morgue. They had John. He was found in a vacant lot. He had died of a heroin overdose.

Again I was left to deal with the pain of losing another child. I had not yet come to terms with Dennis's death. Some days I am so overwhelmed with grief. I feel like my heart has been ripped out of my chest.

If I could have only one wish to come true, it would be to hold my sons, if only for a minute. Some people say they are at peace now. The only peace I have is knowing they are just sleeping and will one day wake up. Until that day I will go on loving and missing them with every beat of my heart.

John had many good traits. He was just so very troubled but he was very kind and everyone who knew him loved him.

John's story as told by his loving mom, Lynne Copeland, Bristol, PA

"Seeing death as the end of life is like seeing the horizon as the end of the ocean."

DENNIS KONEWAL

OCTOBER 8, 1969 – SEPTEMBER 11, 1998
(Age 28)

HEROIN

"GONE BUT NEVER FORGOTTEN"

Dennis was always so full of life. He was always smiling. I remember about a week before he died, we went out to eat. He kept kissing my cheeks and saying how good he was doing. He was in a

half-way house. He seemed so happy.

A few days later he asked my husband, Dennis's step-father, if he could move back home. He said he really didn't need the half-way house, that he wanted to stay with us and then get his own place. My husband told him it was okay.

Dennis tried to call me the next day, but I was in the shower. I tried to call him back. It was too late. The phones were off in the half-way house. That would have been our last conversation.

The next day no one could find him. Then we got a phone call from his best friend. He said they found Denny's van on Kensington Avenue. Someone had OD'd and died. He said he was sure it was Denny.

I will never forget that day. I felt like I had been kicked in my stomach. It had to be a mistake. How could I live without one of my children? I remember feeling like I couldn't breathe. I never felt pain like this. I kept seeing Denny's face only days ago, laughing and saying he was so happy, and that he was gonna be okay.

He cheated death so many times. When he was 12, he was hit by a truck. When he was 17, he was in a bad car accident that took the life of his cousin. Then, when he was 21, he was in another car accident and his friend was killed. He used to say, "Mom, I am never going to die."

I think these accidents affected him and he chose drugs to ease his pain. But he lived through all this and ONE BAG OF HEROIN took his life.

It will be seven years on September 11th and I still can't believe I will never see him or touch him again. I can't help but wonder what he would look like now. What his life would be like. He left behind a lot of people who miss him. He never even got to meet his 2 nieces or 2 nephews. They only know him by his picture. I love him and miss him so much. I will miss him until I die.

Dennis had worked as a carpet installer, and was very good at it. Everybody raved about his work.

Dennis's story as told by his loving mom, Lynne Copeland, Bristol, PA

"When you are sorrowful look again in your heart, and you shall see that in truth you are weeping for that which has been your delight."

I AM YOUR DISEASE

A LETTER TO JOHN AND DENNY

Dear John And Denny,

I miss you both so much. I think about you all the time.

I know you would not want me to be sad and crying all the time. But I cannot help it. I get angry because you left me even though you could not help it. I used to think I knew what pain was. And then you died and now I know. Sometimes I hurt so bad I can hardly breathe. I always say that I have been hurt so bad that no one could ever hurt me again. The pain of losing a child is something that cannot be explained. Only someone who has lived it would know.

Denny,

I wish I would have known you were going to get high. Maybe we could have talked. I know you never meant to die, alone in your van on Kensington Ave. They treated you like just another drug addict. Didn't they know you were my child and I loved you? I hate that you died. I miss you so much.

John,

We were so close. Why didn't you come to me? You knew I would never turn you away. Like Denny you were in a vacant lot. We didn't find you for 19 days; you were in a morgue. Again they treated you like just some junkie. But that's not who you were. You were my first born, my baby. I loved you.

I love you both and miss you so much.

Love always,
Mom

ROBBY NUNES

JULY 17, 1981 – APRIL 16, 2001
(Age 19)

HEROIN

"I HOPE YOU HAVE THE TIME OF YOUR LIFE"

Robby is the youngest of three children. His father Rick and I divorced when Rob was 9-years-old. His father remarried Micki and I remarried Don. Robby has a sister, Shannon, who is 5 years older than him and thinks she's his second mother. His brother, Jeremy, was a year ahead of Robby in school and his mentor. They are as different as night and day.

Robby was average in sports and Jeremy excelled in that area. Robby had a dark complexion with dark hair and eyes while his brother is a blue-eyed blond. Jeremy is out-going and has a temper. Robby played guitar and was more sensitive. The girls used to say he was sweet. Jeremy was a jock who was popular and involved in school activities. Robby never felt he could or should compete, so he was popular with the music-playing, head-banging kids. The brothers, though different, were very close and Shannon mothered them both, whether they liked it or not.

By the time Rob was in 8th Grade, his grades began slipping (he used to have all A's and B's) and he became even more popular. He started getting new friends that no one had ever heard of before! I tried my best to stay on top of his grades, attendance, etc. He attended Summer School every year to make up for goofing off during the school year. By 11th Grade, Robby was grounded more often than not for either missing school, getting caught with cigarettes, or one time because a group of kids were caught with a beer. Rob also seemed to withdraw from the family.

When Robby was 16, he asked me to have a talk with him one night. Since that didn't happen much anymore, I was all ears. Rob began to sob and told me he was addicted to drugs and couldn't stop. I felt like I had been kicked in the gut but tried to remain calm and get more details from him. I asked Robby what kind of drugs he was using and Robby sobbed harder saying it was heroin. Heroin! A death sentence! That's all I could think of. Robby cried that night saying, **"I just want to be a kid again, Mom. I want to stop lying and I want my life back!"**

I had no idea where to turn for help, but promised I would figure it out. Robby wanted to sit up alone in the dark to think. I asked him if this is why he had been sick so often. "Were the drugs making you sick, Rob?"

"Oh my God, Mom! I am sick when I am trying not to use drugs!" and he was.

I lay in bed all night waiting for Don to wake up so I could tell him what was going on. I alternately cried and prayed. Don could hardly believe what he heard and was very worried and angry. I called our family doctor for advice. The advice was to have Rob detox at home so he'd remember how awful it felt and that should take care of it. It didn't sound right to me so I did some calling around and got him an appointment with a doctor who worked with an outpatient addiction program.

I took a week off work to detox Rob at home. He threw up, had the runs, fevers, sweats, leg cramps and nightmares. He could hardly walk due to joint pain. He was so sick I considered buying drugs for him, to ease his pain. When Rob felt better, he began his outpatient treatment twice a week and Don and I attended with him as a family once a week. After 6 weeks, he graduated from this program and attended After Care meetings twice a week in the evenings.

We did it! Robby was cured! Or, so we naively believed. Six months later we noticed some of our checks missing. We discovered that Robby had been forging checks for money. His father, Rick, noticed the same thing at his house. When I confronted Rob, he was too scared to face his father or stepfather and ran away from home. He was 17 years old and a senior in High School.

About 2 weeks later, Rick called me at work to say he had found Robby sleeping on his couch. I told him I would be right over. But first I made arrangements to get him into the hospital with an inpatient facility for addiction. Rick and I talked and decided to intervene together as a united front. We woke Robby up and gave him the choice of going to jail for forged checks, or going to this hospital. Crying and apologizing for hurting his family, Rob chose the hospital.

The hospital wanted money up front. We paid what we could, but could only afford to keep him in there for 10 days, not the recommended 30 day inpatient treatment. The treatment seemed to do him a world of good. He came home a changed boy! This time it worked, we just knew it! Rob was to attend outpatient treatment again and he started working at a new job.

Another six months passed. Rob got fired from his job at a tire shop for his temper. His temper? This is the most easy-going kid you could ever meet! I noticed he was losing weight and spending a lot of time sleeping lately.

I waited for him to leave one night and searched his room, as I had done so many times before. Under the laundry, in his closet, at the bottom of his waste basket, inside a Big Gulp Cup, and inside an empty potato chip bag. I found two syringes and some pawn slips.

When Robby returned home, I confronted him. It was the same scenario. He cried saying he just couldn't stop and that his life was ruined. He said he was afraid and didn't know how to stop.

I took him to the Emergency Room the next morning because he was even sicker this time. They kept him long enough to detox him and sent him home to find further in-patient treatment.

How would we pay for this? There were still bills from previous treatments! Robby and I called the State and got him in for an evaluation. They said he qualified as an IV Drug User, but there was a waiting list. He was placed at the top of the list. After six weeks of waiting, there was still no room through the State Treatment Center. Rob took his name off the list and decided to get a job and start attending church more faithfully. And he did.

Robby got a great job through his bother-in-law, Shane. He was learning to be a glass fitter for a glass company in Salt Lake City. He was so proud of his job and really looked up to Shane. Rob bought himself a nice black Honda Civic that he fixed up really nice and also joined a gym. He worked out regularly and looked so healthy and buff! Robby also got a cute little girlfriend, Alicia, whom he adored. He was regularly in attendance at St. Francis Catholic Church.

We thought this time we turned the corner for sure. One time he cut his hand pretty bad at work and got stitches. He requested no pain medicine. We were so proud of him for that! Six months earlier he would have milked that situation.

On Easter Sunday, 2001, the whole extended family went to church and brunch together. Everyone commented on how wonderful it was to have the " old Robby" back in the family. Robby adored his baby nephew, Ethan, and little niece, Hunter, and they adored him too. It warmed my heart to see my kids hanging out together again, all looking so healthy and happy. That afternoon was a beautiful sunny, spring day. Rob asked me if I minded if he missed dinner and went golfing with a friend. That's a healthy activity; it's exactly what I wanted him to do more of! So, off he went, in his freshly waxed Honda.

When Robby returned home, about 7:30 p.m., he complained of a really bad headache. Headaches run in the family, so no one was alarmed. I gave him some Advil and Rob took the phone upstairs for his usual three-hour phone call with Alicia.

At 10 p.m., Rob got off the phone and I peeked my head in, as I was going to bed, to tell him good night. He said he felt awful and I suggested he stay off the phone and try to get some sleep. About 2 a.m., I could hear Robby in the bathroom, sick. I got up to check on him and he said he had the worst headache he'd ever had in his life. I asked him if he thought he was coming down with something and he said that was probably it. Rob apologized for waking me up, knowing I had to work in the morning. I suggested he not take any more Advil, but lie down and be still for awhile and see if he could sleep. I went back to bed, reminding myself that Robby was healthy now. It had been seven months and I just had to start trusting him now. Rob never once mentioned using drugs that afternoon.

The next morning, I headed straight for the coffee pot, as usual. Next to it was a note from Robby telling me not to wake him up too early. He had a doctor's appointment and wanted to sleep until 8:45 a.m., I was glad he was finally sleeping and tried to be quiet while dressing for work.

At 8:30 a.m., I was ready to leave and decided to check on Robby and see if he felt better. I opened his bedroom door and screamed his name when I noticed how strangely he was lying. No answer. I ran over and shook him, screaming his name. Nothing! I felt for a pulse while screaming "Robby! Don't you do this to me! Robby, you come back to me right now! Don't you do this!"

There was no pulse. I pulled the pillow from under his head and tried CPR. The breath came back out so fast! I kept wondering if I should be doing CPR or calling 911. I was so torn! I ran across the hall to my phone to call 911. "Why hadn't we installed a cordless phone in there yet?"

When 911 answered, I told them my son was not breathing and had no pulse. I could hardly remember my own address when I was asked for it. The 911 officer told me to remain on the phone, but I couldn't. I had to go back and do more CPR! I threw the phone on the floor and went back to Robby. More CPR and more nothing.

In a panic, I ran back to the phone and yelled at them to hurry! They told me to go out front and flag the ambulance down, so I did. Then, I remembered that Robby now had my lipstick all over his mouth. He'd be horrified if anyone saw him like that, so I ran back up to his room to quickly wipe off his face.

The ambulance crew met me in the doorway and I was asked to stay in the living room to speak with a police officer who would arrive soon. What to do? Pray! That's it! I prayed and begged God not to take my baby. " Please, God, don't take my son, please! God, take me if you need to, but not my baby!"

While I waited, I called Shannon. "Honey, I think your brother is dead, he's not breathing!"

"Mom, they'll help him, don't worry, he's probably back on that damn heroin again," she said.

"The ambulance is here, call Don, your dad and your brother and have them get to the hospital," I said.

"Oh, and Shannon, please pray really hard for Robby!"

The police arrived and asked a lot of questions. I told them he was a recovering heroin addict and I suspected an overdose. They asked for any medication he might have taken and I handed it over.

They took Robby away in a quiet ambulance and asked me to have someone drive me over to the hospital. A friend from work happened to be driving by and stopped to see what was happening. He gave me a ride to the hospital and some neighbors made calls and locked up the house.

At the hospital, I was taken into a small room with a social worker. I was amazingly calm, perhaps in shock. Another police officer came in to ask more questions. He told me they did not yet know what happened to him.

I began to pray some more. A doctor came in next and told me he could not save Robby. They did all they could but he was gone. My youngest son was gone! I cried a little, but mostly I was numb. This was not happening. It could not be true, it couldn't!

Robby's father barged into the room demanding to know what was wrong with Robby. "He's gone, Rick, Robby's gone," I told him. Rick punched a wall and became hysterical. They took him outside to calm him down. A couple of friends arrived and I sent them out to be with Rick.

Don arrived at the hospital and he was shocked. The doctors suggested we not go in to see Robby because "he didn't look good." They needed to send him to Salt Lake City for an autopsy because the cause of death was not determined. I said they had to wait. We had to find our priest to bless him.

Robby had become so active in his church that he would want that. And I had to see Robby! This was my son! We waited about a half hour for Father Flegge to arrive and we all went in to see Rob together.

"Oh no, not Robby, not one of our young people!" said Father Flegge. Father blessed his body and the family said their good byes.

So many times I had been angry with Robby for his drug abuse. I worried he might be watching and thinking I was mad at him. I couldn't stand that thought! I cradled his head and said " Robby, Mom's not mad, I love you. You are ok now. Save me a place in Heaven Baby. Good bye for now, Baby, I love you so much."

The rest of the day is a blur. Rick fell apart and had to be medicated. I wanted everything to be perfect. I brought this child into the world and I was going to see to it that I sent him out properly. I planned every detail with Rob and young people in mind. Somehow, it had to make a difference to these young people.

Though the autopsy report was not in yet, in my heart I knew it was an overdose. I asked Father Flegge how this could have happened when I had been praying so hard for three years for God to save my son. Father said that God did save Robby; I just didn't get to tell him how to do it. Robby is ok now. No one can hurt him.

The viewing the night before the funeral was attended by several hundred mostly young people. It took over three hours for the line to get through. Pink Floyd, Robby's favorite, was played during this time. His photos, golf clubs and his guitar were on display near by. It was a warm, beautiful evening. I found myself being strong once again, hugging so many young people as they sobbed through the viewing. So many kids hurting! Robby had no idea how many friends he really had. Three months and one day shy of his nineteenth birthday, he just wanted to be popular and he didn't seem to know that he already was.

The morning of Robby's funeral it was raining very hard. The funeral was Catholic and a friend played Rob's favorite hymns on guitar. As we approached the burial site, the rain stopped and the sun shone. We all sang " Good Riddance-It's Something Unpredictable" by Green Day. Rick released a crate of white birds into the sky. We knew Robby must have been watching. He loved his father's birds. As we drove off, the rain began again. My heart rains tears every day now. A part of me went to Heaven with my youngest son, Robby.

Robby's story as told by his loving mom, Sandi Daoust, Salt Lake City, UT

"It's something unpredictable, but in the end it's right. I hope you have the time of your life."

http://www.geocities.com/dyingtogethigh/robbynunes.html

LENNY ORLANDELLO, JR.

JULY 10, 1964 – JULY 16, 2003
(AGE 39)

HEROIN

"An Angel's Face"

How do you start a story that changes your life forever? I've decided to start at the end.

On July 20, 2003, I got a phone call from my daughter. I'll never forget the words that we exchanged. She said " Ma, I need to talk to dad right away."

I said "Lisa, please don't say it's Lenny."

My precious son had been sitting at his kitchen table for four days. He had overdosed on heroin.

Lenny had been an addict on and off for 20 years. When I look back, I realize that it was my husband and I who kept him alive.

Lenny had sat at his kitchen table for four days. My sweet boy was beyond recognition. They couldn't even ID him by a picture.

Those days will forever remain with me for the rest of my life. I never got the chance to say good-bye or to hug him again. I still to this day wake up in the middle of the night thinking that the phone is ringing. The pain of that night will live with me forever just like the hole in my heart that will never heal.

We should have seen something coming. He was always a good student until he went to high school. He ended up quitting and getting his GED. He went to college, (and made the dean's list) and ended up quitting that too. It seems he quit all the good things that life had to offer him.

Then he found Ms. Heroin. She took him on a journey where there was no return.

We sent him to so many detoxes. We thought that we could win this war on drugs. What a price we paid! Lenny would get clean and then get a good job and relapse again and lose everything he worked for. The worst day was when we told him that he couldn't live here any more. I'll never forget the look on his face.

He called me one day and told me that he couldn't stop throwing up. I, of course, told him he was drug sick. Two days later he went to the hospital and that's when we found out that he was in kidney failure.

He was in hospitals for his kidney failure and on dialysis for a couple of weeks. Those days made me realize that this drug had such a hold on him. How could he ever do heroin again? Nothing stops her from coming back into your life. She rules your every move and then she destroys you.

Ms. Heroin wraps her arms around you and doesn't let go. She brings you down evil paths and turns you into a person that you never thought that you could be. And when she lets go it's too late!

She turns you into a liar, and a thief and robs all your loved ones. When Lenny was at the end of his journey he had hepatitis C and kidney failure and through it all that Ms. Heroin still hung on.

On July 10, 1964 I gave birth to a beautiful baby boy. He weighed 7 lbs, 11 ounces. It was one of the happiest days of my life.

Lenny's story as told by his loving mother, Lucille Orlandello,
Revere, MA

"Death ends a life, not a relationship." ---Jack Lemmon

I AM YOUR DISEASE

LENNY

In your brief length of time
in the ordinary place
we were blessed with the sight
of an angel's face

You were truly sent to us
from God up above
to hold, to teach,
and to give you our love

The days and the nights
were all sweet and dear,
and we'll always thank God
for sending you here

Now that you're gone
from this ordinary place
I know that one day
we will see your face

Love, Ma

Lenny's website:
http://www.geocities.com/dyingtogethigh/lennyorlandello.html

BOBBY MEHLBERGER

AUGUST 18, 1980 – JULY 22, 2005
(Age 24)

HEROIN

"MY BOBBY"

It was Saturday, July 23rd, 2005, when I heard the horrible news that my Bobby was dead! I had been out shopping that morning for Bobby's birthday. He would be 25 on August 18th. The last time I saw my baby was on Thursday July 19th, when I left for work and I kissed him good-bye and told him I loved him.

Bobby had a problem with drugs from the time he was 14 years old, that I knew of. He and I fought the demons for a long time. Bobby had been doing so good for about 4 months, then two weeks to the day that I last saw him, he was not acting right. I asked him what was going on. He told me "Nothing, don't worry." But I worried every minute, every hour of every day about Bobby.

The last time we talked was on the 18th of July. He was so excited and happy. He had been at the Oz Fest, a big outdoor concert, with his older brother. The top of his head was sunburned, still things I remember. So I wasn't too worried when he wasn't home on Thursday, then again on Friday, after all he was 24 years old. But by Friday night, I felt that there was something wrong.

I started calling all of his friends to see if they had heard from him.

It wasn't like him not to call home. Bobby always called me and told me when he would be home and that he loved me. Yes...he was a momma's boy; a loving, caring, talented, compassionate young man. He had a disease. Bobby was a loving dad to his 6-year-old son, Derick, a loving brother, son, and friend.

Back to that day...I kept calling home, hoping he would answer, hoping he would be making up some excuse why he hadn't been home, but he never did. So I called my answering machine and there was a message from his father...telling me to call him, that it was important! I thought, "Oh God...Bobby got into trouble...maybe locked up, but why would he call his dad?"

I called his dad and my oldest son answered. Bobby sounds just like him, so I said "Bobby where have you been?---I've been worried sick about you." My son Jimmy said, "It's not Bobby mom, it's me Jimmy, here is dad."

His dad got on the phone and told me to get home...BOBBY WAS DEAD! All I remember was screaming---"No! No! No! Not my baby!! You are a liar!"

I went to his house and there were my two sons and his dad and when I walked in they told me it was true, Bobby was gone. He was found in an abandoned house. He was identified by his tattoos and his piercings.

He was there for over twenty-four hours. My beautiful son...all alone for all that time. My baby died alone!

The next few days were a blur. I keep reliving that day. Did he suffer? Did he call out for me? Why would someone leave him there alone? Now I know why I was feeling uneasy on Friday. There was a reason...my Bobby was dead!

Bobby was born on August 18th 1980. He was my baby, and such a good baby. Bobby was fine until he reached school age then all hell broke loose, he didn't want to be separated from me.

When he was 10, he was diagnosed with ADD. He was a very sensitive child, always needed me more than his brothers did. When

I AM YOUR DISEASE

Bobby was 9, I divorced his dad. I always wonder if that led him to his addiction. Then when he was 14, it was a life of rehabs and overdoses.

His father gave up on him. I told him, I could never, and would never, give up on him. He was my child for God's sake. How can you give up on your child?

Bobby became a dad when he was 17 years old. He finished high school when he was 19. He was so proud of himself for graduating and I was as proud as a peacock.

Bobby always wanted to be famous with his musical abilities. He also wanted to be a tattoo artist. I told him he could do and be anything he wanted to do but he was the one who would have to work for it. I would be there for him.

How horrible it is to think Bobby will never fulfill his dreams…never see his son grow up, never meet the right woman and marry and have a home and family, that I will never see his beautiful face, see his smile, hear his laugh. How can this be?

The day that my Bobby was put in the ground, my heart and soul went with him. There is not much to laugh about anymore, no more plans and dreams. Just emptiness, and memories.

Bobby's story as told by his loving mom, Michele Mehlberger, Bristol, PA

"I lost my heart. I lost my joy. I lost it all when I lost my boy"

SHERYL LETZGUS MCGINNIS WITH HEIKO GANZER

Bobby's favorite poem

Nothing Gold Can Stay
Nature's first green is gold,
Her hardest hue to hold.
Her early leaf's a flower;
But only so an hour.
Then leaf subsides to leaf.
So Eden sank to grief,
So dawn goes down to day.
Nothing gold can stay.
----Robert Frost

KARA EDELMAN

AUGUST 30, 1975 – MARCH 4, 2001
(AGE 25)

HEROIN

"A MOTHER'S GREATEST FEAR"

My daughter Kara died from heart failure 3-4-01 on my living room couch. Kara had been ill for a couple of years, from all her drug use since the age of 12 years old.

Kara was 25 years old when she died. We went through a lot of years of drug abuse with her. Dropping out of school 3 months before graduation, running away, and lots more. Before she died she was very much wanting to get off the drugs but did not want to give up most of her friends.

She would write on the back of books and loose paper her goals. On 12-31-00 she wrote 10 goals...she met 9 and the last one was to get off and away from a few of the people she felt were the ones most hurtful to her and the suppliers...she had to die to meet that one.

I believe God knew it was too much and brought her back home. She had herself baptized 9-00 as a Christian...she felt it very important then to be forgiven. I feel that was one time she actually listened to the voice...I miss her so much.

Kara was born 8-30-75 in San Diego, CA. A beautiful curly haired girl. Kara was shy growing up, but had many friends.

At the age of 12 her brother was struggling with some drug abuse and I admitted him to a treatment center. Part of the program was the family counseling. We participated weekly and Kara did also. During this time she decided that she was to start using also!

Her journey was to be 12 years long. We went through counseling, changing schools, restrictions, etc.

I was a single mother and had to support myself, and two children. I must say the divorce was very hurtful to Kara; she was a pawn in the revenge her father felt for me.

Drugs and alcohol addiction were very prominent on his side and I wanted out of that and everything that goes with it. Kara continued to live in the life with that world.

At the age of 17, two months before graduation she dropped out of school. The life she chose was totally taking over. The friends she chose were into really bad things. She lived a very secretive life protecting her friends and their doings. I learned later she was trying to protect me, because her boyfriend had threatened to do something if she revealed any of his doings.

Kara did get away from him in 2000. But she found another guy very much the same.

She became ill with heart problems and was admitted to the hospital. We were told she would need a heart transplant eventually but would not be considered unless she was clean. DENIAL was the word. Kara took heart medication and did her drugs. This went on for 3 years and it finally started to show the signs of the end.

Kara came back home to me September of 2000. She was getting very weak and had weekly visits with the doctor. Kara began then to look at her life and very much to feel well again, and started writing goals for herself. She felt very much the need to attend my church and get herself baptized in September of 2000.

Kara fought hard off and on those months, but could not stay off the drugs. She quit her job in January of 2001, because of her health. She became very weak and had to stay in bed. But on better days, she got up and went out and used.

The goals she wrote were all met but one; to get away from the drugs and the people who were part of it.

On 3-04-2001, she passed away in my living room. She was sleeping and stopped breathing. Her brother found her dead when he went downstairs that night. He has felt that he heard her "call him."

The coroner told us she died in a few seconds. I believe that her last goal was completed by Jesus; he knew this was too much for her.

She left me her dog, Chelsea. She loved her so much and so do I.

Kara is so missed. The comfort I must feel is that she is not of that world anymore. One last thing...on March 3, 2001, she told me none of this was my fault and her favorite color was yellow. What did she know?

Parents, do not blame yourself. Our children make their own choices.

Kara's story as told by her loving mom Kim Edelman, San Diego, CA

"God, grant me the serenity to accept the things I cannot change."

BRANDON JAMES HAGNER

JULY 4, 1980 – MARCH 6, 2003
(Age 22)

HEROIN

"BROKEN DREAMS, LOST PROMISE"

Brandon was born a healthy, beautiful baby on July 4th 1980. Having a 13-year-old brother and an 11-year-old sister, he was an extremely spoiled, and therefore happy baby. Always having one of us carrying him around or playing with him made him the center of the family and we all indulged him---(maybe over-indulged).

He was a happy, bright child growing up with no problems until around the age of 11 or 12 when he began questioning authority and experimenting with marijuana. I didn't know then that this would be the beginning of years of addiction and pain for him.

Whenever and wherever there was excitement or trouble, there was Brandon. Although extremely loyal to his family and friends, somehow the drug took over and we all took a back seat to them.

He became increasingly depressed and anxious. My beautiful son became someone I didn't know. Our tears and prayers couldn't help him. He couldn't help himself. I know there are some who believe in tough love, but how do you enforce tough love with a child who is in so much pain that it breaks your heart to see them hurting so badly? If only I could've taken the pain away. We spent years of trying and crying together to stop this demon that had a hold on him.

From a very young age he always took on too much responsibility for everyone else. Never blaming anyone for their sometimes bad treatment of him. He always understood their problems and tried his best to help, even if this meant hurting himself. Maybe if he had blamed someone, anyone else, he could have forgiven himself for causing so much hurt.

Brandon lost his stepfather to suicide in May 1995, when he was only 15 years old. His best friend Clint, died in his arms of a heroin overdose in December the same year. I don't believe he ever really recovered from this. In March 1997, he lost his friend Randy and shortly after that his friend Jeremy. As time went on and the loss of his friends continued, life didn't seem to mean as much to him. Death was not to be feared. As hard as he tried for a normal life, he was not destined to have one.

Years stretched on and rehab after rehab did not help. He spent 9 months in a school in upstate PA (court ordered). At age 17 he graduated high school while in a boot camp (again court ordered)in the Pocono Mountains. He always excelled while away. Somehow, it sounds strange, he actually seemed to find freedom while incarcerated: Freedom from addiction, freedom from pain and confusion.

I don't know if there are any answers for them other than an end to them. Children become addicted and their childhood is over.

Our life as we always knew it is over too. So many lives are forever changed. Brothers, sisters, grandparents, no one escaped the pain of losing a loved child.

We remember Brandon when he was Brandon: A loving, beautiful boy. An IQ of 140, talented, active, everyone's friend. Gone so fast. Too fast.

I heard that when your child decides to take a drug, that is the last decision they will ever make. The drug makes all the choices after that and I think most families of a lost child will agree that they lost him or her long before their actual death. We tried everything we had to get him back but it wasn't going to happen.

That last day I spoke to Brandon, he was high and we argued as we so often did. My biggest regret is the fights we had. He walked out the door and was gone. Now, looking back, I can't be sure it could have been different but I pray everyday to relieve some of this guilt I carry around and give me my boy back.

The next morning, his friend came to the door and told me she couldn't get him to wake up. We rushed to the hospital, where he lay in a coma due to an overdose of heroin.

We never got a chance to speak to Brandon again or hear him laugh. Dear God, I miss that laugh. Eleven days later we had to say goodbye. The doctors said the brain damage was extensive due to lack of air and he would never breathe on his own again.

The boy lying in that bed was not my Brandon. Not the young man struggling to get straight. I have to believe that he is at peace now.

He did leave part of himself here. He was an organ donor and now three people are alive today, living through Brandon's heart.

We, his family, will go on but the suffering will probably never stop for me. I just hope with all my being that his suffering is now over. I wish life could have been easier for him. I need to believe I will see him again and he will be his pre-drug self. Smiling.

Thank you for letting me tell his story. I keep talking about him. It keeps him alive. Alive in me and all the people who knew, loved, and remember him. The real Bran, Uncle Bo Bo, Bizo, Player, Cuz. All in one very special Boy.

Brandon's story as told by his loving mother, Celeste Dale, Phila., PA

"I'm just in the other room"

GINO VENTIMIGLIA

OCTOBER 8, 1977 – OCTOBER 23, 2002
(Age 25)

HEROIN

"SHATTERED LIVES"

I remember October 8th, 1977, like it was yesterday.

That was the day my first-born child, my son Gino was born.

From the moment I knew I was pregnant with him, I loved him with all of my heart.

The moment Gino was born, a connection, a special bond between the two of us was there.

As a child Gino was very sickly and I was the over-protective mom who didn't let him leave my side.

He was quiet and sweet and so smart. He and I were best friends.

When His sister Liz was born they had each other. We lived on a very small dead end street and being overprotective, I didn't let the two out of my sight. As a result they played with each other. The three of us had each other.

We spent summer days in the back yard and in the pool. We spent weekends camping as a family.

I couldn't have been happier if I had won the lottery.

As Gino and his sister grew up we had two more children, another boy and then another girl.

Gino started high school and I was busy with the younger ones in pre-school.

Not once was Gino any kind of problem. He was such a good son. I had no complaints whatsoever.

One afternoon, a week before Gino was about to get out of school for the summer (junior year), I got a call from the EP cops telling me Gino was smoking pot behind a church at lunch time and was at the police station.

I thought, "They have to have the wrong kid. Not Gino."

Not that I was naive, it's just that he gave me absolutely NO reason to even think he smoked pot. I didn't make much of the pot incident. After all, everyone tries pot, right??

I swear, from that point on, it was one thing after another with Gino. He had the worst driving record and was forever being arrested for unpaid tickets. Fines, not showing up for court.

That following winter Gino jumped over a wall at a concert and smashed his heel bone and had to have surgery on it to repair it.

I think that is where his love of opiates started, with the pain meds he had while recuperating.

Gino finished out the rest of his senior year partying with a new group of friends and I wasn't happy about it.

Following graduation, Gino received a full paid scholarship to Wayne State University for academics. I was so proud of him. I will never forget the first day he went to college.

Gino started college and my little one started preschool at the same time. What could be better then that? My house was filled with so much commotion and craziness and I loved it all.

Little by little, with Gino going to Wayne State, he wasn't the same person. I was getting calls from professors telling me they didn't know why Gino even bothered to sign up for their class; he didn't even show up.

He would have every excuse in the world why he couldn't get to class and why he cut classes, etc.

He was spending more and more time at "raves" and online looking for "raves" to go to in other cities.

Although I pleaded with him about Ecstasy he swore he wasn't using it.

He would go from one dead-end job to another making enough money to party on the weekends. Around this time he got a job at a place near our house called Sun Corporation.

That is where he was introduced to heroin.

I kept telling him he needed to get out of those small shops he was working in; I knew they were filled with drugs.

I kept on him about going back to school and the more time that went by the more afraid I was that he would never go back. He needed to go to school. He was so smart and was wasting his intelligence.

He told me once, "It's too late for me. I screwed up and there is NO way I'm going to be able to make everything all right again."

I told Gino "It's never too late in life for anything."

To show him how right I was I enrolled in school myself.

I went for a year and a half and Gino was so proud of me.

Just before Gino died he got a grant to go back to school.

The judge put him on an electronic tether a few weeks later and suspended his license indefinitely. So once again he couldn't go to school.

In the late fall of 2001, Joe and I celebrated our 25th wedding anniversary. We went on a trip together and when we got back we could see Gino wasn't well. He had been on some kind of strung out drug trip. We were so stupid. We knew Gino partied but we had NO idea he had a drug addiction.

He came to us and told us he was addicted to heroin and wanted to go to rehab.

HEROIN???? No one does heroin. Only "street people" do

heroin. NOT MY SON!

Gino found a place in rehab in the spring of 2002. I sobbed when he walked out the door with his stuff. I was looking at someone else's son, not mine.

I couldn't see him for the first week because he was in detox but my mind was on him morning, noon, and night. I was filled with so much hope.

The first visiting day after detox I saw clear eyes for the first time in a long, long time. I was so happy and thought our life was going to be like the Lifetime movies. Kid goes to rehab, comes home and the addiction is cured and they all live happily ever after.

The problem was it wasn't like that.

It was one catastrophe after another as I watched my son try to stay sober.

He attempted suicide once a few months before he died but was found by a person who called EMS. He was then placed in a mental ward at the hospital for a week until they could find him a bed in a half-way house.

From there he went to jail, back home, and finally three weeks before Gino died he went to court on a probation violation and his PO, who hated Gino, recommended 9 months in county jail.

We had a sweet-talking attorney and Gino got 9 months probation on an electronic tether. I was so happy he wasn't going to jail but I soon realized that I was physically in jail in my home and I was the warden.

Gino reported with his Probation Officer once a week.

The guy kept telling Gino he "wanted his A** badly" and he will be waiting for when Gino screws up. When Gino told me that I couldn't believe it.

I told Gino he better stay sober and not slip because he would go directly to jail if he failed any drug tests.

Three days before Gino died he relapsed. I caught him smoking crack at four in the morning in our garage with a friend. I couldn't believe it.

I AM YOUR DISEASE

I wanted so badly to call his Probation Officer and have him picked up but I didn't want my son to go to jail with that bastard.

I was so upset with Gino. Here he was on an electronic tether from the courts, had to drug test once a week, and was smoking crack??

I didn't know then how strong addiction is and couldn't understand.

I told him I hated him and told him if he didn't go back to jail he was going to go to rehab or he couldn't live here.

The next few days little was said between Gino and me.

The night before he died he was sitting in the dark in a room all by himself. He was crying. He wouldn't tell me why but I knew why.

He felt so awful, knew he screwed up and didn't know how to go about fixing it all. I never saw anyone that down before.

He came upstairs and the last few hours we spent with him alive we watched Forensic Files on television.

He was so smart, he could have been in forensic medicine or been anything he wanted if he didn't choose the drugs.

He said he was going to fix things. He was not going to live like this anymore.

The next day, instead of going to his probation meeting, he skipped it and was found dead all alone in a hotel room by himself.

Twelve empty packets of heroin and several needles scattered around and seventy-seven dollars were all they found.

The police were called in and they called the morgue to come get Gino's body.

I wish I could say it ends there but it doesn't. What happened next is what happens all the time in America.

He was taken to the morgue where his body laid for nine days until a funeral home called to ask us what we wanted done with our son's body!

At that point we didn't even know he had died…Can you imagine the shock??

For nine days he laid in a stainless steel drawer, while I paced the floor. Gino's dad spent hours out looking for him in every pawn shop, crack house and abandoned building in Detroit.

They treated him like just another "junkie." Well damn it, this junkie had a family: A family who loved him with all of their hearts:

A family who prayed every night that Gino would get well again.

It's been almost four years since that awful day in October, 2002. It's been a hell of a road, a journey I would never wish on anyone.

I have spent the last three years mentoring addicts; educating myself on addiction and learning every thing there is to learn about heroin.

In the future I would like to get into Methadone advocacy work.

I made a promise the day I buried my son that his life and death would not be in vain.

Gino's story as told by his loving mom, Karen Ventimiglia, Chesterfield Township, MI

"Suffering has been stronger than all other teaching, and has taught me to understand what your heart used to be. I have been bent and broken but I hope into a better shape." ...Author unknown.

http://www.geocities.com/dyingtogethigh/ginoventimiglia.html

MARK DANIEL BAUER

FEBRUARY 12, 1986 – MAY 28, 2004

(Age 18)

ACCIDENTAL OVERDOSE OF PRESCRIPTION DRUGS (INCLUDING MORPHINE AND OXYCODONE)

"LIVING A PARENT'S WORST NIGHTMARE"

If you were to ask any parent what their biggest fear in life is, their worst nightmare, most would say that it would be losing a child. We are living that nightmare, and it is worse than anyone could have imagined.

I still can't believe that Mark is gone. There is no way to explain the pain and devastation of losing a child. Only those who have lost a child can understand.

A week before graduating from high school, Mark went to school, played in a student/staff basketball game, lifted weights, and went to work. A great day!

The next day he never woke up. It is a day that lives with us always. I can't tell you what it's like to try to revive your child and then to hear those dreadful words; "I'm sorry, but your son didn't make it".

Then to hold your child's lifeless body…plan his funeral…go to graduation to see his cap and gown and a picture on the chair where he should have been sitting. There are no words that can even come close to describing that feeling.

Throughout his life, Mark was quiet and an introvert. He didn't let many people into his life; you had to bring him into yours. When people took the time to get to know him they found a wonderful, caring person. Never much for words, he had a terrific sense of humor and could make you laugh just by his expressions and mannerisms. It was devastating to the many people who loved him when he tragically died just one week before his high school graduation.

Mark is the younger of our two boys. When our children were born they became the focal point of our lives. Their mom quit work and became a stay-at-home mom. Mark and Brian were less than two years apart in age and were best friends during much of their pre-teen years. They were constant companions and Mark followed Brian everywhere. We did everything as a family. Mark seemed to be very happy growing up.

Up until the time Mark was two, we lived thirty miles from the ocean. We used to go to the beach often and he always loved it there. This love continued throughout his life. He was always comfortable in and around the ocean. Even when we moved away from the ocean, we would travel to the Outer Banks of North Carolina on vacations. We all enjoyed it so much that we even spent some time there over the winter holidays. Mark had a great time there even in the winter. He would ride bikes, tour lighthouses, shoot pool, look for shells and just hang out.

His love and compassion for animals was evident early on and can best be described from an event that occurred when he was six or seven. Our dog found a rabbit's nest and killed the mother. We found her eating one of the babies. When we looked into the nest there were still two live baby bunnies. We realized that they were doomed to die without their mother and also knew that they could not survive as pets. Mark wanted to take care of them and didn't want them to die alone. We took them in and he fed them with an eyedropper and cared for them. If love could have saved them they would have lived. Mark was devastated when they died. We buried them in our yard (with

I AM YOUR DISEASE

markers for each grave) and had a funeral.

Mark's early school years were happy ones. He did well in school and had many friends. He participated in karate and enjoyed shopping with his mom and fishing with his brother and dad, and was also active in the youth group at church. Some of his other enjoyments in life were playing video games, hiking, the ocean, and animals. He also developed a love of basketball during this time. Everything in Mark's life appeared to be going well.

The biggest disappointment in his life was when he didn't make the basketball team. Although seemingly insignificant, he grew increasingly more withdrawn when this occurred. Each year that he didn't make the team, he withdrew even more until finally he abandoned many of his friendships (or some friends abandoned him).

Mark was extremely athletic and loved sports, and basketball was his true passion. When he was younger, he would tape every game when Michael Jordan was on TV. We used to tape some movies that came on TV and had a movie "library." Many times we would go to watch one of them only to find that a Bull's game was taped over it. We also had a driveway basketball court and would play all of the time. Packing for vacations was incomplete unless a basketball went with us. Although Mark was only 5'9" tall, he realized his lifelong dream shortly before he died…he was able to dunk a basketball. He also played in the student/staff basketball game at school, which is an event that is very significant to us now. That game was played on May 27, 2004. Mark died the next day.

Mark's passion for basketball in life has now turned into a tribute to him. His basketball backboard is now a driveway memorial. His portrait is on the backboard (complete with lights at night) and there is a cross and flowers at the base. His school now plays the annual student/staff basketball game in his memory complete with T-shirts with his name on them, and a plaque in the school office.

He was also an avid weightlifter from the time he was twelve years old until the day before he died. He would sometimes lift seven days a week. Although he only weighed 180 lbs, he could bench-press almost 400 lbs. He sometimes lifted in the middle of the night because he also had trouble sleeping. We can remember the many times during the middle of the night when we would be awakened by the sound of the weights "clanking." Even when he started to have chronic back pain, he would continue to work out.

In April of 2004, Mark was experiencing pain in his lower back (a chronic condition), a sore knee (diagnosed as bursitis), and a sprained wrist. His doctor prescribed Naproxen for pain. Early on, Mark told us that the medication was not helping the pain. He never said anything else about the pain after that and did not return to the doctor for a follow-up. Looking back, we sometimes wonder if Mark had found his own method of treating the pain.

Perhaps the signs of Mark's addictive personality surfaced early in life. We remember when the boys received candy for Easter or Halloween and Mark's "stash" could disappear the same day. He would tend to go off by himself and all we would find later would be empty candy wrappers in a pile. We started to get concerned when this trait was also exhibited with household medicines when he was in his early teens. Cough medicine and acetaminophen had to be hidden and sometimes even diluted with water.

When Mark was a sophomore in high school we received a phone call from his school telling us that they had found marijuana in his possession and that they had called the police. He received probation before trial and also went to drug and alcohol evaluation and counseling.

Over the next year or so, there were occasional issues related to marijuana usage or beer consumption. The signs were much more evident to us by then and we could look at his eyes or listen to his speech to tell when he had been "using."

In the months preceding his death, Mark seemed to have turned things around. He was happy, talking about the future, and looking forward to his upcoming graduation from high school. His self-confidence was also on the rise. The faculty and staff at his school also noticed this change. From all appearances, he had won his personal battle with addiction. His eyes were clear and his speech was sharp.

On May 27, 2004, Mark's day went something like this. He woke up and went to school and played in the student/staff basketball game.

When he came home from school he lifted weights and ate dinner. He then went to work and got home at about 9:30 that night. When he got home, Mark talked to us about the game that day and we knew what a special day it had been for him.

That was the last conversation we ever had with Mark he never woke up the next day. On Friday May 28, 2004, Mark died from an accidental overdose of prescription drugs.

Mark was so strong and seemingly invincible. After he died, we found out that he had taken prescription painkillers for his back pain. We believe that he may have gotten the drugs from a co-worker.

Mark's mom, dad, and brother are devastated and heartbroken. Life is not the same anymore. Maybe someday the memories of Mark will bring laughter and joy to our heart, but right now it just hurts. It's amazing how every facet of daily life brings a reminder of Mark.

As with all families, Cookie and I have dealt with, and shared, many issues of grief within the family. We have faced family illnesses…Cookie's near-death battle with colon cancer in the late '80's, and Brian's acute respiratory problem when he was just 6. We have dealt with the death of my dad in 1983, the death of Cookie's dad in 1989, and the death of her mom in 1996. We have even dealt with the death of our dog in 2004. Cookie and Brian survived their medical issues…and we were o.k. We also shared the loss of our parents together, which may have actually brought us closer together.

The grief due to Mark's death is like no other grief imaginable, however. It is not the normal course of life. Kids shouldn't die before their parents. There are no words to describe the devastation and emptiness. It's not something that you "get over" and the emptiness will always be there.

The way in which Cookie and I have dealt with Mark's death is as different as you can imagine. It's amazing how two people can share the same loss, the death of our son, yet deal with it in such opposite ways. Here are a few examples:

Cookie's faith does not seem to have wavered at all since Mark's death. My faith (shaky even before Mark's death) has caused more questions than answers.

Someone can be with Cookie for hours without knowing about Mark...however, you can't be with me more than 5 minutes without knowing about Mark.

Cookie seems to gain comfort in strong relationships with extended family and close friends whereas I have pushed friends and family away (or vice-versa) and would mostly rather be alone (except for Cookie & Brian and his family and very few others).

If people don't talk about Mark, I believe it's because they don't care. On the other hand, Cookie believes that people do care and think about Mark, but don't always know what to say to us.

In our opinion, grief is an emotion that we all have experienced (or are experiencing) many times in our lives. It can actually be a positive emotion in many cases. It's a reminder of just how special and significant the person has been in our lives. It can also give us a stronger appreciation of life and what we have. Unfortunately, for some of us, it can take over our life and we are consumed with sadness and emptiness. Time does not "heal all wounds".

There seems to be a stigma attached to those who have died a drug related death. Many think that they are bad people who probably deserved their fate. Our son and many other kids who have suffered this fate are caring and wonderful people. Mark gave us so much during his short life and we are so thankful that he is our son. This is not just something that happens to others. This can happen to a friend, a neighbor, or your own child. Sometimes the signs of addiction are obvious, and sometimes they're much more subtle.

Mark's story as written by his loving mom and dad, Phil and Cookie Bauer, York, PA

"*The truth is, everyone's life ends in tragedy...if you believe that death is final*"

Dennis Ray, Minister, York Christian Church

Mark's website:

http://mark-bauer.virtual-memorials.com

MATTHEW GUASTAMACCHIA

JULY 9, 1983 – FEBRUARY 11, 2005
(Age 21)

HEROIN

"IN A NEW YORK MINUTE, EVERYTHING CAN CHANGE"

I lost my son and only child, Matthew Guastamacchia, on February 11, 2005 to a heroin overdose. He was 21 years old.

Matt was a very kind, loving person. He always had a smile on his face and was one of those people that everybody loved. He always loved animals, and over the years brought home every stray he could find. He was extremely intelligent, a talented photographer and a wonderful son.

As Matt became a teenager, he thought he was invincible. Although he never got into any trouble, he tested every rule and boundary. At 16 he began going to clubs in Manhattan (without permission, of course) and he loved the city and the party atmosphere. Although I worried constantly about where he was and what he was doing, he thought he had everything under control. While I know Matt experimented with drugs during his teenage years and did things that would make any parent crazy, he always seemed to land on his feet and rarely faced any consequences for his behavior.

When I would try to talk to him about his risky behavior, he would just brush me off with, "Oh, mom, stop worrying, I'm fine."

It was almost always followed by a smile and a kiss on my cheek. As he grew a little older, he started to mature and seemed to outgrow his teenage rebellion.

Matt was a sophomore at Pace University when he first tried heroin in August of 2003, and he was dead within 18 months. He did not use it continually and had stopped many times by himself. But he always went back after 6-8 weeks of being clean.

I know my son did not want to continue to use drugs, but he was unable to stop. At the time of his death, he had been clean for at least 6 weeks after only one relapse in December. He was going to NA meetings and had just started an outpatient drug program the week before he died. He had never been to rehab. When we asked about it, they told us he didn't do enough! He seemed to be doing very well and I think he convinced himself, as always, that he had it under control. That he could do it "just one more time."

The morning he died, he was still awake when I got up, having gone out the night before. He looked like he may have done drugs, but when I asked him, he hugged and kissed me, told me not to worry, that he was fine. He had just been up all night.

Although I was skeptical, I guess I wanted to believe him. He came out in the kitchen with me and I made him breakfast, which he took in his room. An hour later I went to tell him something and he was face down on his bed, his breakfast lying next to him untouched. They were never able to revive him and I take some (although very little) comfort in knowing he died peacefully at home.

There is a perception that kids use drugs as a way of dealing with pain in their lives and I'm sure that is true for many of them. My son was a very happy person and I think he tried heroin because it was fun and he thought he was invincible. Once he tried heroin, he was unable to stop. He underestimated how dangerous heroin was and he paid for it with his life.

Dealing with the loss of my son is the hardest thing I have ever tried to do. Although I try to tell myself that Matt would not want me to be so unhappy, I am completely consumed with sadness and I just don't know where to go from here. He is all I think about. I miss him terribly and my life will never be the same.

Matt's story as told by his loving mom, Susan Brogan, Holmdel, NJ

"*Remember how I laughed, remember how I loved. Use me as the reason you embrace life, not the reason you don't*".

Read about Matt on My Space:

www.myspace.com\matthewguastamacchia

DONALD CHARLES PARENT

AUGUST 19, 1975 – JULY 18, 2002
(Age 26)

HEROIN

"MY PRECIOUS SON"

We moved to PA and the kids went to a new school. They met new friends but Morrisville is a small town and half the kids were doing some drugs. Don graduated high school, got a job and wasn't home much.

I was worried about my other son Jay. It was very apparent that he was on some heavy drugs and drinking. He wouldn't go to school and he dropped out when he was 16. I found out Jason was doing heroin, the last of the line of drugs and I was terrified. I kept thinking I would get a call telling me he was dead, and I tried to talk to him, but it didn't do much good.

When they were 23, 21, and 17, Don and Jay were doing drugs in the basement, where all their friends would come to party, and my youngest would get home from his part time job, and one of his brothers would drive him to get beer and other alcoholic drinks. I was living a nightmare. My two oldest were doing hard drugs and my baby was drinking himself stoned every night.

One day I had just stepped out on my front porch and a thought came to me that one of my sons was going to die. I thought---which one? But didn't get an answer.

And then one day I came home from work early and caught my middle son Jason, shoving something in his jacket pocket. He looked purple-blue, and I thought he would die right then. I was horrified and asked what he had done, and he said, "You know I get high." But I didn't know how, so when he left the room I looked in his pocket and pulled out a syringe. More horror! I didn't know he was injecting.

Soon after that I found out that my Don asked his brother to inject him. He had been snorting heroin and wanted to inject. Oh my God! I pleaded, cried, screamed that they had to stop, that they had to go to The Detox Center and not do any more drugs.

I would get calls in the middle of the night from Don, saying he was in a Philadelphia Emergency Room, or a jail in Philly and can I come and get him.

I was seeing a therapist and taking meds, anti-anxiety, and they kept trying different antidepressants, but I never took the antidepressants.

I was also trying to go to my part time school bus driving job, which I did end up quitting.

The therapist told me I had to do something and I knew things couldn't go on this way so my husband and I ended up moving to a much smaller place, which was a good thing as far as getting my two sons into a detox. They would not take brothers in, sisters, or anyone who had a friend in there. I soon found out why.

After we moved, Don and Jay were staying at an apartment, but lost it in a couple of months for non payment of the rent. Then they each moved in with separate friends, and Jay was the first to finally say he was going to The Detox Center to detox. Don wanted to go too, finally, as he was wearing out his welcome where he was staying and almost OD'd one night on the front steps. I was married before and they had different last names so it was perfect! Jay's friend drove him to The Detox Center and I took Don. They both got in. I'll always remember the relief I felt that night knowing they were finally safe.

I went to an Alanon meeting at the same building, but in a different room and thought everything was going to be ok. Well, 4 days later they called me to tell me that Don left the detox with another kid. That kid was his brother Jason.

Don went back again a week later but could not get in because he hid some pot in his shoe and they found it during the search. So they recommended he go far away, to a place in Williamsport, PA. The Detox Center said that would be his best chance, so they got someone to drive him there, about 6-8 hrs away. I was hysterical but wanted to give him what he needed and I desperately wanted him off the drugs.

He seemed to do well there and when the time was up he went to a halfway house in the Poconos and did well there for awhile. I would get him almost every weekend and drive him back.

He wanted all his stuff so we would bring some each time. After he had everything, I got a call from him saying he was in a motel. He had relapsed with another kid and gotten kicked out. Of course I went to get him but he almost OD'd again, and I got him into The Detox Center one last time.

The third morning he called me and said he was detoxed and doing good, but that same night at around 8:00 I got a call from the nurse that Don had tried cutting himself and they do not handle that kind of thing so they took him to the ER.

My husband and I went to the ER right away and I asked Don what happened? Why was he cutting himself? We went outside to smoke a cigarette and he said he heard someone telling him to do it and he felt worthless.

Oh my God. Was this my beautiful, handsome, charismatic, smart son who I thought I never had to worry about because he seemed so street smart? I didn't know anything about cutting.

They sent my son to a psychiatric hospital where they diagnosed him with severe bipolar disorder and had him on heavy meds. I called the doctor and asked why my son was on so much as the other residents didn't seem as groggy as Don, and he told me it was because Don had a very high tolerance for drugs.

Well, when the insurance wouldn't pay anymore for the hospital they recommended a place that treated dual disorders, so we went there.

They had to detox my son from the drugs they were giving him at the hospital, but he looked so good a few days later, was more like himself instead of a zombie. They also had a dual diagnosis house right on the premises, one for the males and a house for females. They were right next door to the main detox and again, I felt so hopeful.

Don seemed happy and got a job, and we both felt that he was finally in the right place. They had gym equipment and a Bowflex there, and drivers to drive the residents to their job, the store, etc.

We would go up to visit Don and go out to eat. On Mother's Day that year, 2002, he gave me a pair of garnet earrings, which is my birthstone and made us coffee.

One day in June I had an inclination to pull into a sport store and bought my son an early birthday present, a pair of Nike's and a baseball hat. I'm so glad I did because he never made it to his birthday, which was August 19. I didn't know he would be dead one month later.

Don came home for a weekend visit on June 29th to the 30th. But he wanted to go back early on Sunday, saying he had a headache. I told him I had Tylenol but he wouldn't take it, saying he had to get back. Something wasn't right. But we took him back. That was the last time I ever saw my son alive. How I wish I would have just grabbed onto him, tied him up, kept him from doing what I thought was impossible.

Don and I talked on the phone the next week. He went to the dentist and had an appointment to get his wisdom tooth pulled, but he seemed to be stressing that they would give him drugs. I told him the dentist would only give him certain drugs for pain, knowing he was in a dual disorder house.

He was on the upswing again. I had just brought up the last of his things to him. It seemed to be a pattern. Then on July 16th, he called me and told me he had been messing up and they were going to kick him out. I spoke to the House Manager and he said Don could stay, and they would try to get him back in one of the programs he was in before but it would take awhile because Don left that program after only two weeks.

On July 19th, I woke up, got a cup of coffee and someone knocked on the door. It was a police officer. He asked if I had a son living down the road. It was very confusing but I told him no one was living there. I gave him my phone number and he left. "What was that all about?" Was someone trying to play a joke?"

Fran, my youngest son, had just moved back and was sleeping in the next room. Well about 15 minutes later the cop came back. He asked if I had a son who was in the Penn Foundation, and he came in and told me that my son, my Don was dead.

I felt like someone had punched me in the stomach. How could that be? He was in such a safe place!

The rest is a blur. He told me to call my husband and to call the Penn Foundation. Oh my God, if I call there, then it must be true. I didn't want to call there. I just kept saying, "NO! NO! NO! I can't do this!"

Fran woke up, and heard but went right back to sleep. I called Jay and we drove to the hospital to see Don. I could not believe it. I had to see. I never ever thought I would see one of my sons dead. Not really.

The day before, Thursday, July 18th, 2002, a girl from the female house was going to visit her family. One of the van drivers was taking her and Don told the van driver, Ted, that he had permission to go along, that he was going to visit us. The van driver never checked and let Don go. They dropped the girl off at her family's in Bristol and Don gave directions to "our" house. But he didn't come here.

He took the van driver, Ted, to Trenton, N.J., where he went to a pawn shop to pawn his gold bracelet. The driver waited. They then went to a house where Don went around back while Ted waited. Then Don took him back over the bridge to PA and asked to stop at a restaurant, where he was in the bathroom for a "long" time, at least half an hour.

Don had snorted 1 1/2 bags of heroin. The van driver noticed Don wasn't acting right on the way back and he couldn't get him out of the van and had to get help. Don denied using at first but then admitted it.

They put him to bed but told him he had to leave the next day. They said they heard him snoring, and the next time they checked, he wasn't breathing.

One of the girls who worked there was attempting CPR, but it was not effective. I talked to the ambulance driver and he said that Don was down too long to try CPR, that it would have been abuse to a corpse.

There are times that I still cannot believe it. This is the worst thing that has ever happened to me. Even worse than my husband of 17 years leaving two weeks later with just a note.

I miss my son so much and think of him every day. This cannot be fixed. My heart is broken forever and I will never be 'all' right again. Most days I have no will to live, I want to be where my Don is.

Don's story as told by his loving mom, Dottie Proler, Morrisville, PA

"Til we meet again."

I AM YOUR DISEASE

TO DON

God looked around his garden
and found an empty place
He then looked down upon the earth
and saw your tired face.

He put his arms around you
and lifted you to rest
God's garden must be beautiful
He only takes the best.

He knew that you were suffering
He knew you were in pain
He knew that you would never
get well on earth again.

He saw the road was getting rough
The hills were hard to climb
So he closed your weary eyelids
And whispered "Peace Be Thine."

It broke our hearts to lose you
but you didn't go alone
for part of us went with you
the day God called you home.
----Anonymous

JUSTIN LUKE SCANCARELLO

JUNE 9, 1982 – APRIL 17, 2004
(Age 21)

ADVERSE REACTION TO COCAINE AND OPIATES

"FOREVER JUSTIN IN MY HEART"

My beautiful son, Justin Luke, was born on June 9, 1982 at 11:31 a.m. He was such a joy to have. He made us laugh and he was just one of a kind.

I could never imagine Justin taking to the dark side of drugs. However, it was quite quick for him. As a teen he started smoking marijuana. He was in trouble with the law as a juvenile. He spent time in detention centers and had a rough few years.

By the age of 20, Justin turned to crack. In one year he was gone. He spent his 21st birthday in jail and stayed there for four months.

In October, 2003, he was sent to a half-way house to complete a program. In one month he took off in the middle of the night with somebody by the name of Hal.

They went for drugs and Justin called me for help in getting him home via taxi. He made it home but had to deal with his violation. They sent him to Florida for three months.

The end of February he came home. He was so handsome. So absolutely healthy and handsome. I never saw Justin look and feel better. That lasted for one month. By April 17, 2004, he was gone.

I can't begin to tell you all of the heartache our family is enduring. The loss of my beautiful son left me lifeless. I still cannot believe I will never see that beautiful smile or hear him laugh.

The night before he passed, he was complaining of a severe headache, and pain in the neck and back. I offered to bring him to the hospital but he just wanted to go to sleep. He kissed me goodnight, hugged me and his final words were "I love you mom, see you tomorrow."

When I woke up in the early morning, I immediately went into his room to see if he was okay. When I found him in his bed, cold as ice, I nearly died myself.

Justin didn't die from an overdose. He had an adverse reaction to cocaine and opiates. He was also a very bad asthmatic.

I will never forget that moment in my life when I too died. I wish I did.

To lose a child is the worst pain anyone could imagine.

Justin Luke never made it to his 22nd birthday. My world will never ever be the same. I cry everyday for my son. Life as I once knew, will never be the same. I will cry and miss him 'til the day I die. Then and only then, do I hope we will meet again and I will see my beautiful son once again.

Justin Luke's story as told by his loving mom, Linda Scancarello, Clifton, NJ

"*The sun will rise, the sun will set, but you my son I shall never forget.*"

eternallyjustin@optonline.net

DAVID DILL

NOVEMBER 2, 1965 – JANUARY 3, 2000
(Age 34)

SUICIDE

"FOR THE LOVE OF DAVID – OUR BRIGHT AND SHINING STAR"

January 3, 2000, started like any other day for me. I got up and went to work and on my way home I stopped at McDonald's Restaurant and picked up fast food as my son, David, loved their fries and burgers.

When I got home, I called down to David who I assumed was in his basement bedroom, that I had his favorite food and to come and get it. He didn't answer so I called again. Still no answer, but the lights were all on down there and I figured he was playing a video game or watching TV. It wasn't uncommon for him to just come when he felt like it so I wasn't worried.

My husband Al and I ate and then I got ready to go to a meeting. I started down the basement steps to the outside door but something told me to go down and check on David.

I went down a few steps so I could see into his room and there, in the doorway, lay my beautiful son; face up with a rifle on the floor beside him. I ran up the stairs screaming, "Oh, God, he's killed himself."

Al hurried down to David's room. It seemed like he was down there forever before he finally came up and told me that David was dead. Oh my God, this can't have happened. How could he do such a horrible thing?

We called the police and they summoned an ambulance to our house. When the police officers arrived they both went down to David's room. A little later one officer came up to talk with us. He was very kind and compassionate and asked us many questions. He wanted to know if we knew where David had gotten the rifle. We didn't know then, but found out later that he had taken it from his dad's gun cabinet.

Al continued talking to the officer and I drove to my daughter Tina's, having the terrible task of telling her what had happened. It was one of the hardest things I have ever had to do in my life. She and David were our only children. Not only were they very close to each other but were also best friends.

My poor Tina was home alone. Her husband was at work and my granddaughter was gone out with her friends. I thought my daughter was going to collapse when I told her and I was in such shock instead of bringing her home with me, I told her I had to go and tell my mom that David was dead.

When I got back home the police were gone and had taken that damn rifle with them. The ambulance had gone too taking away the horribly mutilated body of my precious son.

I had seen and talked to him the night before and that was the last time I would ever see him alive. That was only the beginning of the nightmare.

Al, Tina and I went to the funeral home to make the arrangements and to pick out a casket for our baby. Tina chose the clothes he would wear in his casket and she and my granddaughter did several beautiful collages which included some of our favorite photos of David and photos of some of the people and things that meant so much to him.

The day of the wake many people came to say goodbye to him. I remember very little about that day except that my son was in that closed casket and I couldn't even see him or touch him or kiss him or hold him one more time. The funeral director advised against my seeing him because of the method he had used to end his life. David's funeral Mass was that evening.

The following morning we laid our son to rest. It was so cold when we buried him and said our final goodbyes to our precious, beautiful boy.

It had been a suicide, that ugly word that no one wants to speak. Our son had committed suicide and was gone from us forever. We were all crushed and broken and left with so many questions. Why? Was it because of something we did or didn't do? What could we have done to prevent it? God, if you please let us have him back we'll do anything.

The guilt was, and is, overwhelming and it goes on forever.

David's precious life began on November 2, 1965. He was a beautiful, chubby, happy little baby with beautiful auburn curls.

He was 2 ½ years younger than his sister, Tina. They had so much fun together and remained close as they grew up. Tina was outgoing like her dad and David was shy like me.

When he got into Jr. High School, kids started making fun of his red hair and glasses and pushing him around. He was very hurt by all of this. When he entered Sr. High School, he had shot up to a lanky 6' 3" tall and from then on the kids didn't bother him anymore.

He loved auto mechanics and was very good at it. He had several jobs, his favorite being an assistant machinist at a local auto supply store. When he wasn't working or tinkering with cars or small engines he loved listening to rock music.

He taught himself how to play electric guitar quite well and took great pride in his collection of guitars and musical equipment. He followed the group, KISS, until he died. He purchased a signed, limited edition of a Gene Simmons Axe Bass guitar, which we still have.

Our home is very old and was in much need of repair. David remodeled almost every room for us before he died. He loved helping other people.

In June, 1992, David lost two of his best friends. One was his beautiful Sheltie, Brandy, which he had for 12 years and a week later his best friend Stan committed suicide. Stan had been a best friend since third grade. Oh, the anguish poor David must have felt.

We were sad too, because Stan spent a lot of time at our home, but we never realized how David must have felt until he died himself and left us in such pain and grief. David became very depressed and introverted after their deaths.

He had smoked pot for many years but now he needed more. He became obsessed with certain things. He thought he was ugly, that no one liked him and that he was fat. In reality, he was very handsome. He tried to change his appearance in so many ways. He lost so much weight that he actually looked gaunt. He cut his curly hair into a buzz cut, which I liked very much and he lifted weights relentlessly. He had Lasik surgery on his eyes so he no longer needed glasses, got several tattoos and had his tongue pierced but nothing made him happy.

The pot he smoked didn't help soften the mental anguish anymore so he started drinking whatever he could find in our house. He sold his car that meant so much to him and practically everything else he owned. What he didn't sell he gave away. We knew he had sold the car but not about the other things. After he died we were told that sometimes when someone is planning suicide, they do those things.

David was lonely, but had only dated a few girls because he was so shy. The summer before he died he became obsessed with a young woman and would send her flowers at work. She never acknowledged him nor thanked him. He was very hurt over her.

That fall he met a woman online and soon decided he was in love with her. He wanted to marry her and she said she loved him too and yes, she would marry him. He seemed really happy for once. However, she suddenly stopped emailing him and talking to him on the phone. She broke his heart and we believe that this was the straw that broke the camel's back. I went into his email after he died and copied some of the email they had written to each other and what I read broke my heart.

Around Christmas he told me he would kill himself but he didn't have the guts. I pleaded with him not to say such a terrible thing and that if he died, I would too because I couldn't stand to live without him. We tried to convince him to seek some professional help, but he wouldn't. He was 34 years old and we couldn't force him.

I will never understand why he couldn't confide in us, or someone. If only we could have talked about what was making him so sad, maybe things would have turned out differently, but David just kept it all inside until everything completely overwhelmed him and the emotional pain was unbearable.

Our lives will never be the same. David's pain is over. We, the survivors left behind, are the ones who will live on with pain in our hearts forever.

He was a wonderful son and brother. He had a generous heart and was talented in so many ways. In our eyes he had so much to live for. We are proud and blessed to have had him for our son for the 34 short years God gave him to us. No son could have been more loved. We miss you David. Fly with the Angels sweetheart.

David's story as told by his loving mom, Kay Dill, Kingsford, MI

"Suicide is not chosen. It happens when pain exceeds the resources to cope with the pain."

CINDY M.

JUNE 9, 1964 – SEPTEMBER 23, 2005
(AGE 41)

ACCIDENTAL DRUG OVERDOSE

"AND I DON'T TAKE DRUGS"

Cindy desperately wanted recovery. She was clean and sober several times in recent years, but ultimately fell back into addiction's fatal grasp. This was included in a collection of poetry she wrote while in recovery, during one of many attempts to break free of her addiction. She shared this with me (her mother) when she was drug-free, several months before she died. She was a prolific writer and putting her words down on paper gave her some relief from her struggles. This shows the anguish, torment, and pain of trying to break free.

"...And I don't take drugs"

The pain is worse than I can ever remember. I look up and say the Serenity Prayer and nothing happens. I pace the floor and then sit down and then go take another warm bath and then take a deep breath and wait. "This too shall pass" is like a scratched record in my brain and I wonder: When? And I don't take drugs.

I drive and turn the radio up loud to drown out the thoughts. I stop to look over the city from the park. I cry and I hurt.

Each day after each sleepless night, I ask, "Is this the day God? Is this the day when it will be over?" And each day it isn't.

I stay in when it rains. I consider returning to the clinic but it's too early. I stay in when the sun shines. I don't notice the difference. Food doesn't go down. I go to meetings.

I cover up and I smile and I ache. I call a friend and it doesn't help. I feel as if I will explode if I don't unload on someone. I can't, I am alone. There is no relief. And I don't take Drugs.

I say the Serenity Prayer 10 more times, eyes closed and fists clenched. I beat my pillow with my fists. I look at the clock and know I have made it through one more day, one minute at a time. I hurt some more.

Then the day comes. I wake up, open the door and the sun is shining and warm. I see the trees. And I say, "Is this the day God?" And it is.

---- Cindy

Cindy's story as told by her loving mom, Jan, California

I AM YOUR DISEASE

"God grant us the serenity to accept the things we cannot change,

the courage to change the things we can,

and the wisdom to know the difference."

-----*The Serenity Prayer*

RICKY AARON PHILLIPS

AUGUST 11, 1979 – NOVEMBER 16, 2001
(AGE 22)

"CEREBRAL HEMORRHAGE FROM CRYSTAL METH"

"UNTIL YOU BEAT THIS THING CALLED ADDICTION, IT WILL DESTROY ALL UNTIL IT IS FICTION"

(Found in his notes after his death)

My son Ricky was born on August 11, 1979. It was a Saturday, and he already had a sister who was 3 1/2yrs old. We had to find a babysitter so I could go to the hospital. It was an easy birth, even though he weighed 10 lb 4 1/2oz. So beautiful.

He was a good baby, and his sister loved him so much, and was such a great help. Unfortunately, my husband was an abusive alcoholic, so at 6 months I took both children and moved into my mother's. I honestly thought that if I get my children away from him, that they wouldn't be drinkers.

As the years went by, Ricky was so active, got into some trouble at school, nothing serious, just active.

When he was six, I met and married my second husband, and the children just loved him so much. My husband was very active also, so Ricky and he rode motorcycles, snowboards, surfboards, and went hiking, camping and all that. My daughter wanted nothing to do with any of it. She was a girlie girl. Ricky rode a two-wheeled bicycle at the age of two, and his grandma taught him how to swim at age one.

As time went on, we moved up into the mountains in northern California on Shasta Lake. Ricky was eight years old. We felt that Southern California wasn't a good place to raise the kids.

Ricky met his girlfriend at age sixteen. She was only fourteen, but he was very immature, so it was a match. They were inseparable.

He still got into trouble at school, mainly just not doing work. I finally moved him into a continuation school. I suspected he was smoking marijuana, but wasn't really concerned. I did know he was smoking cigarettes, and that broke my heart, as he begged me when he was 12 not to smoke, so I quit. Anyway, Ricky wouldn't cut it at continuation school either. He decided to quit. I, thinking I was so smart, told him that he had to work, or move out. My son Ricky always called my bluff. He moved into his girlfriend's house with her mom and dad. I couldn't believe it.

Of course I saw him almost daily, giving money, and groceries as her family were poor. The girlfriend and mother were good people, but we knew the father was an addict. What kind we didn't know, but does it really matter?

Two months before Ricky turned 18, we had an opportunity to move back to southern California for a job for my husband. Ricky wouldn't go with us. We thought he really was in good hands, so we left.

Within a year, I developed breast cancer. We had already visited with Ricky several times, and we knew he was still smoking marijuana, but didn't most kids? (This is where I want to go back to).

We brought Ricky home to us so he could be with me during my treatments for breast cancer. I picked him up at the airport, and for the first time in his life I didn't recognize him when he got off the plane.

I begged and cried and yelled for him to tell me what was wrong with him. He finally started crying and told me he was addicted to heroin. You could have knocked me over with a feather. Not heroin. Not my sweet lovable boy. He would NEVER do that! Well, I moved into action and called all drug information places so I could find out what to do. I cared for him at home, and between his dad and me, he kicked the heroin. He looked fantastic.

Two months later he went back up to his girlfriend's family's house, and within two weeks he was back using again. We found out at that time that the father showed him how to use. Even used to shoot my son up because Ricky didn't like needles.

My husband drove eight hours straight to get him, and brought him back home. We went through the process again to clean him up. Now all the while I am still going through chemotherapy and radiation treatments for the breast cancer.

Ricky was clean for a few months and went back up there again. Yes, within a few weeks he was again back on heroin. This time we paid for him to go to a methadone clinic, while I was in close contact with the people in charge, it seemed to go very well.

Ricky soon came back home. This was in late 2000. He was doing great. He got a job, his sister gave him her car. He met new friends and also had a new girlfriend. He soon started going to parties, "raves," and staying out all night.

Now even though Ricky was 21 at this time, he still had to obey our rules. My husband and he fought all the time. The tension in the house was thick. We started suspecting that he was doing ecstasy. We were right and the battles continued. He still was my boy. Loved us so unconditionally. Tried to help all, but couldn't help any.

The beginning of 2001, we finally bought our very first house and were so excited. We had a pool and Ricky had his very own room with a bathroom and all the privacy he could want.

But then I started finding glass pipes. I didn't know what to think of it at first. My husband explained that our son was smoking crystal methamphetamine. I never thought I was so ignorant on drugs, but I had never heard of it. I searched the web and was blown away. How does one go from heroin to speed? My son did.

We fought and fought. Tried tough love, but I usually gave in. I just loved him so much that I couldn't put him out in his need. My husband threatened to leave. He just couldn't take it anymore.

Ricky was no longer working. He was just chasing the drug. The strange thing is, that his girlfriends never did the drugs, just the guys he hung out with.

I joined Nar-anon. I was going insane. I didn't have anyone to turn to. I couldn't talk to anyone about this. I needed to learn how to distance myself from my son without losing my mind.

On Tuesday, the 13th of November, 2001, my son had been clean for about two weeks. He was behaving like the boy that I knew. No rages, no sleeping all day, and no all-nighters. He also just started a new job. I was breathing again.

Ricky was off on Wednesday the 14th of November so Tuesday night he asked me if I would take him to his friend's house. It was a new friend and they were just going to drink some beers. He was going to spend the night. I was on my way to my meeting and the apartment was on the way so I said yes. When Ricky got to the top of the stairs, he waved and said, "I love you."

I said "I love you too, son." I left.

I guess around noon the next day I had expected him to call for a ride home. No call came. I called the friend and was told that Ricky was still sleeping. Around 3:00 p.m., I called again. He was still sleeping. I got busy, and thinking maybe Ricky drank too much, I figured he was sleeping it off.

Well 7 p.m., came and I just about came out of my chair. Ricky ALWAYS called. I called there again, and was told very frantically that Ricky wouldn't wake up.

I rushed over and my boy was lying on the living room floor. I grabbed him and tried to wake him. No response. I did notice he was breathing, but when I opened his eyes, his left pupil was completely black.

We called 911. The ambulance took him to the Emergency Room and the doctor intubated him. The doctor explained that he had a bleed in his brain, but that he would probably be fine. Unfortunately, he didn't have a neurosurgeon available, so they had to transfer my son to another hospital with one. This took five hours!

When we reached the new hospital, we were greeted by the neurosurgeon. I had this grin on my face thinking the doctor would tell me good news. The words came out of his mouth so matter of fact, like he said it a hundred times a day. He said, "Your son is brain dead." Wow!

Helplessly and sadly, my son Ricky was on life support for two days. We had to shut it off. He wasn't coming back to us. He did his last drug on November 13th, 2001. This time it caused a cerebral hemorrhage to his brain.

So, on November 16th, 2001, we turned off my son's breathing machine and watched and listened to his heart stop. No more Ricky. No more drugs. No more nothing. My life ended with his. I am his mother, and I couldn't save him. Deep down I knew he could die, but never really believed it. Well, believe it! If my son could die, so could anyone else's.

Ricky's story, as told by his loving mom, Toni House of Murrieta, CA

"Death is nothing else but going home to God, the bond of love will be unbroken for all eternity." ~Mother Teresa~

http://www.geocities.com/dyingtogethigh/rickyphillips.

SHERYL LETZGUS MCGINNIS WITH HEIKO GANZER

For Ricky, My precious Angel

It was just an average day,
in the middle of November
Everyone in the house was at work,
at least that's what I remember

You came home for dinner as usual,
you hardly missed a meal
when all of a sudden you said to me,
 Mom, I'd like to make a deal

If you take me to my friends house,
as tomorrow I don't work you see
I'll come home in the morning,
and do all the chores you have for me

I knew you were working hard,
and you were definitely due some fun
so I took you to his house ,and said
" I love you, see you tomorrow son."

I slept real peaceful that night,
for I knew where you would be
I woke in the morning quite rested,
looking forward to a day about me

I AM YOUR DISEASE

I started cleaning the house,
getting on with my day
doing some laundry and dishes,
then had some bills to pay

All of a sudden I realized,
that it was getting close to noon
I kept looking out the window,
knowing you'd be home soon.

I called the house where you were,
they said you were still asleep
I told them when you woke to call me,
as you had a promise to keep

At three o'clock I called again,
so unusual that you hadn't called
Your friend said you're still sleeping,
and you haven't moved at all

I jokingly had asked him,
is he breathing, have you checked?
he said he's breathing fine,
I said I'm going to ring his neck

Suddenly my stomach
was getting pretty upset

SHERYL LETZGUS MCGINNIS WITH HEIKO GANZER

it was seven o'clock in the evening,
and you haven't called as yet

So I picked up the phone to call,
I wanted to talk to you right now
the frantic voice on the other end
said we can't wake him up at all

We've tried and tried, we lifted him up,
he will not budge an inch
we poured some water on his face,
we even gave him a pinch

I put on some shoes, rushed out of the house
and flew into their front door
There I saw my baby son,
lying on the floor

I grabbed you quickly screaming,
Ricky wake up please
I held you close, then slapped your face,
as I fell down to my knees

you were breathing, but when I opened your eyes,
one pupil was completely black
I screamed at your friend, call 911,
and he waited for them out in the back

I AM YOUR DISEASE

They came real quick, started to work on you,
and they threw many questions at me.
I didn't have any answers,
I didn't know what had happened you see

they put you in the ambulance,
I followed them in my car
I called your daddy on his cell,
he wasn't very far

I met him in the parking lot,
near the emergency door
The ambulance had just arrived,
only minutes before

They wouldn't let us in,
the doctor had to see you first
The waiting seemed forever,
I thought my heart would burst

The doctor said we could see you now,
he said you had a brain bleed
I asked if it was serious,
he said not to worry, no need

you were intubated when I saw you,
I asked the doctor why

SHERYL LETZGUS MCGINNIS WITH HEIKO GANZER

He felt you were having trouble breathing,
then I started to cry

The doctor said he had to transfer you,
to a hospital with a brain specialist
He would get on the phone, and find one,
and then I gave you a great big kiss

I called your sister and told her,
she didn't have to come up tonight
The doctor said you would be ok,
I would see her in the morning light.

So five hours later they transferred you,
to a hospital close by
We sat in the CCU waiting room,
and prayed that you wouldn't die

The doctor walked in to talk to us,
your dad stood up so I did too
He looked us straight in the eyes, and said I'm sorry
there's nothing I can do

I looked at your dad in shock,
I saw that he started to cry
I looked back at the doctor,
and all I could say was why?

I AM YOUR DISEASE

He was talking but I couldn't hear him,
I don't know what he had said
then all of a sudden I heard him say,
"I'm sorry, your son is brain dead"

I couldn't speak, not a word came out,
then finally I said " you're wrong"
"You do not know my son that well,
he's a survivor he is so strong"

Then I said well, do something,
you can't just let him die!
"I can do some surgery to stop the bleed,
I don't think it will work, but I'll try"
They prepped you for the surgery,
I talked to you and wept
I prayed to God to save you,
then out the door they left

Your sister came running in,
she didn't know what was going on
I had to tell her as best I could,
that her brother may be gone

The surgery lasted until six am,
we patiently waited for some news
The doctor finally walked over to us,

SHERYL LETZGUS MCGINNIS WITH HEIKO GANZER

and said we would have to choose

The brain was swollen way too much,
the damage is too severe
We'll have to disconnect the machine,
then I started to tear

He also said, the machine could stay on,
but he would have a tube to be fed
HE'LL NEVER COME BACK, HE'LL NEVER WAKE UP,
you can choose this option instead

I just went blank, He can't do this,
where is my God, I need You
I felt this scream, deep inside.
What am I going to do?

This was Thursday morning,
"I want to give it another day"
I called the family to tell them,
they should be on their way

As the day went on, family and friends
came to say their goodbyes
I held them all and left them alone,
to speak to you before you die

I AM YOUR DISEASE

So now its Friday, and the time has come,
we're all standing around your bed
I whisper special things to you,
while my arms are around your head

We are holding you and praying,
my mom is rubbing your feet
I talk to you so lovingly,
until I feel your last heartbeat.

Toni House
7/18/2003
Ricky Phillips' mom
8-11-79 - 11-16-01

In Loving memory of my son Ricky Aaron Phillips
My son, my friend, my life

JOSEPH SMERKER

DECEMBER 1, 1982 – DECEMBER 16, 2002
(AGE 20)

HEROIN

"MY BEAUTIFUL SON"

My beautiful son was an honor student 1st thru 8th grade although he made it quite clear that he hated school. He didn't act out. He knew that education...at the least a high school diploma... was something that both his dad and I expected.

During the last semester of his junior year he began to "flounder." During senior year he was in danger of not graduating. I'm sure now that his drug use had begun during this time and that his bad marks prove that out.

During his freshman year, Joe played football. He would stay after school and work out at the school gym. He suddenly lost interest and withdrew from the team after his freshman year. When I questioned him as to why, he seemed uncomfortable and unwilling to answer. I have my own suspicions about why he withdrew but I can't confirm them.

Joe taught himself to play the guitar and was a member of his brother's band. He was very talented. We discovered a song he wrote and recorded on his computer a year after he died. The song is called "Always." We play the recording when we talk at schools. The kids seem to connect to the song.

In hindsight, when he withdrew from football, my antenna should have been up. He had multiple stresses that year. Both his brothers moved out of our home during Joe's 16th year, leaving Joe an "only child." That same summer he lost the dog we got for him when he was a small child due to a stroke.

Joe also questioned me as to why his biological father never wanted to see him or his brothers. The last time bio-father saw my sons was when Joe was 2 years old. Bio father lives 5 blocks from our home.

I think my working and being caught up in my own struggles (health, high stress career etc.) drew so much of my attention away from what was more precious to me than life itself...my children. I still blame myself for not paying more attention, for not seeing the signs of sadness/addiction in Joe. He had too many losses in a very short time for such a sensitive person.

When I meet kids today, kids who knew Joe, when I read his yearbooks etc., the same word is used over and over and over. Joe was "sweet." And he was. He had a softness of his soul that radiated outward. I never ONCE heard him speak negatively about ANYONE! Never once did he poke fun at those less unfortunate. He never teased or bullied.

I'm not glorifying him because he's gone now. He truly was so very special. A light shone from him and because of that I choose to believe that he was an angel God put into our lives. I am a better person because Joe touched my life. I speak at schools now and tell Joe's story. In that way he lives on through me.

I never had a clue that he was doing drugs. My husband is in law enforcement (he spent years in the worst drug area of Philadelphia, fighting crime) and got a phone call from someone he knew in the court system. Joe has been arrested for shop lifting several times over the few months preceding that call. We weren't aware of those arrests because he was 18. The person who called told my husband of Joe's arrests and asked us if we knew he was drug addicted. That is how we learned.

The Joe we knew ceased to exist. He became a shell of himself. He didn't radiate the softness and innocence I loved so much about him. His eyes were empty. He would have "fits" of anger which was so unlike him but would always end up apologizing afterward. My Joe, the son I loved so much died twice...my Joe passed away long before the drug addicted Joe left this earth.

He was on probation for retail theft for many months. He reported to a probation officer twice a week and was tested for drugs via urine each visit.

Joe went to rehab in Florida for a three week period. I think the whole Florida rehab thing is a scam. He also was court ordered to attend an outpatient program.

I think the fact that his biological father not being interested in seeing him and his brothers as they grew up, and the losses listed above, and I'm not sure what else, were contributing factors to Joe's taking drugs.

Joe started using weed and some pills in his senior year. He graduated in 2001. Deceased in December, 2002. Heroin took his life and was his drug of choice.

My family is presently in group therapy. Even though Joe is deceased, the effects of his addiction and death linger and I imagine always will. I became a different person the day my son died.

My advice for others who think their kids may be doing drugs would be to find a therapist who has a specialty in addiction treatment. I would also encourage parents of younger teens/teens to read "Yes! Your Kids Are Crazy" and their children should read, "Yes! Your Parents Are Crazy." Both books are written by Dr. Michael Bradley.

If I could have my son back for just five minutes I would tell him that I am sorry if there was anything I did or didn't do that led to his drug use. I'd also tell him how very much I loved him and what a pleasure he was in my life. We had a special tie to each other that wasn't obvious to others. But Joe and I both knew it was there. I would tell him that he is always with me no matter where I go or what I do. And lastly, I would hold him to my heart so that I could have that memory to hold onto until the time comes when I've left this life and we're together again, forever.

Joe's story as told by his loving mom, Barbara Fitzgerald, Philadelphia, PA

"We should all be so lucky to have someone who will never let us go. The ultimate legacy is to leave behind someone who will love you forever."

RICKY WELDON, JR.

SEPTEMBER 29, 1978 – JULY 14, 2003
(AGE 24)

MULTIPLE DRUG OVERDOSE

"THE BEGINNING OF A BAD DREAM"

Ricky was in recovery for his addiction for around 3 months. He and his father and brother and sister went out on July 5, 2003, to dirt bike ride in the woods about an hour from home. They unloaded the motorcycles and off Ricky went.

Ricky hit a rut in the dirt and the back wheel hit it and flipped him over the handlebars. He came walking back to the truck saying he broke his back and maybe his foot.

Well no one really believed him as he always had some ailment or another and also he was walking so they thought he was faking. I probably would have too.

My husband took him to the Emergency Room down where they were and he was in so much pain that finally after 5 hours they gave him something. But Ricky explained to the nurse he was a recovering addict and not to give him narcotics for pain. They said ok thank you for letting us know. Ricky also told my husband whose name is Rick also, to make sure the doctors know that he does not want narcotics for pain. That was July 5th, and he was in the hospital until July 9th. He had a broken back and a broken foot. He did fine in the hospital and he looked good other than the pain.

He came home from the hospital at 6:00 p.m. It was a long drive. He had prescriptions and guess what the doctor had prescribed---60 Percocets for the pain! Ricky kept saying he is going to have to go to rehab for pain meds when this was all over.

He and his girlfriend had an apartment. It was on the second floor and he wanted to go there. We were going away in a couple of days so it was probably best he went home there. He barely could get up the steps. He had to use a walker and it took a long time to get up to the second floor.

I went over there the next day while his girlfriend was working and he looked all drugged up. I was mad and said "How many pain pills are you taking?"

He was over-doing it. Well he overdosed on July 14, 2003. They say it was "benzo," marijuana and heroin. But I would like the toxicology report and also the autopsy.

His girlfriend had no idea he was doing that again. She thought it was the Percocets. Well, if it was heroin, someone had to bring it to him. My husband thinks the doctors should not have given him those drugs and all this stuff.

He keeps talking to lawyers that he does work for, so then he wants me to get involved and talk to them. I don't care---it is not going to change anything and I don't like talking about it to those kind of people. Not that my husband wants money, he doesn't. He feels Ricky would still be here if it wasn't for the doctors' choice in drugs.

Well I believe that it was his time. As sad as that is, I believe that. I didn't want it to be his time, but God wanted him. I can't do anything about that.

I AM YOUR DISEASE

Ricky's story as told by his loving mom, Chris Weldon, *Maple Shade, NJ*

"I have fought a good fight. I have finished my course, I have kept the faith."

http://www.geocities.com/dyingtogethigh/rickyweldon.html

JASON EUGENE MITCHELL

JANUARY 2, 1978 – NOVEMBER 7, 2002
(AGE 24)

HEROIN/COCAINE

"MY PRECIOUS ANGEL JASON"

When I was told that someone wanted to know how I got to this web-site, the tears started to come. I know that I was going out of my mind, and I was trying so hard to find some group here in Stockton, Ca. where I could fit in. One night I was crying and talking with my Jason, and I don't know how, but I pulled up RememberMe, and talked a lot with two ladies. One who lost a brother and one who lost a son.

The web-site became my world. I could cry and laugh and talk with others about anything, and most important I could tell them who I was and what I used to be. My son, I feel, and the other angels guided me to that web-site. I can't have it any other way.

Here I'm a recovering addict for almost 9 years now, give a few months. And I was sitting in groups with women and men that hated people like me.

I was a recovering addict, and they have lost their child, their loved ones and I was still alive. I know that feeling, how could I tell them that for awhile I felt the same way? I should say the person I used to be was dead. Now I'm just a mother who has lost her child to this illness of addiction.

My son Jason died on November 3, 2002, at about 10 a.m., from a drug overdose of heroin and cocaine. He was given a "hot shot" I was told on the back of his neck. He was released from county honor farm in Stockton, at 12 midnight on the 2nd of November 2002, and died the following day, the 3rd.

I remember holding him close to me and saying "Please don't go." (He wanted to be with this young lady that had been writing him in jail, that he met though another inmate).

He wanted to show someone that he can love, and that he wanted them to help him stay clean. "It doesn't work that way," I would tell him. "You have to do it for yourself Jason."

I was the working parent and his father worked on cars and didn't do drugs. Jason was his only son, and I have another son, Ismel that is clean now for over 15 years.

I'm the only one in my family of siblings that used drugs out of the six of us, I was the only one who left home. Incest wasn't looked down on, but just turned away from. I was the baby of the family, the youngest, the one.

My sons are so much like myself, they wanted love, and to make their own family. All we had was the tools that were put before us, and we all were in for change. Jason mostly because he was from a mixed marriage, and he knew he had the best of both worlds. But he was so much a good young man.

I guess what I'm trying to say is, that no matter how bad we feel we have been treated in this world, when drugs came into our lives, we treated ourselves more like crap than anyone ever could, and that, for my sons and I was the hardest road back.

Some don't make it. My Jason, I prayed for him every night, and he was going to go to college to be a cook and signed up and had the half way house ready to move in, but that one more time... hang out with old friends and thinking he could do it one last time...

He looked like my baby boy, sleeping, when I went to him at that hotel, he was so soft and clean, he had his clothing taken, shoes, everything but one sock and underwear.

The tears I'm crying now are because I know my son has no more

I AM YOUR DISEASE

pain, that life where they rob the dead to go on with their habits, their fix, he didn't have to live like that anymore.

To have party with him, and then to try and save him, so I prayed that God take him home, take him home God if he's not done. That next morning my son was gone.

I carry his ashes around my neck as I go to the jails and work with different treatment programs. I tell his friends some that are still out there, that I will take you when you're ready. I feed the homeless and some are doing well and come with me and some have died, and some are still out there.

The values and morals, and self-esteem, we lose when we are out there, makes it hard to come back. I told my son when I got clean for a year that I never thought anyone would love me if they knew the things I did. He told me he loved me even if he couldn't love himself. So I do what I must. I love me today and help others like my son and me.

My oldest is going to be a nurse practitioner, and he will be getting his AA in 2006. I'm in college going for my AA in Substance Abuse and I will have my real estate business degree in 2007.

Jason's father, Ernest Mitchell, has kept Jason's ashes, and he has coffee with Jason every morning just like he did when Jason was alive, and he fixes cars for people in recovery , their first auto. How cool. We can't change the past. They tell us in recovery that if nothing changes in your life, then nothing changes.

"Jason, this one is for you and your angels of brothers and sisters. You finally found your rainbow." Told by Jason's loving mom, Rebie, Stockton, CA

http://www.geocities.com/dyingtogethigh/jasonmitchell

DEMONS

Demons all in my head, can't seem to shake them they're always there.

Always watching me, waiting for me.

See there was a time when I was one of them!

Doing the things that demons do.

Terrorizing my fellow man, why-o-why I think this way is beyond me.

Can't seem to see the light, and find my way.

Darkness is most definitely swallowing me!

Jason Eugene Mitchell

~AFTERMATH~

They say a mind is a terrible thing to waste!

But what about a man's soul?

Help me find the light that guides us to humanity.

Jason Eugene Mitchell

WILLIAM ELLIOTT SOMMER

SEPTEMBER 24, 1980 – MAY 4, 2004
(AGE 23)

"ACCIDENTAL HEROIN OVERDOSE"

"LOSING WILL"

There was a late night knock at the door. I was asleep, but my husband Tim was up. When he heard the knock, he thought that Will must have forgotten his key.

Tim opened the door to find three people in uniform standing on our porch. They asked if this was " the Sommer residence, the home of William Sommer, are you his father, is your wife at home, would you please get her, may we come in to talk to you about William?"

I remember being awoken from a sound sleep. Tim was talking, telling me I had to get up, there were people downstairs who wanted to talk to us about Will.

I followed Tim downstairs into our living room where the three stood. Tim and I sat on the couch together; the three took chairs facing us.

I remember the somber faces staring at us. I'll never forget the look in their eyes. "We have some bad news," said the one whose uniform was somehow different from the police officers. Her uniform said county coroner. She went on, "Your son was found unresponsive this evening at the home of Ron Haywood on Packer Court."

We sat. Who were these people? What are they doing in my house?

Whatever were they talking about?

They keep talking. We sit, we stare, and we try to understand.

We don't move, we can't move.

"Did you know your son was a drug user?"

"We suspect heroin overdose, we'll know more after the autopsy."

They hand us Will's wallet and cell phone. They offer their condolences.

We have just entered hell.

Will was my second child, my second son. He was born 3 years and 10 days after his older brother, Ethan. He was named after my father who had passed the month before his birth.

Will was a beautiful baby, but a fussy one. Ethan called him "the Fusser." He always wanted to be held, not just held, but moving, too. I used to joke that I held Will for the first two years of his life.

Will and I were very close. We shared a special bond. I still feel it now. He was my sunny day. Big blue eyes and a light up the world, smile.

He was loving, kind, thoughtful, fun to be with, smart, silly and sensitive. He loved to laugh and had that gift of making others laugh at his wit and humor. Will enjoyed people, and always had lots of different friends. He liked school and sports and excelled at both.

When Will was 12 years old he was molested by a pedophile, Tom Gregg. This man was a scout leader in the same troop that Tim was head scoutmaster and both my sons were active scout members. This monster was a friend of the family. He abused four other boys in the group.

Will had the courage to speak, to tell. He told Ethan, and they came forward to the other adults in the troop. Will testified before the Grand Jury. The perpetrator only served an eighteen months sentence. Looking back on these events we realize this to be the pivotal time in

I AM YOUR DISEASE

Will's life.

There was a slow turn in Will's world. We can only see it clearly now, years later. We know that Will turned to drugs to escape. He could no longer stand the pain and shame. He needed to escape, forget, at least for periods of time. He was self medicating. His drug use eventually led to heroin. It took his life. He was left alone to die while his "so called friends" cleaned up the drugs and paraphernalia before calling 911.

I can only begin to try to put into words how Will's death has affected my family and me. In every fathomable way, in every fiber of our being we feel his loss.

He took parts of Tim, Ethan and me with him when he left this Earth. Ethan lost his only brother, his only sibling. His friend. Tim and I lost our precious son, our baby, our friend, and part of our future. I grieve not only for what I lost, but for what my husband and surviving son have lost, too. We are broken people, the walking wounded, wearing our masks, trying to live in this new world.

We have been given a sentence to relive each year as Will's heaven date comes. We feel it all again. The horror, the regret, the "what if," the "if only," the pain that crushes your heart and takes your breath away. It is raw and real, there is no denying it. This nightmare happened, it is our reality.

We take one moment at a time. We try to move forward. It's hard. It hurts. We find comfort in each other, in our families, our faith, and our friends. We talk about our Will.

We have found people who care and try to understand. The Compassionate Friends in our town have been a lifeline. I belong to two online groups, Angels of Addiction and Remember Me in Heaven. These people have lifted me up, encouraged, supported and loved me. I thank God for that.

Life changed for us on that warm spring night with a full moon.

Somehow two years have gone by, we are still here. It seems like yesterday, it seems like an eternity. We miss him so.

Rest in peace sweet Will. We'll see you when we cross over.

Until then, I love you, Mom.

Memorials

Money was raised and donated in Will's name to The Children's Advocacy Center of the Bluegrass, Inc. This agency helps child victims of sexual abuse as their case moves through the criminal justice system.

Will's cousin and his wife named their child in memory of Will. They made the name Wilsom, by combining the first three letters of Will's name. Baby Jacob Wilsom was born on February 11, 2006.

Two songs were written for Will. The people he made music with, The Placated Forms, wrote Loveable Scoundrel and Catch You on the Other Side in his memory.

The Will Sommer Memorial Labyrinth (a Chartres style labyrinth), at Cedar Hill Retreat Center, Carlisle, KY was dedicated on May 29, 2006.

Will's story as told by his loving mom, Rita Sommer, Lexington, KY

"Everyone shall be remembered, but everyone was great wholly in proportion to the magnitude of that which he struggled."

Soren Kierkegaard

http://www.geocities.com/dyingtogethigh/willsommer.html

SHAUNA PATRICIA MIKULA

AUGUST 13, 1985 – AUGUST 25, 2005
(AGE 20)

HEROIN

"MY DAUGHTER, MY BEST FRIEND"

I'd like to tell you my story. My name is Madonna. I lost my beautiful daughter Shauna to heroin on August 25, 2005, 12 days after her 20th birthday.

I did all I could to try to help her; counseling, boot camp, psychiatrist, doctors, rehabs, and even jail, but she was not strong enough to fight it.

I feel such a loss.

She was so multi-talented. She was an actress, artist, a writer and a musician. She could have had the world in the palm of her hand.

She was my daughter and my best friend.

Starting with pot at age 12, she progressed to stronger and more dangerous drugs, as she got older. She decided to try the one drug that would lead her to her untimely death: Heroin.

Shauna was 16, when she first tried heroin in September of 2001, not believing that one time would cause her to be addicted for life.

In December she came to me crying and told me she was addicted. I immediately took her to the first of 5 rehabs.

She found that she had contracted hepatitis C within those 4 short months of use.

You all know how the story ends…" the phone call," the drive to the hospital. Only in my case I did not know her condition. I thought it was a trip to pick her up after she overdid it…yet again.

Enter the hospital and I ask where she is…a woman in black comes and takes me to a private room…in walks the doctor…I'm totally oblivious to what is going on here.

The doctor tells me they worked on her for 45 minutes and could not get her to breathe, and then her heart stopped and they did CPR.

I asked, "OK, where is she then?"

The doctor says, "She is gone."

I think to myself, *OK, did you take her to another hospital? Where is she, damn it?*

He has to be blunt and tell me that she is dead.

I was all alone there when this happened. I did not expect it. I went to the hospital fully expecting to pick her up and bitch at her all the way home. It wasn't supposed to be like this.

Oh my God! How I wanted to die that night.

Well, I have made it 10 months so far. As each holiday passes, I grieve again.

My Mother's Day was very nice as I received something from Shauna, believe it or not.

Now, I don't know if you believe in signs. I never did until Shauna died. The Thursday before Mother's Day, I visited Shauna's grave. I was feeling really sad and crying a lot as Mother's Day approached. As I talked to Shauna, I asked her for a little sign for Mother's Day. I know, silly, huh?

Well, on the Saturday before Mother's Day, I got home from work and went to my bedroom. Now, my dresser is a little messy, but I know where everything is, right? I noticed a pile of my junk had fallen over. I thought *darn those cats!* But the door to my room was closed, so no cat could have gotten in there.

Well, in front of my jewelry box, leaning up against it was a blue envelope with "to my mother" written on it in Shauna's writing. I opened it, and it was the Mother's Day card that she had given me last year.

The big pile of junk sat where it was, kind of half falling over, but still in place, and that one card fell out of the pile for me to see it. Coincidence? I don't think so!

Also it was so like Shauna to give that to me the day before. She never could wait to give her surprises on the given day. Be it Christmas, a birthday or whatever, she could never wait. So I know this was my Mother's Day surprise from her.

Shauna's story as told by her loving mom, Madonna Mikula, Brighton, MI

"*Death leaves a heartache no one can heal, love leaves a memory no one can steal. From a headstone in Ireland.*

Shauna's Website -
http://www.angelfire.com/my/cleardayzpage/Shauna.html

DAVID CHARLES HALL

APRIL 21, 1978 – JULY 3, 2001
(Age 23)

ACCIDENTAL DRUG OVERDOSE-UNKNOWN TYPE

"MY HONEY BOY"

My son, my Honey Boy as I always called him, David Hall, of Kokomo, Indiana, went to be with the Lord on July 3, 2001. He was just 23 years old.

I can still hear the words from his dad on the phone. He was crying and I KNEW something bad had happened. Never did I dream it was David.

I had just talked to David the night before. We talked almost every day. He sometimes would get upset because I called so much, but after all, I'm a Mom.

David's dad and I adopted David when he was two months old. He was so sweet, what a cute baby. He had blue eyes and dark hair just like his " dad." As he grew up he even looked like his dad, strange how this works.

When David was 3 years old and 3 days, we adopted his sister, Dyan. Both were from Indiana but from different towns. How lucky can two people be, to get two children so sweet.

We had it all. I quit work to stay home and raise our children.

David and I were very close. He clung to me everywhere we went, but he loved his dad as well.

David's dad and I divorced when David was 16. I will never forgive myself for this. It was the WRONG thing to do. I look back now, and wonder "if" this is the reason for the drugs. I will never know.

I remarried and we moved to South Carolina. David and Dyan did not like this much but seemed to be ok. Then David and his stepfather did not get along. I was always in the middle. It was terrible. I won't go into all this, but I should have known better. The move was good for Dyan, but bad for David.

The school called one day and said to come and get David. I called his stepfather and he then called the school to see what was wrong. David had gone to lunch and smoked pot.

I did not know anything before this but I did not see what was ahead. I NEVER saw the drugs. I knew he smoked cigarettes but not anything else. I figured the pot was a one-time thing…little did I know!

He finally moved back to Kokomo, Indiana, to live with his dad…what a sad day for me, and I'm sure him too. Things only got worse.

The last few months before David passed, his dad would call and say things like, "David passed out, just figured you would want to know." Again, little did I know it was drugs.

This happened several times. He ended up in the ER and I called the hospital. They would not tell me anything because he was of " age" and they could not release any information. That was in May of 2001.

David was working for Chrysler but he was "on leave" for falling asleep on the job. His dad was kind and did not tell me what all David was into when he passed. I only know the police were involved for months.

David's tires were slashed. "Strange" people would show up at the house. All this I learned from his dad after the fact.

Another thing I learned that I would like to share with all parents, as a warning, is that David had so-called friends who had friends who worked for various doctors. These girls would write prescriptions for drugs and forge the doctors' names. This went on for a couple of years. Sadly, I didn't learn this until after the fact.

It's been 5 LONG years. It still seems like yesterday.

I still want to tell the world! I had business cards made that have David's picture and information about his passing on them. I give them to everyone I can. I want everyone to know it CAN happen to them.

Drugs don't care if you're poor or rich, what color you are, where you live, how smart you are, what kind of person you are, what church you belong to or don't belong to if you have a family who loves you or you're just living on the streets. I do believe that this is a disease, not a choice in most cases.

I have now made a brochure and have sent it to funeral homes in the area. I want to start a support group to help other parents. I don't know how to help except to be there for them to vent, to know they are not alone.

I still cry. I still visit his web site daily. I still miss him every day, and now his dad has gone to be with him; he went to Heaven on May 8, 2006. I miss them both very much.

Each year over David's Heaven date I go to the mountains in North Carolina. There I "feel" a little closer to Heaven and my son.

I am so thankful to have found such a wonderful support site as Angels of Addiction, started by Sandy LaCagnina in memory of her son Jason.

I'm thankful for every mom who has been there for me, and they all have. I would not have made it without the online support group. Thank you to Sheryl (Sherry) McGinnis for writing this book, to let parents and other young people know that this can happen to ANYONE, no matter where you live.

David's story as told by his loving mom, Ann Long, South Carolina

David's Website http://members.fortunecity.com/davidhall23/

KEITH MONTAMBO

FEBRUARY 4, 1985 – NOVEMBER 13, 2004
(Age 19)

COCAINE/HEROIN

"IGNORANT OF THE TRUTH"

In the early hours of November 14th, 2004, my husband, Bill and I received a knock at our door. This was the kind of knock that every parent fears but, in their heart, never really thinks will happen to them. The officer told us that our 19 year old son, Keith, had died, but that he did not have any details. We were forced to wait some 20 minutes until the coroner called us with more information.

Within those 20 minutes, Bill and I speculated as to what might have happened. We had agreed that a car accident was the most obvious thing we could think of. Knowing our son had a habit of drinking on the weekends, we only hoped that he didn't hurt someone else. What the coroner finally told us tilted our world. Keith had died of a drug overdose. "This couldn't be," we thought. "Our son doesn't do hard drugs."

This began the journey to learn about our son. We knew a smart, vibrant, loving young man who had turned the corner of a troubled past; the son who was on his way to making his life right. What we didn't know was that there was a part of Keith that he had chosen to keep from us.

Keith was born in 1985, and raised in a small Michigan town filled with lots of friends and extended family. He had a sister, Jennifer, who was two and a half years older. They were the best of friends, and we were a close family.

Bill and I were always doing things with our kids. By the time the kids started school, they were playing baseball and softball with their dad as coach. They learned, early on, to bowl and were part of leagues well into their teens. Camping, drives to Lake Michigan, walking the Mackinaw Bridge, and attending hockey games were just a few of the many family things we enjoyed.

Keith became a good student, often having a " straight A" report card. By the time he had finished eighth grade, he had fulfilled his high school requirements for math. In sixth grade, Keith joined the school band and played the cornet. During his freshman and sophomore years he played Junior Varsity Baseball, played in the band, and was part of the Science Olympiad team.

One day, Bill and I found a used electric guitar at a yard sale and decided to get it for Keith. It was love at first sight! He taught himself to play and became very good at it, with his long fingers being perfect for that type of instrument. His love of music expanded when he and two of his high school friends started a garage band. They would play the popular rock music and toyed with writing their own songs. In Keith's sophomore year, the band competed and had won a slot in a local school talent show.

For Keith's 16th birthday, Bill and I bought tickets to a Green Day concert. At the time, that was Keith's favorite band. He was even lucky enough to become one of three young men asked to go up on stage with the band, and play the instruments. Keith got to play Billy Joe's guitar.

Keith was the "boy next door" really. He was a good kid. He was quick witted and quick with a smile. He showed his love for Bill and me openly with hugs, often given in front of his friends. He had lots of friends, including his sister. He was just the average kid from an average family.

But sometime after Keith turned 15, he began to change, nothing sudden, nothing dramatic. His taste in music changed; he met new friends.

By 16, he had his driver's license so his world expanded. Bill and I didn't think much about these changes. After all, he was a teen, and the teenage years are a time of discovery and change.

Toward the end of Keith's sophomore year, his grades started to slip. By the summer, he no longer was interested in sports. He thought competition was "dumb." His new friends, not from his home town or high school, frequented an "underground" teen nightclub. That soon became Keith's favorite Saturday night hangout. With the different taste in music came a new band. This one was Punk Rock.

One Friday night, in the fall of 2001, Keith failed to come home at his appointed curfew. In fact, he didn't come home until the following Sunday night. I had called around to his friends' houses, but no one seemed to know where he was. When Keith came home, his only explanation was that he was hanging around town with his friends. For those who wonder; yes, we had met the parents of his friends. We knew the environments where Keith was supposed to be. There was no reason for concern there.

The following spring, Keith and his best friend came upon someone's credit card, on the ground, outside a local fast food restaurant. Being young and stupid, the two boys used the card to purchase some electronics for themselves. They thought they could then get some cash by returning a couple items to the store. Finding out that the money would only be put back on the credit card, the boys gave up and left the store. By then, the store clerk had become suspicious. Keith and his friend were followed to the parking lot, and the description and license plate of their vehicle were given to local police. The vehicle they had used was registered in my husband's name, so we were called.

This was Keith's first encounter with the law, and his friend was the one that had signed the credit card receipts. So his friend, who was a juvenile, was charged with the crime. He would not receive any time in detention if the boys paid back the money spent. This was a break for Keith since he was now 17, and basically, considered an adult in the eyes of the law.

We continued to have discipline problems with Keith, so Bill and I decided to go to family counseling. The counselor, which I would like to point out had never had children of her own, told us that Keith wanted more boundaries from us. We took her advice and started grounding Keith more severely than we had in the past: Basically, "tough love". The result of this advice was that Keith started disappearing whenever he finally got a chance to be free.

We became aware of Keith's drinking alcohol when he came home one night acting crazy. It was obvious he was drunk. He had finally admitted that he had downed a fifth of whiskey. We didn't like the way he was talking, almost suicidal, so we called our doctor. He suggested that we take him to the local hospital that had a department for mental illness because of the suicidal thoughts. In the ER of that hospital, Keith's blood alcohol level was taken. It was very high: No big revelation at this point. They did not test for any drugs, but then again, we never asked them to. Why should we? We had talked to our children, since they were old enough to understand, about the dangers of drugs. Our children were very close to us, and openly discussed things with us. We didn't think drugs were an issue. Understand that Keith was showing some of the " signs" to look for in regards to drug use, but many of those signs can also pertain to just being a teen. We trusted Keith to tell us the truth when asked about drug use.

A counselor was called into the ER to talk with Keith. After talking with our drunken son, the counselor told us that, " This is just a teen thing. He is a smart kid and knows right from wrong. He'll out grow it. I wouldn't be too concerned." Fine, the expert told us not to be too concerned, so we weren't.

We took our son home, and in the morning had another discussion about the dangers of drinking and drugs. We asked Keith if he took drugs. He told us that he didn't; that people who did drugs were dumb. He said he could never do drugs because he could never stick a needle in his arm. We believed our son. Even after he had gotten drunk, we still didn't feel that he couldn't be trusted to tell us the truth. We were still very close to Keith, and he to us.

In school, Keith managed to keep his grades high enough that he was allowed to become "dual enrolled." That meant that half of his school day was spent taking classes at the local college. Keith chose to take piano and music theory. He started to write his own music. Even though Bill and I didn't like the kind of music Keith wrote and played, we were proud of his talent. He formed another band, which became very popular locally. Now, instead of going to the "underground" nightclub to hear other bands, his was the one everyone came to hear.

Some time late in his junior year, I was called by Keith's school and told that he was caught smoking marijuana behind the school. He was suspended for three days and grounded, once again, by us. I searched his bedroom, and found some marijuana...more discussions and more grounding.

After that, things seemed to smooth out a little with Keith, and we thought maybe we had gotten through the worst of the teen years. We were wrong. Keith disappeared again for several days.

I was getting frantic and thought to call on the police officer who had handled Keith with the credit card incident. I wanted to know if he could help us find our son. All he could do at that point was to check to see if he had gotten in trouble with the law and check with the hospitals.

To our horror, we were told that Keith had shown up at the ER with a cut to his forearm that resulted in 19 stitches. The story given to the police, at the hospital, was that Keith and some friends had gotten into an altercation in an abandoned building in town. This story would later turn out to be false.

Keith called home a couple of days later asking if he could come home. He knew he was in real hot water with us now. Bill had taken the phone call and promptly hung up on Keith. After about the third attempt on Keith's part to talk with us, we told him he could come home. More discussions, more grounding.

Things got progressively worse at school, during Keith's senior year and three weeks before graduation, he was informed that he would not have enough credits to graduate. We weren't told this, and not knowing that our son was distraught, saw no dark clouds on the horizon. The day Keith was told, he went off to his college classes, and simply didn't come home. He was gone for a week. Within that week, we had found out that he had gotten arrested, in a city about 40 miles away, for "a minor in possession" . The van Keith was driving, registered in our name, had been impounded.

Keith didn't bother to call and ask us to bail him out. We had told him not to bother, if he had gotten in trouble with the law again. When Keith finally came home, he took the money from his bank account earmarked for college and moved out.

At this point in our lives, Bill and I had been through three long years of problems with Keith. Both of us were on high blood pressure medicine, and we were under considerable stress. We couldn't stop Keith. He was now 18 years old. We thought maybe being on his own was what Keith needed to grow up. He had gotten a couple of jobs and lost them for one reason or another. We didn't know how he was going to keep his apartment.

One day, once again, I received a phone call from a police detective. Keith and another of his friends had been caught on security cameras cashing forged payroll checks.

There was a warrant out for our son's arrest. When Keith was arrested, he wasn't put in a holding cell for a couple of days. What he had done was a felony. He was placed in the general population of the county jail, and that is where Bill and I went to visit him.

It was so hard to see my son, behind glass, crying for us to bail him out and take him home. He had told us that he was afraid to sleep for fear of what would happen to him. Bill and I had already decided to make Keith stay in jail for at least one night. We wanted him to get a good dose of reality. We thought maybe that would scare him into changing his life. I had cried so hard when we left him there, pleading with us not to leave him.

We came back the next day with a contract for Keith to sign. It contained strict guidelines as to what we expected out of Keith. We told him he had to move back home and get a job. We told him enough was enough. He had to change his life. Keith signed the contract and came home.

In January of 2004, just before Keith turned 19, he landed a good paying, full time job. Part of the pre-employment procedure was a drug test. Keith passed it. We had checked. Ok, we now had proof that he wasn't doing drugs.

At the end of February, Keith had his court hearing on the felony charge. I sat in the courtroom to give our son support. It looked like he was turning the corner. He had a job. He was facing up to things he had done wrong and taking the consequences.

After Keith was sentenced, because it was policy for a felony charge, he was shackled, both hands and feet and led away. At the time, I thought that was the hardest thing I would ever have to do, watch them shackle my son and take him away.

Keith received a sentence of 90 days in jail and 18 months probation. He was lucky enough that he was granted work release, thus keeping him employed. Because of jail overcrowding and Keith being a good inmate, he was released after 60 days. He had to serve the other 30 days on a tether at our house.

Over nine months had passed since Keith had been first arrested for the felony charge, and we had bailed him out. He had served his time. He was paying back the money spent from the forged checks, fines, and court costs. The same day Keith was taken off the tether, he moved out. This time, however, he found an apartment in a better neighborhood than the previous one. He had a good job to support himself, a girlfriend and dreams for the future. Still wanting to further his music career, Keith had also started to save money to move to Oakland, California as soon as his probation was over.

On May 15th, Keith stood up with his sister in her wedding. Jennifer's husband, Frank, considered Keith his best friend, and the three, along with Keith's girlfriend saw a lot of each other. After all we had been through, our family, now growing, was as close as ever. We had made it though the hard times, and life fell into a good routine.

Keith, being on probation, was being drug tested every other week. He was tested a total of 18 times and had passed all of them.

During the first week of November, Bill had received a phone call from Keith's probation officer. She had wanted to know our views on Keith's life. Bill had told her that it looked like Keith had turned the corner in his life. The probation officer told Bill about Keith passing all of his drug tests, and that he was doing everything that was asked of him. Two weeks later, our son was dead from a drug overdose!

Keith's band was set to play at the local nightclub on the evening of November 13, 2004. Keith usually arrived at the club a couple of hours early, to check the equipment. Keith never arrived, and some of the band members went looking for him. He didn't answer the repeated knocks at his door, so one of his friends climbed to Keith's third floor balcony and went in the sliding doors. He found Keith, sitting on his couch. He had been gone for about 12 hours. He had apparently sat down to roll and smoke a cigarette and passed out. He never woke up.

The days following Keith's death are somewhat of a blur. There was to be an autopsy, but the police had said that the reason for Keith's death was pretty obvious. I remember having to become Executor of Keith's estate just so I could enter his apartment to get the suit I wanted for his burial. (It is the suit in the photo. I had made it for his senior pictures.)

During the visitation, the mother of Keith's best friend came up to me and hugged me tightly. She cried so very hard on my shoulder and just said, "It could be me here just as easily as it is you." Apparently she had known a lot more than I had.

The autopsy results would not be available for another eleven weeks, but we were told that there were two spoons on the table in front of Keith. One contained residue of cocaine. The other, heroin. This, I learned, was a common combination among drug users known as a "Speedball." Before rolling the cigarette, Keith had shot up. The autopsy would later reveal that, prior to shooting up, Keith had ingested or smoked five other drugs, some of them prescription.

To this day, I'm not sure if Bill understands why I had to find out everything I could about Keith and the life he had been keeping from us. I was driven to find out when Keith had started using and what he had been using. I was going to have to deal with the overwhelming guilt I felt for not knowing what Keith was doing.

There are still days when that demon comes calling. With the exception of two different six month periods, Keith had lived at home. I didn't understand how we missed it. I didn't understand why this young man, who had been told, from the cradle, how bad drugs were, had ever started using.

Keith apparently had been experimenting with all types of hard drugs for about two years. His girlfriend had told me that about two weeks before Keith died, he had become very " reckless." He was shooting up cocaine or heroin at least twice a day.

Bill and I became angry. We are angry that we had sought out the professionals, the experts, to help us when we didn't know how to handle Keith. One told us " It's a teen thing and he'll get over it" for God's sake. We found out that the so-called drug testing that Keith had passed 18 times was only for alcohol and marijuana, nothing more.

All that time, Keith knew when he was going to be tested and for what drug. He simply went on to other drugs and ones that couldn't be found in simple urine tests.

We are angry that we did everything the television ads still preach today. They tell you to talk to your kids about drugs, be involved in your kid's lives. Tell me, what more could we have done!

The only answer now is to forgive Keith and forgive ourselves. We have done both. Our son, like so many other youth, became entangled in something they thought they could control, only to find out that it controls them.

If you come away from our story with nothing else, please take this. We still believe in being close to our children. Still talk to them often about drugs. Don't take the answers from the experts at face value. Sometimes you just have to go with your gut instinct. Don't expect the school or the justice system to help.

Early on, Keith just became one more troubled teen, and thus a number to those who didn't care. If your child is being tested for drugs, make sure you know the extent of the test. We were very naive in that department. We thought testing for drugs meant testing for drugs. Don't assume that, just because your child has been told about drugs, or that they go to a good school, or that your child says they don't do drugs, that all is well. We had no reason to think Keith would lie to us, and yet he led a double life for about two years. The drug users of today are not skid-row bums. They are the faces you see at the dinner table. Drug use crosses all gender, social, ethnic, and economical boundaries.

For those who will judge us, and Keith because of the Punk Rock music, let me say this. There were so many people in attendance at Keith's funeral that many had to stand and the crowd went out the door of the funeral home. A large part of the people attending sported tattoos and several piercings.

I was approached by a family friend who is in her eighties, and she told me that her generation was taught something that day. They realized that these "different" looking kids are good kids. Keith's friends were devastated when Keith died and showed their love and respect for him by saying goodbye that day.

I had thought that watching Keith being shackled in that court room was the worst thing I had ever been through as a mother. I have now found out just how much worse it can get. As of this writing, it has been a year and a half since Keith died. As much trouble he put us through in those three or so years, I would rather have those problems instead of this hole in my heart.

With the help of our family and friends, we are making it through our grief journey. Our daughter, Jennifer and her husband, Frank, have been and continue to be especially comforting. During the week following Keith's death, they found out that they were going to have a baby. They now have a beautiful daughter, Kaylis Danielle, and Keith has a niece. (Keith's middle name was Daniel and so they honored their brother by making Keith his niece's namesake.) We can only continue to keep Keith alive by telling Jennifer and Frank's children about Uncle Keith, both the good and the bad, with hopes that they learn about his love and his mistakes.

As with other things I do now, I write this story in hopes that other parents wake up to the fact that even the "boy next door" can get themselves into the world of drugs.

Keith's story as told by his loving mom, Pam Montambo, Shelby, MI

"What we have once enjoyed and deeply loved, we can never lose, for all that we love deeply becomes a part of us." ~Helen Keller

SARA JO CORBETT

April 25, 1988 – August 8, 2004
(Age 16)

METHADONE OVERDOSE

"YOU ARE SO BEAUTIFUL TO ME"

Sara was born on April 25, 1988. She was born on my brother's 19th birthday. What a gift!

Everyone loved Sara. She had so many friends, kids her age and adults alike. I was told by all of the adults she touched in her life what a beautiful, kind, thoughtful person she was. She loved little kids, especially her 3-year-old sister Sabrina.

Before I got pregnant with Sara, I myself fought the demons of addiction. I was a drug addict and alcoholic. Once Sara was born, I stopped doing most drugs, but I couldn't seem to put down the bottle.

Sara's first seven years were filled with turmoil. I would send her to a babysitter every chance I got so I could go out and party. When I was around, I was either on my way to getting drunk or so hung over I couldn't even get out of bed. Don't get me wrong. I loved my little girl with all of my heart. The addiction had me in its grip, not Sara. Her dad wasn't any better. We were not together and he didn't put too much effort into seeing Sara, never mind help raise her. He was also a drug addict and alcoholic. So that really put Sara in the high-risk group of becoming addicted to something herself.

I finally quit drinking when Sara was 7 years old. The only positive thing that came out of my drinking were the bad memories she had of her mom drinking, which in turn kept her from touching any alcohol. Even when her friends would get drunk, Sara was the one to stay sober and make sure her friends were OK.

Sara suffered from depression, low self esteem; she had no self worth at all. She always sold herself short. She always let people walk all over her. I wish I could say that it was one of her "ad choice" friends that gave her the drugs that cost her, her life, but I can't. The drugs were my brother-in-law's.

I knew that Sara was fighting her addiction to pot; she was attending NA meetings, seeing a therapist, and really trying to get her grades up and change the path she was starting to go down. But as I said, she suffered from depression, and with her addictive personality, it was just temptation when she spent the night at my sister's house and got ahold of my brother-in-law's Methadone. From what I have been told, she was watching a movie, fell asleep on the couch, and never woke up.

My life will never be the same. I miss my beautiful daughter. Even though we fought all the time, (she was 16, which is par for the course), I would trade both of my arms just to argue with her one more time.

Being a recovering addict myself, I just cannot grasp that my daughter lost her life to drugs. To think there may have been signs that I missed, just tears me up inside. I know that this wasn't a drug that Sara knew about. She didn't know how potent this drug was. We had been through so much in the last two years of her life; I know that she would not have wanted to hurt me. The pain of losing her is just indescribable. I have lost half of myself.

"You are so beautiful to me." That was my song to her ever since she was born. The day before she died, I picked her up at my sister's and she said " Hey Mom, I have a surprise for you." She took my hand, brought me into the living room, went to the stereo, turned on a CD that she had made by downloading music, skipped a few songs, then Joe Cocker comes on and she took my hand and we danced to the song holding each other very close. Eighteen hours later, she was gone.

When I think about Sara, which is about 24 hours a day, I just try to know that she is no longer in pain and she is waiting for me. Those are the only thoughts that give me any type of solace.

I know that I have an angel watching over me now. I talk to her all the time, I receive signs from her, and she seems to help comfort me with happy memories when I'm feeling down.

I LOVE YOU Sara, until we meet again…

"Once you lose a child, no parent is particularly concerned about their own life anymore. Losing a child is truly the worst thing that can happen to a parent in his or her lifetime, and although there are so many reasons to continue on earth - other children, loved ones and friends - many parents (say) with sobering clarity that the prospect of dying, ending the pain, and seeing their children again would not be such a bad thing after all. Feelings of a life with no perceived worth is the best-kept secret of parents who have lost children. A secret to all but their children in the hereafter, who truly become guardians of their parents resolve to continue here, despite the want not to."

George Anderson and Andrew Barone ~ <u>Walking in the Garden of Souls</u>

"It is so hard to watch your child grow up in your mind."

- Compassionate Friends Parent

Sara's website: http://sara-corbett.memory-of.com/

Sara's story as told by her loving mom, Robin DeBaise, Hartford, CT

RANDOM THOUGHTS AND POEMS

On the following pages you will find some poems that I've chosen for the book along with some original thoughts by the moms whose children's stories are contained herein.

Some of the poems are chilling and sobering. Others may bring a smile to your face, and a tear to your eye. All are by unknown authors (with an exception or two as noted), whose poems I found on the internet.

While they may not be great works of literature, they are great works of the heart.

I've included them in the book because I know most of you will relate to them and also because there is something comforting about reading the words of others who share our grief.

A Mom's Thought

"I dreaded picking up the phone and answering the door for fear of what new heartache was waiting to spring.

And now, we've exchanged all our worries and depression for grief so strong that it makes our previous anxiety-ridden lives seem almost pleasant to what we now face every day." ---- Joy Farmer

I Never Thought...

I never thought I would survive after burying you, but ~ I did.

I never thought I'd get through those first days, weeks and months, but ~ I did.

I never thought I would be able to endure the first anniversary of your death, but ~ I did.

I never thought I would let myself love my new grandchild, but ~ I did.

I never thought tomorrow would be different, but ~ it was.

I never thought I would stop crying for you, but ~ I have.

I never thought that I would ever sing again, but ~ I have.

I never thought the pain would "soften," but ~ it has.

I never thought I would care if the sun shone again, but ~ I do.

I never thought I would be able to entertain again, but ~ I have.

I never thought I would be able to control my grief, but ~ I can.

I never thought I could function without medication again, but ~ I can.

I never thought I'd smile again, but ~ I do.

I never thought I would laugh out loud again, but ~ I do.

I never thought I would look forward to tomorrow, but ~ I do.

I never thought I'd reconcile your death, but ~ I have.

I never thought I would be able to create that "new normal," but ~ I have.

I never thought I'd want to go on living after you died, but ~ I do.

Always missing you,
always loving you,
and thinking of you daily,
with a smile on my face ~
and tears in my heart.

   ---Author unknown

COMETS

"Some people are like comets,
They streak through our lives in a flash
Of excitement, love, and awe.
Then they are gone, never to be seen again,
Although we think of them often.

Comet-like people cannot be held onto or controlled,
They need to keep loving, lighting up yet another sky.
Sadly, some comet types die too young,
And we miss them and grieve deeply in their absence.

But the angels know that each comet person
Who has left the earth at a young age
Exists in a burst of light that remains
For the good of those left behind.

A comet would never want
Us to mourn its disappearance.
So comet people want us to remember
The joy they left behind and to allow the love
We have for them to continue to grow,
Blessing others in its path." – Author unknown

Grief Wish List

If you have been through grief, you will relate to this. If you are going through it, you will relate. If you have never been through this type of grief, keep this handy…it may help you one day.

My Grief Wish List

1. I wish you would not be afraid to speak my loved one's name. They lived and were important and I need to hear their name.

2. If I cry or get emotional when we talk about my loved one, I wish you knew it isn't because you have hurt me; the fact they have died has caused my tears. You have allowed me to cry and I thank you. Crying and emotional outbursts are healing.

3. I wish you wouldn't let my loved one die again by removing from your home his/her pictures, artwork or other remembrances.

4. I will have emotional highs and lows, ups and downs. I wish you wouldn't think that if I have a good day my grief is all over, or that if I have a bad day, I need psychiatric counseling.

5. I wish you knew that the death of a child is different from other losses and must be viewed separately. It is the ultimate tragedy and I wish you wouldn't compare it to your loss of a parent, a spouse or a pet.

6. Being a bereaved person is not contagious, so I wish you wouldn't stay away from me.

7. I wish you knew all the crazy grief reactions that I am having are in fact very normal. Depression, anger, frustration, and hopelessness and the questioning of values and beliefs are to be expected following the death of a child.

8. I wish you wouldn't expect my grief to be over in six months. The first few years are going to be exceedingly traumatic for me. As with alcoholics, I will never be "cured" or a "formerly bereaved", but will forever be "recovering" from my bereavement.

I AM YOUR DISEASE

9. I wish you understood the physical reaction to grief. I may gain weight or lose weight, sleep all the time or not at all, develop a lot of illnesses and be accident prone, all of which are related to my grief.

10. My loved one's birthday, the anniversary of his/her death and the holidays are terrible times for me. I wish you could tell me that you are thinking about them on these days and if I get quiet and withdrawn, just know that I am thinking about them and don't try to coerce me into being cheerful.

11. I wish you wouldn't offer to take me out for a drink, or to a party, this is just a temporary crutch and the only way I can get through this grief is to experience it. I have hurt before and I can heal.

12. I wish you understood that grief changes people. I am not the same person I was before my loved one died and I never will be that person again. If you keep waiting for me to get back to "my old self", you will stay frustrated. I am a new creature with new thoughts, dreams, aspirations, values and beliefs. Please try to get to know the new me: maybe you will still like me.

Author unknown

SHERYL LETZGUS MCGINNIS WITH HEIKO GANZER

Meet Mr. & Mrs. Crystal Meth

I destroy homes, I tear families apart,
I take your children and that's just the start.
I'm more valued than diamonds, more precious than gold.
The sorrow I bring is a sight to behold.
If you need me, remember, I'm easily found.
I live all around you, in school and in town.
I live with the rich, I live with the poor,
I live just down the street and maybe next door.
I'm made in a lab, but not one like you think:
I can be made under the kitchen sink,
In your child's closet, and even out in the woods.
If this scares you to death, then it certainly should.
I have many names, but there's one you'll know best.
I'm sure you heard of me. My name is Crystal Meth.
My power is awesome, try me, you'll see;
But if you do, you may never break free.
Just try me once and I might let you go.
But if you try me twice, then I'll own your soul.
When I possess you, you'll steal and you'll lie.
You'll do what you have to do, just to get high.
The crimes you'll commit for my narcotic charms
Will be worth the pleasures you feel in my arms.
You'll lie to your mother, you'll steal from your dad.
When you see their tears, you must feel sad.
Just forget your morals and how you were raised.
I'll be your conscience, I'll teach you my ways.
I take kids from their parents, I take parents from their kids.

I turn people from God. I separate friends.
I'll take everything from you, your looks and your pride.
I'll be with you always, right by your side.
You'll give up everything, your family, your home,
Your money, your true friend then you'll be alone.
I'll take and take til you have no more to give.
When I finish with you, you'll be lucky to live.

I AM YOUR DISEASE

If you try me, be warned: this is not a game.
If I'm given the chance, I'll drive you insane.
I'll ravage your body, I'll control your mind.
I'll own you completely. Your soul will be mine.
The nightmares I'll give you when you're lying in bed
And the voices you'll hear from inside your head,
The sweats, the shakes, and the visions you'll see:
I want you to know these things are gifts from me.
By then it's too late, and you'll know in your heart
That you are now mine and we shall not part.
You'll regret that you tried me (they always do),
But you come to me, not I to you.
You knew this would happen. Many times you were told.
But you challenged my power. You chose to be bold.
You could have said no and then walked away.
If you could live that day over now, what would you say?
My power is awesome, as I told you before.
I can take your life and make it so dim and sore.
I'll be your master and you'll be my slave.
I'll even go with you when you go to your grave.
Now that you've met me, what will you do?
Will you try me or not? It's all up to you.
I can show you more misery than words can tell.
Come take my hand, let me lead you to HELL

    Author unknown

SHERYL LETZGUS MCGINNIS WITH HEIKO GANZER

TAKE ME IN YOUR ARMS, MS. HEROIN

So now, little man, you've grown tired of grass
LSD, goofballs, cocaine and hash,
and someone, pretending to be a true friend,
said, " I'll introduce you to Miss Heroin."

Well honey, before you start fooling with me,
just let me inform you of how it will be.

For I will seduce you and make you my slave,
I've sent men much stronger than you to their graves.
You think you could never become a disgrace,
and end up addicted to Poppy seed waste.

So you'll start inhaling me one afternoon,
you'll take me into your arms very soon.
And once I've entered deep down in your veins,
The craving will nearly drive you insane.

You'll swindle your mother and just for a buck.
You'll turn into something vile and corrupt.
You'll mug and you'll steal for my narcotic charm,
and feel contentment when I'm in your arms.

The day, when you realize the monster you've grown,
you'll solemnly swear to leave me alone.
If you think you've got that mystical knack,
then sweetie, just try getting me off your back.

The vomit, the cramps, your gut tied in knots.
The jangling nerves screaming for one more shot.
The hot chills and cold sweats, withdrawal pains,
can only be saved by my little white grains.

There's no other way, and there's no need to look,
for deep down inside you know you are hooked.
You'll desperately run to the pushers and then,
you'll welcome me back to your arms once again.

I AM YOUR DISEASE

And you will return just as I foretold!
I know that you'll give me your body and soul.
You'll give up your morals, your conscience, your heart.
And you will be mine until, "Death Do Us Part"

~~~**Author unknown**

Nothing really ever dies
That is not born anew.
The miracles of nature
All tell us this is true.

The flowers sleeping peacefully
Beneath the winter's snow
Awaken from their icy grave
When spring winds start to blow.

And little brooks and singing streams,
Icebound beneath the snow,
Begin to babble merrily
Beneath the sun's warm glow.

And all around on every side
New life and joy appear
To tell us nothing ever dies
And we should have no fear.

For death is just a detour
Along life's wending way
That leads God's chosen children
To a bright and glorious day.

~ Helen Steiner Rice

I AM YOUR DISEASE

MY MOM LIES

My mom, she tells a lot of lies,
She never did before.
From now on until she dies
She'll tell a whole lot more.
Ask my mom how she is
And because she can't explain,
She will tell a little lie
Because she can't describe the pain.

Ask my mom how she is,
She'll say, "I'm alright."
If that's the truth then tell me
Why does she cry each night?
Ask my mom how she is
She seems to cope so well
She didn't have a choice, you see
Nor the strength to yell.

Ask my mom how she is,
"I'm fine, I'm well, I'm coping,"
For God's sake, mom
Just tell the truth
Just say your heart is broken.
She'll love me all her life,
I loved her all of mine.

SHERYL LETZGUS MCGINNIS WITH HEIKO GANZER

But if you ask her how she is,
She'll lie and say she's fine.

I am here in Heaven,
I cannot hug from here,
If she lies to you don't listen,
Hug her and hold her near.
On the day we meet again,
We'll smile and I'll be bold,
I'll say "You're lucky to get in here, mom
With all the lies you told."
Author unknown

I AM YOUR DISEASE

It's Okay to Let Me Go, Mom

Mom, you have to let me go,
Because it was meant to be.
And just because you let me go,
Doesn't mean you'll ever lose me.

You hold my hand and stroke my cheek,
As your heart is breaking in two.
And my spirit is still right there, you see,
I'll always be there within you.

I see your tears and I feel your pain,
And I know you just want to die.
But it's not your time to come here yet,
And right now I can't tell you why.

There's more you have to do there,
More lives and hearts you must touch.
There's others there around you,
Who still need and love you so much.

So please don't feel like you've lost me,
For you haven't I'm still by your side.
Now I'm holding YOUR hand and stroking YOUR cheek,
So you'll want to live and not die.

Oh Mom, I want you to live now,
And I need you to let my body go.
The part of me you love so much,
Is now in the breeze as it blows.

When you're in the kitchen `cooking',
Or simply just combing your hair.
When the light in the room flickers a bit,
Know it is me, and I'm there.

When I was hurting and I was in pain,

SHERYL LETZGUS MCGINNIS WITH HEIKO GANZER

You were there with your comfort and love.
Now let me do the same for you,
Let me give you those things, from above.

I'm walking and smiling, and happy.
And I want you to know this is true.
I'm with you and around you still.
And I'll be here to help you get through.

Close your eyes and you'll hear me talking.
Open your heart and you'll then feel me there.
It's not a `trick' or just `your mind',
It's " me" that you feel on the air.

So it's okay to let me go, Mom,
I'm not in my body, you see.
Cause I'm in your heart and in the air,
And I promise You'll never lose me.

~~~Author unknown

I AM YOUR DISEASE

"Heroin is only a CHOICE you make the FIRST time!"
----Brigitte G.

SHERYL LETZGUS MCGINNIS WITH HEIKO GANZER

The Missing Page

A page is missing
From our history
It's all about one
So dear to me

Our book was filled
With laughter and joy
So much of it from
Our darling boy

Each chapter and verse
Contained his song
We thought it would last
We were so wrong

For when he died
The page was torn
I cried and cried
For my second born

The mischievous child
The beautiful young man
Born to be wild
In his VW van

I AM YOUR DISEASE

The guitar he played
Strummed a song in my heart
The memory won't fade
Even though we're apart

I still hear him say
I love you mom
Don't cry for me
When I'm gone

The monster has me
In its control
I know I won't live
To be very old

No, no my son
Don't say that to me
This is not how
It's supposed to be

You're young and so strong
You can beat this, I know
I was so wrong
It's a formidable foe

No matter how tough

SHERYL LETZGUS MCGINNIS WITH HEIKO GANZER

And determined you are
The Addiction Monster
Is tougher by far

Stronger than diamonds
Cunning and cruel
He laughs at you
And makes you a fool

You promise yourself
You'll beat it this time
But the monster knows
"He is mine."

How many books
In this country so wide
Are missing pages
Because someone has died

From the disease of addiction
That holds them so tight
Try as they will
They have no more fight

The Monster will win
There's no denying
Its power so strong

I AM YOUR DISEASE

So many are dying

Leaving our families
With a torn page
As we are consumed
With unyielding rage

Torment and grief
The guilt of the living
The Addiction Monster
Is unforgiving

Life is unfair
So we've been told
The Monster takes all
The young and the old

Our once happy book
With pages of joy
Is missing the chapter
Of our little boy

May your book stay complete
With its pages all there
So that your heart will never
Experience that tear.
~~~Sherry McGinnis

SHERYL LETZGUS MCGINNIS WITH HEIKO GANZER

Death Be Not Proud

Death be not proud, though some have called thee
Mighty and dreadfull, for, thou art not soe,
For, those, whom thou think'st, thou dost overthrow,
Die not, poore death, nor yet canst thou kill mee.
From rest and sleepe, which but thy pictures bee,
Much pleasure, then from thee, much more must flow,
And soonest our best men with thee doe goe,
Rest of their bones, and soules deliverie.
Thou art slave to Fate, Chance, kings, and desperate men,
And dost with poyson, warre, and sicknesse dwell,
And poppie, or charmes can make us sleepe as well,
And better than thy stroake; why swell'st thou then?
One short sleepe past, wee wake eternally,
And death shall be no more; death, thou shalt die.

~John Donne 17th century English poet

I AM YOUR DISEASE

~I LOST MY CHILD TODAY~

I lost my child today
People came to weep and cry
As I just sat and stared, dry eyed.
They struggled to find words to say,
To try and make the pain go away,
I walked the floor in disbelief
I lost my child today

I lost my child last month
Most of the people went away,
Some still call and some still stay.
I wait to wake up from the dream.
This can't be real. I want to scream.
Yet everything is locked inside,
God, help me, I want to die.
I lost my child last month

I lost my child last year
Now people who had come, have gone,
I sit and struggle all day long,
To bear the pain so deep inside.
And now my friends just question, "Why?"
Why does this mother not move on?
Just sits and sings the same old song.
Good heavens, it has been so long.
I lost my child last year

Time has not moved on for me.
The numbness it has disappeared.
My eyes have now cried many tears.
I see the look upon your face,
"She must move on and leave this place."
Yet I am trapped right here in time.
The song's the same, as is the rhyme,
I lost my child....Today.
~~~Netta Wilson (from the Internet)

SHERYL LETZGUS MCGINNIS WITH HEIKO GANZER

WILL YOU GO OR WILL YOU STAY?

My precious child has a disease
It's destroying him day by day
Oh I'm so sorry you earnestly tell me
I just don't know what to say

The disease came on so slowly
Without a hint or a clue
By the time we felt its impact
There was nothing that we could do

My friend, I am so sorry
In me you can confide
I know that you must worry
So I'll always be by your side

Please let me help in any way
Just tell me and I'll be there
You shouldn't have to suffer so
This is more than you should bear

Thank you very much, I say
As my eyes fill to the brim
This disease is like no other
And it's slowly destroying him

I AM YOUR DISEASE

Tell me, is it cancer
Or something with his brain
What kind of horrible disease is it
To cause everyone so much pain

Was it caused by a virus
Or some genetic disease
Something that he couldn't help
That's brought him to his knees

No child should have to suffer
They have so much to give
So much learning and so much joy
So much life to live

Well my friend I'll tell you
Our little family secret,
Our child is a drug addict
We've tried so hard to keep it

For when people come to know
The reason for our despair
They don their self-imposed judicial robes
And pass judgment without a care

What kind of parents must we be

SHERYL LETZGUS MCGINNIS WITH HEIKO GANZER

I see the question in your eyes
Well we were parents just like you
Believing all the lies

For when addiction enters your life
No matter how you've raised them
It'll turn your world upside down
And you are powerless to save them

That beautiful body is now just a shell
Masking what lives inside
The Addiction Monster has invaded our son
His heart and soul have died

But we still love him with all of our being
For we remember when
He was more than "just a drug addict"
He was a loving and caring young man

Now that you know the awful truth
Will you stay or will you leave
Or were they just hollow words you said
That we wanted so to believe

I see the shocked look that you're trying to hide
And the words that you dare not say
If the disease was socially acceptable

I AM YOUR DISEASE

You would never go away

But if you go I'll understand
Though saddened I will be
That you can't look beyond the disease
To see what he means to me. ~~~Sherry McGinnis

SHERYL LETZGUS MCGINNIS WITH HEIKO GANZER

THE 'EVERYTHING-WE-COULD' BRIGADE

We did Everything We Could

But Everything We Could was not enough

Everything We Could did not work

Our sons and daughters died anyway

*****

We did Everything We Could

We got the Shrinks n' Rehabs--Innies and Outies--kicked them out, kept them in, Fresh Starts, re-starts, fits and starts, new jobs, new abodes, as a cacophony of "I-love-you's! Don't-do this-to-yourselves!" cry out in unison.

How could Everything We Could not be good enough?

How could Everything We Could not be 'could' enough?

How could Everything We Could not work?

Everything We Could did not keep them alive and kicking in our neck of the woods

I AM YOUR DISEASE

Our neck of the woods is all we know

*****

Everything We Could had nothing to do with it and Nothing We Could had everything to do with it.

Because it wasn't about us.

We wanted to be God and get inside them and cure them

We love them and so wanted them to live and thrive

God loves us and admires us

So do the kids

Because Everything We Could was done with love and well meaning

*****

Once Upon A Time, we set out to do Everything We Could

But our children had something to learn from this--beyond our Everything We Coulds-- and Everything We Shoulds--and Everything We Woulds

And, perhaps, so did we

We don't know what that is, but they do

Because they are in the pure love zone

We are close to them in prayer and feel them with us

Until we get to where they are

And then we don't have to do a damn Could

Because Some One will have brought their healing to perfection...

...and with it our Everything We Coulds.

.

For all parents
anonymous author

I AM YOUR DISEASE

The Cord

We are connected,
My child and I,
by An invisible cord
Not seen by the eye.

It's not like the cord
That connects us 'til birth
This cord can't been seen
By any on Earth.

This cord does its work
Right from the start.
It binds us together
Attached to my heart.

I know that it's there
Though no one can see
The invisible cord
From my child to me.

The strength of this cord
Is hard to describe.
It can't be destroyed
It can't be denied.

It's stronger than any cord
Man could create
It withstands the test
Can hold any weight.

And though you are gone,
Though you're not here with me,
The cord is still there
But no one can see.

It pulls at my heart
I am bruised...
I am sore,
But this cord is my lifeline
As never before.

SHERYL LETZGUS MCGINNIS WITH HEIKO GANZER

I am thankful that God
Connects us this way
A mother and child
Death can't take it away!

~ Author Unknown ~

WE REMEMBER THEM

In the rising of the sun and in its going down,
We remember them.
In the blowing of the wind and in the chill of winter,
We remember them.
In the opening of the buds and in the rebirth of spring,
We remember them.
In the blueness of the sky and in the warmth of summer,
We remember them.
In the rustling of leaves and in the beauty of autumn,
We remember them.
In the beginning of the year and when it ends,
We remember them.
When we are weary and in need of strength,
We remember them.
When we are lost and sick at heart,
We remember them.
When we have joys we yearn to share,
We remember them.
So long as we live, they shall too,
For they are now a part of us,
As we remember them.

From The Reform Jewish Prayer book

SHERYL LETZGUS MCGINNIS WITH HEIKO GANZER

A CHILD'S VIEW OF PEER PRESSURE

This book would not be complete without hearing from the most vulnerable segment of our drug-entrenched society---our children.

Children today face a startling amount of pressure to do drugs, drink, have sex, join gangs, beat up other kids, and participate in law-breaking behavior. Never before have children had so much freedom, money, independence and accessibility to things that were once considered only the realm of the adult world.

Little kids as young as five and six are encouraged to "grow up" by their parents and by the advertising world. Parents who dress them in the style of their favorite singers, encouraging them to act more mature, thus denying them their exclusive right to be just a kid.

My husband is an 8th grade science teacher. When he asks his students how many children are in the class, not one hand is raised. When he asks how many adults are in the class, all hands go up simultaneously. These are 14-year-old children who think they are adults! Why? Because our society has led them to believe, and in fact encouraged them to believe, that they are indeed adults.

Look at most TV commercials today. Have you noticed how they depict the children as being smarter than their parents?

We have taken the most precious commodity from our children---their childhood. No eighth-grade child, (and even younger grade children) should be concerned about these things at such a young age.

What kind of childhood memories will these kids have to look back upon? What kind of experiences are they having today that we adults don't know about?

Read the following excerpts from essays written by 8th grade students. Read these sentiments with your child. Encourage dialogue with your child about these pressures, but above all---**Listen** to your child!

Following are descriptions of peer pressure written by children from average, and middle class, to upper middle class families.

What they have to say may shock you!

I AM YOUR DISEASE

#1. "Mike" – " Hey man put this in your pocket," my friend said. " But I didn't pay for it" I said, as I put it in my pocket anyway. This is an example of peer pressure that us teens have to go through. Three pressures that teens have to go through are the pressure to look good, the pressure to do drugs, and the pressure to steal.

If you don't wear the right clothes or look the right way, then you're not cool.

Another example is the pressure to do drugs. My cousin was a great track runner. She even got a scholarship for it until one day her best friend offered her drugs. She gave into peer pressure and she took the drug. Ever since then that's all she could think about!

#2. "Harry" – Peer pressure is like a voice in the back of your head. You want it to go away.

#3. "Dusty" – Pressure to fit in and be popular. This means having the right clothes or the right gadgets, for example having a cell phone or an Ipod. This kind of peer pressure can lower a teen's self-esteem. Peer pressure is like being trapped in a burning building---if you go the right way you'll be OK, but if you go the wrong way, you'll be burned alive.

#4. "Benny" – Probably the biggest peer pressure today is to do drugs. I was walking home and saw two 10-year-olds smoking. I asked them where they got the stuff and they said some guy just kept asking them until they did it. Today though kids aren't being asked to smoke cigarettes. Oh no, it's worse than that. They're being asked to do crack cocaine, joints, pot, and ecstasy. Most kids don't even care for cigarettes.

Teens go along with the crowd because if they don't, their popularity goes down and to a teen, popularity is important. Why? Because popularity gives you respect and respect gives you power and power gives you control. I'd like to say stay away from the bad crowd. Don't ever do drugs because once you start, it's hard to quit. Please don't sell or try to put peer pressure on anyone because my guess is that they probably have enough already.

#5. "Danny" – Peer pressure can make you lose friends, get you hurt or into a lot of trouble with your parents. You wanna fit in but you don't wanna do it. If your friends are doing drugs and you never tried them and they try to get you to do it but you don't. Then they don't think that they should be friends with you. But if you do them, then they think you're cool. If you don't do the drugs, they will go to school and tell everyone that you were the biggest chicken and no one would want to hang out with you. Then you will be as lonely as the cave man sobbing in his cave. Trust me you don't want that to happen.

#6. "Tony" – Smoking, drinking and drugs are the biggest peer pressures with the pressure to do drugs as the #1 pressure. Why? Because parents don't tell kids not to do drugs because they think they are too young! My conclusion is that kids don't know that these things are bad because their parents don't tell them.

#7. "Laura" – Sex on TV is at an all-time high, along with the number of teens who are sexually active. When teens see everyday young, pretty, successful people having fun and sleeping around, it tells them that it's cool. At least six out of ten kids has tried at least four drugs!! My friend is a great example. Her other friends told her it was harmless fun. Now six months later, she's stuck in rehab. Society plays a big role also. On a lot of teen shows, the characters smoke and do drugs and have no consequences.

#8. "Marie" – The most common peer pressure facing teens today is to do drugs. I bet you that most people take drugs as a result of peer pressure. Because you think it's cool to get high.

#9. "Alycea" – Never do drugs. We are told about drugs over and over. You never know when someone will ask if you want any. By not taking it you could get hurt. The pressure put on teens about doing drugs and not doing drugs, seeing friends and loved ones doing drugs is unbearable. You can't tell them to stop. There are so many things that teens are pressured about. One is grade pressure from your parents. Not hanging out with the right people, from friends. The fact that drugs are around us everywhere!

#10. "Jerry" – A big problem kids have today is drugs! My friend and I used to hang out all the time. Then we went over to another friend's house. My friend and I were offered some drugs. At first we both said no. Then the kid kept begging us to try it. He kept going on about how good it is. Only because of the pressure that was on my friend, did he finally give in. My friend now has a serious drug problem because of peer pressure and that he wanted to be " cool."

#11. "Joseph" – Drugs are probably one of the biggest pressures on kids today. Drinking is another pressure. The biggest pressure of all is to be " cool." Kids want everyone to like them, and to get that they might do terrible things. Kids will do anything to be " cool."

#12. "Bob" – People are pressured to do drugs. People who do drugs and drink alcohol usually don't have a good life. So they want to drag other people down with them. For example, there was a kid (who was my friend) who was the smartest kid I knew. But there was the other kid who (with his friends) tormented him because he didn't do drugs. Until one day he started to do drugs, drink and then got bad grades and eventually flunked out. Peer pressure is something that bored, dumb and/or bad people like to do to others to drag them into unhappiness with them.

#13. "Joanie" – The three main peer pressures are alcohol, drugs and sex. They may seem great but they can ruin your life. You may start to feel guilty, sad or want to rewind time. Some effects from doing these things can lead you to the hospital. So before the peer pressure starts, stop it!

#14. "Alayna" – Kids today pressure you not only to do drugs and drink but also to kill people! Some of my friends pressured me into doing drugs. If you ever go into a club and take a drink from someone you don't know, that person might have put a drug in your drink. That's why a lot of people are becoming more addicted to drugs today.

Teens will pressure you to rob someone or kill someone, this is a way to get in a gang. Teens get pressured to do drugs and to have intimate relationships with their boyfriend or girlfriend. Wow! Think real well...is your teenager feeling pressure from any of this or even worse stuff?

#15. "Beth" – There's smoking, drinking, stealing and beating up people, not to mention doing drugs. You will do all these things to be cool because every kid wants to be considered cool.

#16. "Andy" – I think teens feel more pressure from their friends today than ever, because of drugs and gangs and also fighting. Friends sometimes push friends into doing drugs and they end up getting addicted. They get talked into joining gangs because they're told it's safe and they won't get hurt and so they join because they don't want to be alone.

#17. "Maleeka" – Teens today are pressured to do drugs, drink, smoke and to ruin other people's property and even to kill. Let's say one of your friends wants to go and blow up cars, but you say no. They will pressure you until you say yes. Killing. Crying. Police. Life in prison. What does this mean? Some people die from stress, disease and hate. But it's just wrong to take a life from an innocent person. Do you know why people do this? Yeah, that's right---peer pressure!

#18. "Jerome" – Teens are forced into doing drugs that cause them to lose touch with reality. Or to wear stuff so they can fit into a group. And they're forced to fight and to be in gangs to be cool. Teens have friends and enemies so when they join a gang they receive more enemies of that group. So they are forced to fight to stay in that gang. Sometimes when a fight is happening, someone could pull out a weapon and either seriously hurt or kill someone.

Drugs affect teen lives and the choices they make. They are forced to wear stuff or act a certain way to fit in. They are forced to fight and die for a gang.

#19. "James" – Drugs! Alcohol! Stealing! Three of the most common forms of peer pressure today. I only have a few words to say. Don't let your friends decide your future, that's your decision. Make the right choice even if it doesn't make you cool.

#20. "Kelsee" – C'mon do it, it won't hurt you. Have you ever heard those words before? The worst part is that it's your friends peer pressuring you into doing drugs, drinking, stealing or having sex.

But if they are peer pressuring into doing these things then they aren't really your friends. They pressure you into doing drugs, drinking, and getting high. Are you going to be a pressurer or a pressuree? Be above the influence!

#21. "Glenn" – Have you ever thought about what teens go through? Us teens today are always under pressure by many things; school and society. Even home can pressure us. Teens are pressured by school in the form of tests and quizzes. Teens are pressured by their own families by being yelled at or punished. Parents are sometimes way too overbearing. Teens will always be pressured but as time goes by, pressure builds up. I believe that teens need time to relax so that they aren't under stress due to peer pressure.

#22. "Keyshanna" – We teens have a lot of peer pressure –from cursing to drinking, to drugs, even to being rude to adults. Cursing is everywhere. It would be a miracle if we could avoid it. Personally I think people use cursing so they can fit in with everybody else. Where does the cursing start? Maybe it started in a gang or in rap music but wherever it started it is putting serious pressure on kids.

Drinking is a huge pressure on kids. You see all of your friends drinking and you want to be cool. They ask you if you want something to drink. You don't want to but you give in because you want to be popular. Stop the picture right there. You have just given in to peer pressure, all because of something you knew was wrong but because everybody else was doing it. You do it over and over again and now you're a drunk. Now look where peer pressure has gotten you.

Then there's being rude. Just because your friends are rude to their parents does not mean that you have to be rude to yours. But after seeing your friends being rude to their parents over and over you start to do the same to yours. Now you're getting in trouble all the time and won't stop. Peer pressure has just taken over and it won't let go.

#23. "Mychele" – School is a huge part of a teen's life. It's where we find friends and learn stuff too. Yet, it can also be somewhat of a drag especially when you realize that you're failing your courses. The pressure to get good grades is constant. Sometimes these pressures can make you physically sick. Another pressure is trying *to fit in. Because of this pressure, most teens feel like they need to "stress to impress," trying to wear the " right" clothes and being someone who they really are not.*

The biggest pressure nowadays for teens is whether or not to try alcohol and drugs. They feel that their friendship will be in jeopardy if they don't go along with the crowd. Peer pressure will always be around us teens and we have to find a way to handle it the right way.

#24. *"Jennafer" – Cigarettes, joints, crack, these are just a few of what many teens are doing today. At first they know it's wrong but if a friend asks a teen to try one, they will. After that they might get addicted and soon they're the ones asking a new friend to try whatever he has done. There are so many drugs out there today and they are so easy to get! Drugs are an easy way to forget about other pressures in your life.*

Sex is another main pressure many teens face today especially girls. Mostly girls are pressured into having sex with their boyfriends. Sometimes it will be because everyone else is doing it or the girl is scared that if she doesn't have sex, she could lose her boyfriend. Many teens also think that if you haven't had sex, then you are too prissy. So your image is another main factor. Eight out of ten girls have sex before they're eighteen.

Under age drinking is definitely related to peer pressure. Drinking can occur at slumber parties, even in the bathroom at school. Drugs, sex and alcohol are tempting and many teens will give in. In the words of many teachers, parents and counselors, " Just Say No."

#25. *"Ethan" – One example of peer pressure on teens is to do drugs. Teens think that if they do drugs they will be cool. Let me ask you a question. When you were a kid did you think you would be cool if you did drugs? Well that is what your kids think! One of my older friends that I've known my whole life didn't like drugs. But one day he tried some and got hooked on them. Now he doesn't go to school, doesn't go to work and still lives at home. To me, basically when you do drugs, it's saying that you don't care about your life. Teens today do drugs because they want to be cool, they want to fit in and they want to be popular.*

The examples you've just read are just some of the thousands of stories of how children feel about the issues facing them every day. We have to talk to our children. We have to listen acutely to what they have to say.

Most of all, we have to love our children. Tomorrow is not guaranteed. Five minutes from now is not guaranteed for any of us.

We brought our children into this world. We have to give them the tools to cope with the decisions that they face every hour of the day.

We all know the real estate adage: Location, Location, Location. For parents of children in today's world the adage would be, Listen, Listen, Listen!

FENTANYL AND HEROIN: A DEADLY MIX

As if heroin were not deadly enough, recently drug dealers have taken to adding the potent pain killer fentanyl, to heroin. Fentanyl can be about 80 times more powerful than morphine, according to the U.S. Drug Enforcement Administration.

Dealers are adding the fentanyl to heroin to give the addicted person an even higher high. Users may experience extreme euphoria, which of course, is their goal. However, the end result can be a deep sleep, from which they most likely will not awaken.

We parents need to keep our ears open for the many slang expressions for street drugs. One variation of fentanyl is sometimes called China White. (Refer to the links below for a comprehensive list of street drug names).

http://www.whitehousedrugpolicy.gov/streetterms/   A website listing slang names for various drugs.

http://www.addictions.org/slang.htm

We, as parents, can't be expected to memorize every slang term listed but it might not be a bad idea to visit the sites, and print the lists. Familiarize yourself with as many names as you can.

Perhaps you overhear your child who is active in sports, speaking of "half a football field." Sounds innocent enough, right? In reality, they could be speaking instead about 50 rocks of cocaine!

Our children are clever, so we must be vigilant. When I was a child we thought it was so cool to speak in "pig latin" (ig-pay atin-lay, as an example). Such innocence.

Today, our children speak in code much as we did when we were their age. Sadly, a lot of the code today is not innocent. Kids speak of "pharm" parties (we hear "farm" parties). "Pharming." We hear "farming."

A quick look at the list of slang terms will reveal that "pharming" refers to searching for pharmaceuticals, searching for these drugs in your medicine cabinet or in your purse or anywhere that your child knows that you keep your medicine.

Whether it's fentanyl mixed with heroin or fentanyl mixed with cocaine, or "pharming" or any one of a number of drugs and/or words that may be foreign to us parents, we must stay on our toes. We must always listen. We must be alert. The life we save may be our child's.

SHERYL LETZGUS MCGINNIS WITH HEIKO GANZER

SOME GENTLE SUGGESTIONS AND TIPS ON COPING

"After the death of someone you love you Listen for them. You wait for signs of reassurance, help, love, the touch, the sound of any presence." Joan Jullet Buck

"It isn't right for my child to be gone before me," the mother of a dying teenager cried. So how do you survive the death of your child? Regardless of the age of the child, when you lose a son or daughter, part of your self is gone. In the case of mothers, part of your physical self is gone--the body that grew within you means so much. As a parent, you're supposed to be responsible for watching your child's growth; most of all, you do not outlive your child. When tragedy strikes and you do bury a child, no matter the cause of death you're faced with reconstructing a life that has been suddenly robbed of its parental responsibilities and joys. The disease of addiction takes lives. Some will say that the person had a death wish and others will reconstruct the events trying to make sense of it! We in the counseling field offer words of encouragement to help the family make something of their loss. Writing a book, or offering to speak to teens or others are some ways to do closure of this major emotional event.

Those of you who are in self help support groups may have heard of the serenity prayer:

God grant me the serenity
to accept the things I cannot change;
courage to change the things I can;
and wisdom to know the difference.

Living one day at a time;
Enjoying one moment at a time;
Accepting hardships as the pathway to peace;
Taking, as He did, this sinful world
as it is, not as I would have it;

Trusting that He will make all things right
if I surrender to His Will;
That I may be reasonably happy in this life
and supremely happy with Him
Forever in the next.
Amen.

--Reinhold Niebuhr

I find this prayer the most helpful for those dealing with grief. God's wish for you may be to learn and move on so you can help others as we have in this book. Only you can decide what to do about yourself and your grief. But be clear that you are still alive and that you have the choice to move in a healthy direction or not.

One suggestion I have for those of you who have experienced a loss due to addiction is to see a therapist and resolve your grief. Closure is very important for your health. Write your loved one a letter telling him/her of your feelings and thoughts. Then go and take the letter to a body of water like a lake or the ocean and light the letter on fire as a demonstration of your love and closure of this event. Above all pray, pray for your loved one and show them serenity. That is what they probably would hope for if they could speak. *Heiko Ganzer, LCSW, CASAC and loving dad*

Coping is such a relative term. First I always remember the 3 C's; I didn't Cause it, I can't Cure it, and I can't Control it.

Since Josh passed I talk to everyone I can about it. There are so many people out there with kids going through drug problems and they can use our help. Most importantly I have started a foundation to continue the memory of my son. I have a website in his memory, (www.joshjoseph.com) have bought a room in a halfway house in his name, and I give speeches to teens and addicts. Anything to keep his memory alive and give his death some meaning. *Paul Joseph, Josh's loving dad.*

After my son Scott passed away and I was beside myself with grief, a friend who had experienced the same loss just three months earlier, said something to me that helped me get through those awful first days, weeks, months, and years. She said that we, who have lost a child, should treat ourselves as if we are in Intensive Care because indeed this is what we need…Intensive Care.

If I couldn't get up off the couch to cook or even to get out of bed in the morning, her words resonated in my mind…I am in Intensive Care and I will stay here until I have the strength to try to regain some semblance of a normal life. Nobody but me knows how I feel and nobody but me can help me through this. I will try my hardest but I will grieve at my own pace without giving in to the admonitions and pleadings of well-meaning friends and family. It helped. After 3 ½+ years as of the writing of this book, I consider myself to be out of Intensive Care (most of the time, with an occasional foray back into the Unit) and have progressed to the regular floor. It's strange, the little things that help us. *Sherry McGinnis, Scott's loving mom.*

Part of my healing…to keep Brett alive through the memories of others. I made a statement at the first anniversary of his death that so many thought was great…." Each of you has a piece of my son in your brain…it is a memory of his words, actions, and heart…please share those memories with me…or they will be forever lost." It made the kids open up a bit more…and really try to remember the good times they had with him. *Chris Tozzo, Brett's loving mom.*

I think just knowing that this horrible pain is normal and probably will not entirely go away. Crying is OK and people are more understanding and compassionate than I ever gave them credit for. No-one understands unless they have been there but most are willing to listen and let you vent. VENTING is important and CRYING is important. As hard as it is, let the people around you in and let them know what YOU want. We have been such caretakers of our lost children, now we need the same. Accept help from where ever. *Celeste Dale, Brandon's loving mom.*

The thing that helped me the most was to get with other parents who had lost a child. I think people should look for a support group, so that you can be with others who know what you're going through and who will understand your feelings. This helps more than anything. Until, and unless you have lost a child, you really don't know what we are going through. If you can't find a support group in your area you can look one up on the internet or as one mother did where I live, you can start your own group. This mom ran an ad in the paper and asked if any mothers who had lost a child would like to meet and talk and to call her. From these beginnings it has grown into a wonderful support group. *JoAnn, Vernon's loving mom.*

I focus on the things I have control over and what I do not. It really hurts and I miss Kara a lot and I tend to think of "what if." Then I have my faith to realize and to thank that it is wasted time. I have two sons who are alive and they need me to be their model. You keep going on…and that is your choice. *Kim, Kara's loving mom.*

One thing I have found that has helped me enormously is Shauna's friends keep tabs on me and stop by all the time. I also get emails almost daily from one or more of them. We talk of Shauna and share silly stories. This always puts a smile on my face. Just today while at work a young man who used to ride my bus came in. He knew Shauna and asked about her. I had to tell him the horrible news. Well once we got past that, he told me a memory he had of her. I didn't even cry today. Imagine that! I thanked him for sharing the story with me and told him that it made my day. These are the things that get me through each day. I love talking about my girl! Not talking about her makes me cry…it's like she's been forgotten. *Madonna, Shauna's loving mom.*

There are no rules in grieving. You just grieve in your own way, in your own time and don't feel you have to make any excuses to anyone. Those who truly love us understand. The other people do not matter anyway. *Maxine, Lang's loving mom.*

I guess the best I could say is that I find it helpful to do things that will keep my daughter's memory alive, and, I do a lot of that. I also find it helpful to do things that might help other families, other addicts, or fight the "stigma" associated with addictive illnesses. These are the only things that give my life any meaning and purpose. *Sue Shields, loving mom of Katie Kevlove*

How does one cope with the most tragic painful finality of losing a child? Once I got through taking care of details like what type of service to have, how to look through and pass along Jennifer's things, I found that I wanted to just run to and find parents like me, parents who lost a child through a drug overdose. What really saved my sanity was being able to share my thoughts and feelings freely with other parents who knew exactly what I was going through. *Sandi, Jennifer's loving mom*

Keep your son or daughter alive in your heart, honor his/her memory in mind, pray, and realize the essence of your child, the soul, has taken residence elsewhere, and still IS, without suffering, where you will be, too." *Anonymous, by a grieving mom*

I can tell you to expect the grief for the loss of your child to be extremely painful both <u>emotionally</u> and <u>physically</u>. The grief for the loss of our kids will last a lifetime BUT you can learn to cope and actually find that life is beginning to claim your attention again.

NO ONE should tell you how long or in what way to grieve. That is a highly personal experience. There is NO time schedule. Expect to grieve deeply because you loved your child deeply.

When my son passed away I was devastated not only from the loss but more from what I perceived was my failure as a mother to protect my child. As loving parents we tend to blame ourselves for those real or imagined slights we feel must have taken our child down the fatal path they chose. When I realized and was able to accept that I wasn't perfect (no parent is), that I loved my child and did the best that I could raising him, then I was able to let most of the guilt go and move forward through the grief process. If you're struggling with grief, professional counseling should be a serious consideration.

Keep as active as possible! You will begin to heal when you have other things to focus on. *Barbara, Joseph Smerker's loving mom.*

So - You've read some suggestions by people who have been there, done that! These are just gentle hints. You will find your own way of dealing with such a tragedy. Please remember there is no wrong or right way to grieve. Husbands and wives may grieve for the same child in totally opposite ways.

Grief is a very personal journey, one on which we've never wanted to embark. Sadly, we all must walk this path in one form or another in our lifetime. Walking this path due to the death of a child makes the walk that much more difficult. Walking this path due to the death of a child from addiction or suicide makes the walk almost impossible.

We take this walk with the weight of our loss in our hearts pulling us down to the ground. We fear we will never get back up and be able to go on. Yet each day we trudge along, treading that unknown path and hoping at journey's end, we will have found some peace and understanding.

We hope that when we come to that fork in the road we will choose the path that will lead us to some comfort and resolution, and not the path of continual despair. The choice is ours! We may not want to, we may not feel up to it, but we can make a conscious effort to finally accept what has happened. If we don't, then for all intents and purposes our lives will have ended when our child's life did. In the beginning of our grief indeed many of us would not find this to be a bad thing. Some have prayed for deliverance from their suffering wanting desperately to join their child. Others have asked for the strength to carry on, to endure each new day without part of their heart beating in their chest.

We're taught a lot of subjects in school, by our parents, and by society but we aren't taught much about death or how to deal with it. It's almost a taboo subject. It's frightening. Therefore when sudden death is thrust into our lives, we lack the necessary coping skills. Where do we turn for advice? For comfort? For guidance? The people whom we would normally trust the most, and look to for help are probably overcome with grief themselves. Death is not an easy subject to handle. The death of a child leaves even the strongest of people weak in the knees, gasping for breath, making deals with their God, bargaining and pleading, and of course asking over and over again, Why? Why? Why?

At the same time that we're grieving and needing consolation, many of us have other children or family members who need consoling, who more than ever need someone to take care of them. As a parent, that has been our job, to take care of everyone. We're the nurturers, the protectors. Many people feel like failures when their child has died.

A lot of times the males in our society are forgotten…the dads! Friends, family and associates are eager to embrace the forlorn mom and to cry with her. But men are not always accorded that kindness. Not because of any conscious thought to disregard their feelings but because our society teaches us that men are strong and will handle this bravely. We must not forget that they lost a child too! We have to allow them to weep openly and share their feelings. We must let them talk about their loss we have to let them be human! Sometimes a big hug can mean as much as any words.

We know in our hearts that our children would not want us to suffer. We can console ourselves with the knowledge that our children are no longer suffering. No matter whether you believe in an after life or not, one way or the other our suffering will come to an end.

I wish us all a measure of happiness, joy, peace and love for our duration here on earth. We can have this if we will allow ourselves to reach out and grab it without guilt knowing that this would please our child. During our child's life on earth we did everything we could to make him/her happy. Our final act of love for them can be to carry on, keep their memory alive.

We can plant a memorial garden in a corner of our yard. If you live in a condo or apartment with no yard, you can devote a corner of a room in their memory. There is nothing wrong with making a shrine to your child. We do whatever we have to in order to get through this, to lessen our pain. When we're stronger we can speak to students in middle schools about the danger of addiction. We can write letters to newspapers, be guests on local radio shows. There is a lot we can do to educate others about addiction. Writing this book has been very cathartic for me, and if it can help even one family, the pain of reliving the event will have been worthwhile.

Some parents wear their children's clothing. We sniff their scent on their clothing, breathing in the essence of what they were until one day there is nothing left to sniff. Their smell is gone. We've sucked it all in and savored every trace of scent. I know of some parents who placed their child's shoes or other articles of clothing into a tightly sealed plastic bag, opening it on occasion, to breathe their child again.

People who have not experienced our loss may find our new habits and expressions of grief somewhat bizarre to say the least. I'm pretty sure I would have felt that way too. I understand a lot now. I also understand that I can't let myself stay in this intense grief mode forever. I will mourn my son until the day I die but I will go on living…for myself, for my husband, for my living son Dale, for my dad, for my precious pets, and for my friends.

Although in time your grief will soften, try not to place any unrealistic expectations on yourself. Whereas someone may adjust to his/her loss more quickly than you, don't use that as your guide. Take your time. Proceed at your own pace. Ask friends and family members from time to time, how they think you're doing. They may pick up on clues that you're suffering more than a normal reaction to loss. You may be in a deep depression and not realize it. In one form or another we suffer Post-Traumatic Stress Disorder. This colors how we live our life, how we interact with others, how we react to every day situations. Try to keep an open mind.

Finally, accept the fact that your whole world has changed and you will most likely not ever return to your "normal" self. You will now have a new normal. Friends will be waiting for your former self to return. This may never happen. Your ups may not ever again be as high as they once were, and your lows may be lower than before. But unless you're suffering from severe depression (for which you would do well to seek help) you will be able to go on. You will be able to enjoy life again. You will find that you still have a lot to offer the world.

I couldn't have believed my own words almost four years ago

when our tragedy struck. I couldn't see how I would get through the next minute. I honestly believed I would not make it. No, I didn't believe it. I just knew it! Nobody could convince me otherwise.

So I kept a diary for a year, writing to my son, pouring my heart out, telling him what was going on, what he was missing. I recently reread what I had written in the beginning and quite frankly it scared me. Who was this deeply depressed, almost suicidal sounding person who wrote all these things? It was so sad.

I still have very sad days and I know I always will. But nearly four years after December 1, 2002, I can see and feel a progression of strength and resolve. Of course as I write this I'm liable to burst into tears at any moment. I never know when it will happen. I do know that it doesn't happen as often now. This does not mean that I miss my son any less. I would give my life for him to return a whole, happy person. I just know now that I have to go on with the business of living. Because as long as I'm alive, he is alive.

In Memoriam

This page is dedicated to the children here whose parents/siblings were not able to tell their story due either to time limitations or the sadness of recalling their tragedy. We remember them also with love and compassion.

Francisco "Corky" Martinez (Sister Debb)
DOB: January 13, 1970
DOD: November 7, 2002
COD: Lethal dose of Methadone.

Tracey S. Sheridan (Mom Agnes Sparnecht)
DOB: May 28, 1968
DOD: April 4, 2004
COD: Accidental Overdose of Xanax, Oxy-Contin and Cocaine

William (Billy) VanNess (Mom Kathie)
DOB: June 28, 1980
DOD: December 5, 2004
COD: Crashed into a tree after drinking all night.

Robert Allen Brown (Robbie) (Mom Janice)
DOB: February 14,1973
DOD: November 22,2001
COD: Accidental Multiple Prescription Drug Overdose with Methadone being the main one.

James Allen Atkins (Mom Marey)
DOB: August 10, 1978
DOD: July 16, 2005
COD: Cocaine / heroin overdose

Melanie Barasso (Mom Diane)
DOB: FEB 21, 1975
DOD: SEPT 23, 1993
COD: Heroin overdose

Timothy Meacham (Mom Laura)
DOB: March 6, 1978
DOD: March 28, 2005
COD: Black tar Heroin

"Punk" Marshall (Surrogate Mom/Friend Karen)
DOB: July 25, 1987
DOD: August 5, 2004
COD: Intentional Heroin suicide

Elliot Joseph Matos, Jr. (Mom Donna)
DOB: December 27, 1981
DOD: September 8, 2001
COD: Acute Oxycontin Intoxication

Garrett Thomas Scott (Mom Cyndy)
DOB: July 27, 1983
DOB: May 5, 2005
COD: Opiate toxicity

Pamela Saphiloff (Mom Sandy)
DOB: June 24, 1971
DOD: December 30, 1997
COD: Acute opiate intoxication

I AM YOUR DISEASE

PART TWO

PROBLEM GAMBLERS, ADDICTION AND THOSE WHO LOVE THEM

By Heiko Ganzer, LCSW, CASAC

Codependency treatment has been primarily known in the addictions field. Most treatment centers focused their attention on healthy behaviors for the addict.

Family therapy has only recently become a method of treatment in the addictions field, due to the lack of training for treating professionals and the skill level required. Family therapy considers that the entire family is in need of help. The wives and husbands of problem gamblers/addicts face even a larger difficulty in that very few professionals are not only not skilled in family issues, but are not trained as addiction treatment specialists. For the purpose of this book I will call codependents enablers and addicts, addicts.

Right about now you may be wondering why? Why is this man writing about codependents when it's a book about horrible events that occur to addicts?

During the last several years, more and more research has been done on gambling in this society. Although figures vary, research indicates that there are 328,000 gamblers in New York State of which only a handful are in treatment.

Gambling, as a problem, is not a new phenomenon, even the Bible and early historical records tell of its existence. Freud wrote an essay about problem gambling in 1926 concerning the Russian novelist and problem gambler Fyodor Dostoyevsky.

Few therapists have any idea how to treat it, or even recognize when it influences their clients. As a matter of concern it is doubtful to this author whether traditional mental health therapists and addiction specialists are aware of its presence in relationship to the other addictions they treat.

Problem gamblers, as well as being victims themselves, have an adverse impact on those with whom they associate. Employers, relatives, friends and families of gamblers suffer from the effects of pathological gambling. Many man-hours of work are lost because of absenteeism and inefficiency due to compulsive gambling. Relatives and friends are manipulated into concealing the problem from outsiders. The promises of change, although short-lived, are believed because those who care wish to believe them, and, as a result, they unknowingly become part of the denial pattern.

I believe that those who are the closest suffer most of all. The family is influenced negatively when the employer concludes the problem gambler's services. The family is shaped when the relatives and friends can no longer consent to the consequences of problem gambling and withdraw from the gambler and his or her family. Unable, without help, to remedy this, the family members become caught up in the consequences of the problem and may become emotionally ill or at minimum severely stressed themselves.

Hi, my name is Heiko and I've been working with addicts and their family members for years. My best friends are recovering addicts and their loved ones. These people have character and certainly are an interesting bunch. But they also have very serious problems. I've elected to help them, and after being a Fortune 500 executive, changed careers just to do that...that is give back to people in need.

This portion of *"I am your Disease"* (The Many Faces of Addiction) is dedicated to those who suffer from money addictions (gamblers, debtors, spenders, etc.) I work with them and their family members and help to give them hope and resolution.

My first story is from a problem gambler's wife, whom I will call Nadine, she is a great lady who tried so hard to recover the love she once had for Bert her husband. Bert was my client as well and although he still tries to gamble, for him it was escape gambling. Escape from his other disease. Bert was an outstanding client and contributed to my knowledge. We found out that some medications can alter the brain and enhance a gambling problem. Bert, who I called "the dumpster diver" would drive to dumpsters, jump in and recover all sorts of items which he then sold on e-bay. Here is Nadine's story as she wrote it.

Nadine

Wife of a gambler who has advanced Parkinson's disease

I feel it is necessary to write all of you to clear the air. As of July of this summer, Bert and I are separated. I have a real problem with this whole situation on many levels. On the one hand, I know how sick Bert is and leaving him in this state is devastating. For those of you who don't see him too often, I'm sure his deterioration is shocking.

Because of his condition, he is completely dependent upon me. I feel I am letting the whole family down by making this decision. One thing I want to make clear is that my decision to end our marriage has nothing to do with his Parkinson's. I have always loved Bert and knew what I was taking on when I married him. Although this disease has put a definite strain on our relationship, I would never have left him because of it. Actually it is his disease that has kept me hanging on years longer than I would have. The truth is Bert has been compulsively gambling since before Norbert was born.

When Norbert was an infant, he confessed. We wiped out the bank account, settled the debt, and I thought that we would never endure that devastation again. Well, that was just the beginning of this nightmare, and it hasn't ended yet. To be honest, I don't think it ever will.

After a while, Bert sought counseling, and has been through several therapists. We finally found one who understands the compulsive gambling problem completely. Although we have been with this therapist for years, Bert has not made much progress. The therapist says all the right things and is completely supportive of both of us, but no matter what consequence is laid before Bert, he continues to gamble. I have been begging and pleading with Bert to consider what he will lose if he continues to gamble, but nothing stops him.

I have been in a regular Gam-Anon meeting for about three years.

From this group, I have learned there really is nothing anyone can do to stop an addict. They must hit rock bottom, and everyone's bottom is different. I always thought I could recognize when Bert hit his bottom, but I was always wrong. Whenever I thought this time was the worst, he'll certainly stop now, he has gone on. I'm helpless. All I can do is what I can do to save myself, and my son from this devastation. The harm done is not so much financial, although we have certainly felt that burden. I find the worst part of this addiction is that it has taken my husband away from me. There is no other way to put it. Because he is a compulsive gambler, he is not capable of being my partner in this life. It's all about gambling with him. He's just not there for me, and our connection is gone. The sad truth is that I know how much he loves me, and Norbert, but the gambling is bigger than all that. There is nothing he wouldn't do for us, I know. Yet he throws us away with both hands by gambling. He cannot stop himself.

That is the biggest heartbreak of my life, to watch him lose the things he loves the most, one by one, and be unable to stop it. I do have an alternative, to stay on as his wife and continue to provide a loving home for him. I have tried this for years. This took its toll on me. The betrayal and the lies just became too much. There was simply no trust left at all. It is really not possible for a marriage to last with an active addiction. The addiction is all consuming. Bert chose to feed his addiction instead of his marriage and family. We could never make this kind of relationship work. If I did stay on, I could not consider what we have a marriage. There is just no partnership in this relationship. It is one person always wanting and needing more, and the other seeking comfort in an outside source. Honestly, it's like living with a cheating husband. That's the only way I could explain it to people who have not lived with an addict. I made excuses for many years just like Bert did, and allowed this in my life years longer than I should have because he is disabled and because we have a child. The truth is, it is and always will be unacceptable. I gave it a reasonable amount of time, and then decided I had enough.

In our separation, I agreed to allow Bert to live in the house and I would continue to cook and clean and shop for him. My only goal was to be free once and for all from this gambling addiction. Well, the gambling didn't stop, and even this didn't bother me so much because I figured, at least I'm legally separated from him so I really don't have to worry about any gambling he might do. Because we are no longer " husband and wife" he doesn't owe me any explanations, so I don't have to feel betrayed or deceived. I reminded him of this, and assured him that he didn't have to hide anything from me anymore. We were to live " separated" in every sense. We could share our time with Norbert at dinner, and all would be pleasant. It worked for a while.

I naively thought that his gambling could no longer hurt me. That was my first mistake. For all the harm Bert's gambling has done, he had never put me personally at risk. Well, all that changed when I got a letter from his credit card stating that I had applied for a line of credit. When I called the company to find out what happened, it was explained to me that I was the co-applicant on a loan, which means I would be equally responsible for the debt. Luckily, he was denied this loan because of his financial delinquency. Had he been approved, my credit and my future would have been negatively affected without my knowledge or permission. As it is, just being denied a loan is a negative mark on my credit.

That was the final blow. With that, Bert crossed a line I never thought he would. This opened up avenues I never thought possible. Applying for a loan in my name just shows how desperate Bert has gotten. Because of this, I have no idea what to expect with Bert, and I have asked him to move out of the house. I do not trust him with my personal papers and belongings, and he can do whatever he likes all day in the house. I put myself on a credit protection plan to check my credit report regularly for any illegitimate loans or credit cards. I really do worry about the next blow. I don't know how or when the axe will fall, but I do feel like it will. All this happened just before Thanksgiving, which explains my demeanor during that weekend.

We are now living a strained existence because he refuses to leave. I have tried to explain to him why I need to live apart from him, but he will not accept this reality. I would never deny him all the help I could offer him in my life. Norbert will always be accessible to him. I would do all the things I could do for him even under these trying circumstances, but he won't hear of it. He says my request to live separately is unreasonable, and he cannot live anywhere else. What he doesn't realize is that we really should be living separately already because we are legally separated. It looks like things could get a lot *worse if I am forced to sell the house.*

Author's Note: Nadine is now separated, has placed Bert in a Nursing home, and visits Bert weekly with his son. Nadine has gained a life of her own and is happy. She is a wonderful mother and Norbert is doing very well under his mother's care. Other family members have stepped-up to help both Bert and Nadine. The addict Bert is doing well as he has good medical care and loves to see his wife and son on weekends. This is a potential result of addiction. Nadine finally took care of herself after seriously trying to get her husband to see the light. Bert would be in a nursing home whether he was a problem gambler or not. Bert's Parkinson's disease was just another byproduct of a brain disease.

As I said earlier co-dependents feed the disease of addiction without really knowing that they are doing just that. Significant others need to see their own addictive behaviors and how it impacts the addict.

In my practice this is one of my greater accomplishments and when properly aware, the significant others can actually help to turn the situation into a positive. The stories from the significant other truly are an insight to this terrible disease. We have no urine test or breathalyzer test to test when one is gambling. We also know that problem gambling is a hidden disease, one that propels addicts to lie about anything and everything.

Lisa Maria's letter to Me!

Hi Mr. Ganzer,

I am writing to seek help for my boyfriend, Thor, who is a money addict and compulsive gambler. From the time I met him three years ago, he has consistently spiraled downward, gambling more and losing more with each bet. His "drug" of choice: Sports betting with illegal bookmakers. He often loses thousands of dollars at a time during football season. Occasionally, he will drive down to Atlantic City, NJ to play poker. Although he is a skilled player and wins quite a bit, he often puts it all back into a slot machine by the end of the trip.

Thor is 27 years old now, but has had a problem with gambling since he was 14. He has never held a steady job, and has virtually no sense of responsibility. Last year, he filed for Chapter 7 bankruptcy protection after a car repossession and constant hounding by creditors for unpaid credit cards, student loans, and other bills.

The reason I am writing now is that for the past month or so, Thor has found himself homeless - first, in Atlantic City, and now, in Las Vegas.

I'll back up, though.

Thor lost his job in early November; he had been working full time with a friend who owns a carpet cleaning and floor restoration business in NY. Thor didn't mind the work, and the money was just enough for him to get by. He is the type of guy who doesn't want to have a boss, and liked the independence that contract work provided. (Most gamblers like this independence) He was fired (he says) because his cell phone bill had gone unpaid (he blames his brother for this), and his friend could not reach him for an important job. I believe his termination was a culmination of other factors **(see how the significant other can tell a lie)** - i.e.: it was getting too expensive for his friend to keep him on, but I'm not really sure. He spent most of the month at home, in bed. Although he was legitimately sick with one bad head cold after another, he was not even trying to find another job **(depression shows up like this in problem gamblers)**. I became fed up.

Thor and I had gotten back together in December 2004, after going through a major breakup in March. At the time we broke up, I was living in NY (on my own), but had been bailing him out of illegal gambling debts. I racked up a grand total of over $20,000 in debt to help him - money that he promised over and over that he would repay. Instead, it got to the point where I was making all of the payments, and could not afford to continue living on my own while paying off the cash advances I took on my credit cards **(this is the unintentional codependency---she helped him pay his debts)**. After I told him that I *had no choice but to move back in with my parents, he couldn't face me, so he ended our relationship* **(the easy way out).** *I repaid every cent of the debt by June 2005, and able to live on my own again.*

During the time I lived at home, I had to come clean to my family about what I had done. (They thought that it had just gotten too expensive for me to live on my own). I think that was the most difficult moment in my life because I hated myself for lying to them. They didn't understand how I could help someone that way - someone who wasn't even a family member. What they didn't understand (and still don't) is that I had every intention of making Thor a family member; when he wasn't gambling; our relationship was very good **(all *the gamblers are smooth, likable characters*).** *(Unfortunately, though, he was gambling most of the time). My family still maintains that Thor 'used' me, and took advantage of my good heart. Over the course of the year I was living at home, they fueled my attempts to get my money back. All I ever wanted was to prove them wrong, and have Thor make things right. I ultimately filed a complaint in NY civil court. In October 2004, I was shocked to learn that my suit had been dismissed after Thor filed for Chapter 7; he had listed me as a creditor, and legally, I had no claim to the money he owed me once the bankruptcy was discharged. I was livid, but eventually got to the point where I was tired of being angry. I just wanted to move on.*

Thor got in touch with me for the first time after the breakup in November 2004, when he was in very big trouble with a bookie again. Obviously, I didn't offer money, but he just wanted someone to talk to. He told me what a mistake he had made, how much he missed me, and how much he loved me. It was the validation I had been seeking for almost a year. We started talking again, and deep down I knew that everything that had happened was not intentional - it was the classic sign of a compulsive gambler who believes the lies that they tell those they care about in order to keep gambling. By that January 2005, we were together again. He moved into his own place in March 2005, and started working with his friend. He said he planned on paying me back the money he owed me (even though the claim had been discharged). I really thought he was on his way to making a life for himself, and that everything we'd been through had changed him.

But by early December 2005, I wanted out - I told him it was over and that I needed to move on. I explained to him that I wanted to have things in life - a house, a family - and that he had not done anything over the past year to improve his own situation or ours. I recently got a new job, and am doing much better financially and am seeking someone who is as ambitious and motivated to have the kind of life I want. He was just barely getting by.

Thor, who has fallen even more in love with me this time around, did not take the news well. Unbeknownst to me, he drove the car I had helped him to get in August 2005, to Atlantic City; he gambled every dime he had on him (including that month's car payment); and was stranded. He lied to me for three days, telling me he was at a friend's house. I told him that I wanted the car back, but he refused to return it. (He was sleeping in it for two weeks). I was forced to call the police and report it stolen, since I didn't know exactly where it was, and he had the keys. Finally, after about a week of silence, he contacted me to let me know that he left the car with a friend (someone I didn't know), and that he was in Las Vegas. He currently owes a bookie about $15,000, and is running from the debt.

At first I was very angry, and just concentrated on getting the car back. (I did, and am currently in the process of selling it and taking the loss once again). But now I am more concerned about the fact that he is homeless, sleeping on the streets of Las Vegas, and living off casino comps to eat. Something has got to give, but I don't know how to help him. I have been in touch with his family - his mother is completely beside herself. She has been dealing with his problem for almost 16 years now, and has depleted all of her savings bailing him out time after time **(one wonders why she didn't get help long ago)**. She is also homeless - they lost the house over a year ago. His father passed away when he was 13. I believed this to be the root of his problem, since that's about when the gambling really became an issue. However, after talking with him tonight, I believe the gambling is just an indicator of a larger problem - a money addiction **(this is what I believe as well and it should be noted that the money is the drug)**.

Thor told me that he thinks his problem started very early - around age 8. He grew up in an affluent NY suburb. He said he saw all of the 'things' his friends had, and wanted to have everything too. His parents were by no means poor - he never wanted for anything - but it was never enough. He says he was embarrassed to tell people where he lived, and was always begging his parents for things to " keep up" with the other kids (common thoughts of a gambler – " I am never good enough"). He says his attitude is one of " all or nothing." He blames his current predicament on this attitude. Because I had broken up with him, he knew he couldn't keep the car (a Mercedes Benz) and he chose to be homeless (i.e.: nothing), since he couldn't have it all. Of course, he tried to win money gambling first to 'solve' all of his problems (**one final try at even though we all know that a gambler's odds are zero to win in the long term**).

Thor does not believe 'talking to a stranger' will help him. I think he is wrong. I think he needs serious counseling to address his warped attitude towards money **(what seems to me to be an entitlement complex),** as well as his compulsive gambling issues. However, I am not a therapist; I'm just a person who is hurt, concerned, angry, sad, and powerless to do anything in the face of all of this. Virtually no one knows of MY predicament - as I have been (once again) leading a double-life with my family for the past year. They do not know I have any contact with Thor, let alone that we have been together. His mother is the only person I have talked to who understands everything I'm feeling. But I do not know where to turn for help.

If you could provide some guidance, I would be very grateful. Thor has agreed to 'try' to get help, and it would help me if you could advise me on what he/I can do at this point.

Author's note: This letter came to me out of the blue on the internet. I get many letters like this and refer the clients to local clinicians whom I am aware of. Sometimes I also do phone or internet therapy to those who have no specialist in their area. This client was referred to a local clinician. I picked this letter due to the typical nature of those that I get. It is usually the significant others who seek the help for their loved ones. Addicts leave a path of destruction for those who remain. It doesn't make any difference whether it's problem gambling, alcohol, drugs, or eating disorders. Since I treat them all I am very conscious of my clients switching addictions. They will quit one and start another and if you're not careful you won't even recognize it.

I AM YOUR DISEASE

HEIKOTHERAPY TESTIMONIAL

I can honestly say I don't know where my husband & I would be if we hadn't met Heiko (who is even better looking than in his internet picture!---unprofessional yes, did I make you smile---yes, that's because I am finally happy...AHHHHH! Ok moving right along).

It was the last straw that broke the camel's back when it came to my husband's gambling addiction. Ironically, it happened the day we had our first appointment with Heiko. We were ready to sign the papers. Well, that was a little over a year ago & I have to say my husband & I are still together, and dare I say happy (most of the time).

Heiko is different than other counselors. Why? Because he deals with addictions, and has a profound knowledge of the way someone with an addiction/compulsion thinks and acts. This is why other counselors have failed us & Heiko has succeeded.

As with any addiction/compulsion there are two parts. The person who has the addiction & the person who 'thinks' they are the victim. I have learned that although my husband made the choice to gamble I was also a part of the dynamic (yes, I am admitting this).

We didn't know how to fix this. It began with a verbal contract, which was "time to allow this process to work and complete honesty" Heiko has taught us how our relationship works & feeds off a vicious cycle. Only when we began to understand this was when the changes started to be made on both our parts. Heiko not only listened but he gave us suggestions on how to handle a situation differently. This was one of the most precious things we could have received. I call it our toolbox. Now that's not to say that sometimes I don't remember or choose not to use my newly learned tools---I'm only human. However, I can say that when we handle a situation the same way we always did pre-Heiko the outcome is always a disaster.

It has only been a year for us, and we are more than half way 'there'. We are happier and stronger than ever before. I think we are now on the same team a majority of the time, which is something I couldn't say, in I don't remember how long!

15 money addiction warning signs

- Spending more than 25 percent of your net income on credit card bills.

- Borrowing money to pay off other debts.

- Paying your bills on time, but running out of cash between paychecks.

- Using your credit card to pay for necessities because you don't have the cash.

- Paying only the minimum payment on your credit cards. If you can't double the minimum payment, that is a problem!

- Getting turned down for a consolidation loan. This reflects an over-extended money issue -- your debt ratio may be too high.

- Refinancing a loan to reduce your monthly payment. If you're 36 months into a 60-month loan and you're looking to refinance because you're over-extended and need to lower payments, it's a clear-cut warning sign!

- Needing a co-signer. If the lender requires a co-signer to make this loan creditworthy, you are probably over-extended; however, if you lack a credit history, this wouldn't necessarily apply.

- Financing your vehicle for six or more years. Doing it to lower your monthly payment, rather than focusing on reducing your debt is a warning sign...

- Consolidating your loans but not closing the accounts where those loans originated. People may be afraid to do so in case they're in trouble again. You need to close off those other credit cards or you're simply going to compound the debt problem.

- Counting on the next " big deal" to see you through your financial trouble. You need to look at the big deal as extra money for the household instead of it bailing you out.

- Carrying more than three credit cards. There's no reason to have more than two credit cards. Everyone accepts at least one of two cards. Better off with a debit card.
- Waiting until near the end of your credit card's grace period to pay, or requesting a higher credit limit.
- Hiding purchases from your family, or fighting with your spouse about how to deal with your financial problems. Financial problems and domestic problems go hand in hand and are one of the top issues leading to divorce.
- Depending on parents and friends to bail you out.

If you're engaged in two or more of these practices, create a budget immediately, detailing all bills, debts and income.

Suggestions for how to better manage your money:

1. Make yourself accountable to someone you trust regarding your spending, borrowing and gambling practices.
2. Avoid purchasing items just because they are on sale or a really good deal-- buy only the things you absolutely need.
3. Never borrow money when you do not have the means to pay it back within a reasonable amount of time.
4. Keep a record of whom and where you have borrowed money from and who has borrowed money from you.
5. Set limits before you start on how much you are willing to spend or lose when gambling.
6. Try to pay as much as possible with cash or debit card. Paying with a check or credit card can be disillusioning because you are not actually seeing the money you are spending.

Addictions to money can be kept under control, but like any addiction, the spender has to know they have a problem and work at finding a solution.

Heiko's website is www.heiko.com

AFTERWORD

I hope that the stories you've read here have touched you. I trust they've opened your eyes to the problem that hard drugs and gambling are causing all across our country from the heartland to the inner cities.

I hope that you don't judge us in how we handled our individual situations. We all have different views on how to raise our children. We all did the best that we knew how.

It's easy to say that perhaps we made some mistakes. Of course we did. We're human. We all make mistakes. Sometimes we enabled our children but sometimes that enabling was the only thing that kept them alive. Believe me, when your child is dancing with death, you will do anything in your power to give them one more week, one more day, one more hour of life.

Some tried the tough love approach. Didn't work. Others gave everything they had. Didn't work. The point is that we tried! We threw lifelines. We threatened. We cajoled. We begged. We pleaded. We loved. We bargained. We punished. We cried…we cried. We just didn't know how to help.

I offer this caveat: Until and unless you have walked in our shoes, you will have no idea of how you would act in a similar situation, no matter what you might think now. I know I didn't!

I do not speak for all of the parents/siblings in this book. Their stories speak for themselves, beautifully, and eloquently, but the one thing that I can say with absolute certainty is that none of us wants you to walk in our shoes. We belong to a select club that nobody wants to join! Our collective hearts break with each new member.

By recounting our stories, and pouring our hearts out, we hope that something in these pages will help you, if you're dealing with a child who suffers from the Disease of Addiction.

Scientists are discovering that there is an addiction gene. I'm certainly not a physician but I read volumes on addiction. How I wish I had been more knowledgeable while my own child was alive. I know I could not have saved him, but I would have had a better understanding of his suffering.

I've been told that the body's craving for drugs sits squarely in the limbic part of the brain, (the pleasure center). Some findings suggest that the brain can be reprogrammed if drug use is curtailed early on and diligent efforts are made to never use again. This is an ongoing and difficult process to say the least.

For some children though, the need to do drugs is not just physical, it is emotional. This condition would have to be addressed thoroughly before there is any hope of successful treatment.

It is up to us, the cheerleaders for reform, to keep public awareness of addiction first and foremost in society's minds. Everything takes time. Sadly during this time more and more people are losing their life. Research must be done to find ways to control the addiction. Let's face it... people want to alter their mental state. Always have and always will. (The before dinner cocktails, the aperitifs, the "social" drinking, the weekend drinkers, etc.) So work needs to be done to find ways to let those people alter their brains but not become addicted. Many of you will disagree with this concept. I don't judge. I try to understand. It would be great if we could all be mentally healthy and happy in our own skin but that isn't how it always is.

Again, I am not a physician and I can't offer medical advice. I just know what I read and I read voraciously about drug addiction. Find out for yourself. Read and educate yourself. Don't wait until it's too late.

As my husband Jack always says..." If you want the world to be a better place, be a better person." Actively working against drug abuse, and for common sense legislation is one way to make the world a better place. Addicted people need treatment, not punishment. Each teaspoon of water that we put into the research bucket will eventually fill the bucket. So we must keep going to the well and toiling, not letting our resolve falter.

For more information on how drugs reprogram your brain, there are numerous sites on the internet, or at your local library. One site that I found most informative is:

http://www.freevibe.com/Drug_Facts/why_drugs.asp

There are many, many more. Check them out. Check them all out.

Arm yourself with knowledge. Even the child, who is not the most academically gifted, can argue the pros of drug use as eloquently as any orator. They're so convincing so as to make you question your own beliefs and rationale.

We want you to know that you are not alone. There are numerous grief support groups and there are now groups aimed especially at people who have lost someone to addiction and/or suicide. This latter group has been needed for quite some time. Such a group can be a lifeline when you're riding that roller coaster of despair.

Angels of Addiction and Remember Me in Heaven are two excellent support groups on Yahoo that I personally belong to. (Their websites are listed at the end of this book along with a few others). There are other groups on the Internet with people waiting to welcome you into their group and offer you their love and support.

Finally, to the newly bereaved families I offer this message of hope. It is true that our lives will never be the same. How could they? But we do learn to live again in our new "normal."

How long does it take to grieve? I would think forever. I can't possibly imagine living the rest of my life without grieving for my son. But the grief I experience today, going on four years since my son's untimely demise, is a softer grief.

It is not the daily, wracking sobs and gut-wrenching screams, and kicking and throwing things as I did in the beginning. Oh, don't misunderstand. I still shed tears every day for my son. I still think of him constantly. It's as if a radio station is playing in my head…WSGM…All day, all the time, Scott, Scott, Scott. Sometimes the despair is still overwhelming. Knowing that he is gone from our daily lives is still unbelievable, and incomprehensible. I wear some of his ashes in a locket next to my heart. It's the closest that I can get to him.

But now, interspersed between the sad times, are the times of happy remembrances, the mental pictures of his big grin and loving heart, the goodness that was him, the joy and the many laughs that he gave us throughout his brief life.

We are told that life is not fair. Indeed it isn't. It can be cruel beyond imagination. If we are to continue living though, we must try to concentrate on the good times and tuck the bad times in the back of our minds and then bring them out to reflect upon them when we need to, when it's safe, when others aren't around to question why we still mourn our child so.

We don't need to feel guilt the first time we smile again or even laugh. This is our natural instinct emerging from the depths of our despair, to help us survive. We all know that our children would not want us to live a life of sadness. We tell ourselves this all the time, especially after indulging in a much-needed laugh.

Nobody can tell us how to grieve. Oh, they might try to with their platitudes of "It's time to move on." Another is "You need a vacation to get away from this." Get away from what? Where is this place that you can go, to get away from the death of your child? If I could, would I really want to go there? I don't think so.

I need to grieve my child, in my own way, at my own speed. I need to hold him in my heart so delicately as a child would gently hold a butterfly in their hand. I need to love him…always! And I need to make sure that no one ever forgets that he lived, he loved, and he was loved!

We parents who have bared our souls in this book want our children to be remembered for their goodness. We want them to be remembered as loving children, who were also victims of the excesses of our society today. We want everyone to remember that they were just children when they had their first introduction to drugs.

They were more than " drug addicts." We won't allow society to define them as such. They were people with a disease, a debilitating disease and they suffered from it more than any of us can really know.

We know our children are going to make mistakes. They're children. That's what they do! It is our job as parents to be there for them, to protect them from themselves, and to guide them from babyhood, through childhood, and into adulthood.

But unless you keep them tethered to you twenty-four hours a day, you cannot be aware of everything they are going through. You won't be there the first time one of their peers offers them a drink, a joint, a line of cocaine, ecstasy, some pills, an aerosol can to huff, and on and on. It seems like there's a new drug every day, a new way to get high.

We're parents, not super humans. Think about the times that your child has fallen and scraped his or her knee and you weren't there to catch them. They come to you for help and receive a loving kiss on the boo-boo, soothing words, some antiseptic spray and a bandage to remedy the mishap.

But there is no magical solution when your child first experiments with drugs. There is no bandage to cover *this* wound. They are most definitely not going to come to you for help.

Why not? They don't want to be healed, that's why! They have just discovered…Drugs!

There is no kiss for this boo-boo, no soothing words. Everything for them now is all tickety-boo. They're on top of the world, Ma! Drugs are cool.

Over time, however, as they begin experiencing the detriment and degradation of drug abuse, the loss of their parents' respect and trust, their loss of self esteem, seeing their lives slowly start to unravel, this is exactly what they will want from you: The kisses, the soothing touch of their mother's hand caressing their face. The big bear hug from their dad. They will want to turn back the time, and be an innocent child again. Too late! The die has been cast.

There is an approximately 98% recidivism rate for heroin users. Scary, isn't it?

So try to nip it in the bud. Don't question yourself. Go with your gut instinct. If you feel that something isn't right, talk about it. Be honest. Stop, Talk, and Listen! Don't be in denial. Remember, good kids do drugs too!

We all wish a full lifetime of happiness and joy for you and your family. We do not want to welcome you to our group but should you ever need us, we are here for you with open arms, loving hearts and understanding and compassion. We will not judge you or your child.

If someone needs your help in dealing with grief, walk gently by his or her side. If they stumble, be there to pick them up. Offer to help with whatever they need but don't force your personal beliefs on them. This is *their* grief. This is *their* journey. May it not be yours!

I AM YOUR DISEASE

Some Internet Grief Support Sites

1. Angels of Addiction (*www.angelsofaddiction.com*)
2. Remember Me In Heaven
3. (*http://health.groups.yahoo.com/group/RememberMe/*
4. Healing Hearts for Bereaved Parents (*www.healingheart.net*)
5. *www.groww.com*
6. *www.grasphelp.com*
7. *www.vigilforlostpromise.com*
8. *www.griefnet.org*
9. Family and friends of Addicts-

http://health.groups.yahoo.com/group/Family_N_Friends_Of_Addicts/

Attention Reader: After you have read this book and used it to help heal, or gleaned from it whatever you need, please pass it on to someone else in need who can't afford the purchase price. Our goal is to reach as many people as possible with our message. You can help.

Thank you for reading our stories and for letting us share our lives and the lives of our children with you. You are not alone! May you find peace and release from heartache.